Northern Vagabond

Northern Vagabond

The Life and Career of
J.B. Tyrrell

by Alex Inglis

McClelland and Stewart

McClelland and Stewart Limited
The Canadian Publishers
25 Hollinger Road
Toronto, Ontario
M4B 3G2

Canadian Cataloguing in Publication Data

Inglis, Alex I., 1939-
 Northern vagabond

ISBN 0-7710-4357-0

1. Tyrrell, J. Burr, 1858-1957. 2. Geologists –
Canada – Biography. I. Title.

QE22.T8I54   550′.92′4   C77-001752-5

Printed and bound in Canada

Contents

to my mother

Acknowledgments

Although they are not responsible for the faults contained herein, a number of people are responsible for making this book possible and for that I am most appreciative. First among them is Joyce Tyrrell, J. B. Tyrrell's daughter-in-law, who was most helpful in making material available, in offering valuable insight into her father-in-law's personality and in giving encouragement. J. B.'s grand-daughter, Catherine Stewart, also helped me catch a glimpse of the man.

The generous co-operation of the staff of the Thomas Fisher Rare Book Library of the University of Toronto where the Tyrrell Papers reside made the research much easier. Quotations from the Tyrrell Papers are published with the permission of the Thomas Fisher Rare Book Library. I have assumed that copyright to the Munro-Ferguson diary, J. W. Tyrrell's *Across the Sub-Arctic of Canada*, and Edith Tyrrell's *I Was There*, has expired. If in making this assumption I have inadvertently infringed on anyone's rights in the brief quotations I have made from these sources, I offer my apologies.

I also appreciate the assistance of the staff of the National Library and Public Archives of Canada and especially of the External Affairs Library in Ottawa for making their facilities available to me. Mr. William Kerr was a great help with maps and photographs, both in identifying material available and in preparing the maps for publication. The photographs used are drawn from the collection of the Geological Survey of Canada (GSC), the Public Archives of Canada (PAC) and the Thomas Fisher Rare Book Library (TFRBL). Many of Tyrrell's photographs are duplicated in these collections.

My wife and children willingly allowed J. B. Tyrrell to take over my life for a while with hardly a word of complaint and a good many words of support, I thank them. My friend and secretary, Eleanor Shaughnessy, worked wonders in deciphering my scrawl and in typing and retyping the various drafts of the manuscript. She, like my family, was a constant source of encouragement. Finally, I am grateful to my publishers for patience and prodding as well as advice.

To all of them, my thanks.

A. I. I.

CHAPTER 1

The Barren Lands

In the rock strewn desolation of the Barren Lands, J. B. Tyrrell made fast his claim to fame as a Canadian explorer. The work of discovering Canada in the late nineteenth century was a many faceted enterprise. Its primary purpose was to fill in the details of a land already known in outline. It was a matter of surveying and plotting; of pacing and measuring; of tracing rock formations and tracking river courses. There was the search for mineral wealth and the pursuit of information about our prehistoric roots. In short, the goal was to expand and make more precise the knowledge of what this ancient land and new dominion of Canada was all about.

Tyrrell took part in this endeavour and by the time he was thirty, the range and thoroughness of his work had already secured for him a respectable place in the history of Canadian exploration. He was, however, a restless and ambitious man, searching always for new and greater challenges against which he could pit his enquiring mind and his strong body.

The Barren Lands were made for Joe Tyrrell to conquer and Joe Tyrrell was made for the Barren Lands. In 1893 that huge tract of the Canadian north beyond the treeline and west of Hudson Bay in the Keewatin District of the Northwest Territories was the largest unexplored area on the North American continent. When he set out over half a million square miles was just a white space on the map. When he was done the curtain of mystery which shrouded that vast area had been rolled back forever.

The opening of the north has been the task of the twentieth century but a major piece of the groundwork was done by J. B. Tyrrell in 1893. In that year he had made Canadians keenly aware of their northern domain. Although on occasion they have since lost sight of that heritage, whenever their gaze has returned to the north Tyrrell's work, though often unacknowledged, has stood before them as a testimony to the magnitude of his achievement. Always carefully modest when talking about his accomplishments he referred to his 1893 expedition simply as a "rigorous trip." Rigorous it certainly was. It took more than sixty years after Tyrrell pioneered the route before anyone else tried to duplicate his feat – and that ended in tragedy. A brief description makes it sound simple. Essentially Tyrrell led eight men on a canoe trip down the Dubawnt River from Wholdaia Lake to where it joins the Thelon River and thence down the Thelon to its mouth on Chesterfield Inlet of Hudson Bay. Then on to Churchill, Winnipeg and home. But the simplicity lies only in the brief description.

It was, in the fullest sense, an adventure into the unknown that required strength and courage, dedication and determination and, above all, freedom of spirit and a will to survive. Death faced the explorers at every turn. The river would serve as their highway but, uncharted and untamed, it could as easily serve as a watery grave. Wildlife was their food supply. Plentiful at first, they took fish from the river and birds from the air to supplement the deer and caribou that fell before their guns. But, as the season wore on, their sources dwindled until all that was left were the ptarmigan, those hardy little grouse that put on their white plumes to brave out the Arctic winter. On one occasion when even the ptarmigan had given out, they met with a polar bear, also in search of nourishment. And when the battle between man and beast was settled in man's favour the animal posed yet another threat to their survival. Unknown to the travellers the liver of the polar bear is poisonous to man and the famished group devoured every morsel of the northern monarch only to bring one of them to the verge of death.

Nor were the river and bear the only enemies. There was also the weather. The brief though beautiful season in the north that some call summer is in reality a mere respite in an unending winter that never fully releases her grip on the land. There are lakes that are jammed with ice in late July and early August; the ground is permanently frozen; men can die of exposure in midsummer; no month is free of blizzards. Such were the Barren Lands of Canada that Tyrrell crossed in 1893. They have not changed since.

Little was known of the land he was entering. Only Samuel Hearne had been there, and that was over a hundred years before.

In 1769 Hearne was in the employ of the Hudson's Bay Company. Based at Fort Prince of Wales, near the present-day town of Churchill, Hearne ventured forth into the Barren Lands three times in his search for an overland route to the Coppermine River and the Arctic Ocean. To Hearne the Barren Lands were but the obstacle that stood between him and his goal. Never a very exacting geographer, he had done little more than establish the bleak and inhospitable nature of the land he had traversed.

And if little was known of the Barren Lands even less was known of the river that would serve as Tyrrell's highway in 1893 as he crossed and recrossed Hearne's path. Tyrrell first became aware of the river itself during an expedition the year before when, on Black Lake, in what is now northernmost Saskatchewan, he witnessed a large party of Chippewyan Indians from Fond du Lac setting out to hunt the enormous herds of caribou that ran in the Barrens. On that one day nineteen canoes of Chippewyans passed him en route for their traditional hunting grounds. The heavy traffic made its impression on Tyrrell and he questioned the hunters and his own guides. For an answer a spot about two miles east of the mouth of the Chipman River was pointed out to him. There, where a clump of willows draped over the lakeshore, was the beginning of a portage which led to the caribou hunting grounds, and to a great river that wound its way through the land.

Leaving the Indians to continue on their hunt, Tyrrell paddled across Black Lake and down the Stone River to Lake Athabasca for a rendezvous with the other half of his exploration party at Fond du Lac. Waiting there for the others Tyrrell again pursued his enquiries amongst the local Indians about this previously unknown river route into the Barren Lands. This time he managed to persuade an old Chippewyan to draw a crude map showing how to reach the river. But where the river itself led, whether it emptied into the Arctic Ocean or Hudson Bay, no one knew, for while the Indians pursued it to hunt each summer, they had never descended to its mouth. To do so would have been to enter the land of the Eskimo who, in Chippewyan folklore, were cannibals.

Throughout the months of August and September 1892, while continuing the work at hand, Tyrrell gathered all the information he could about the land to the north and pondered upon a great new undertaking for the next year. By the time he returned home in the fall a plan had formed in his mind. He was on the staff of the Geological Survey, the body charged with the task of exploring Canada. At the first opportunity he would put to his chief, A. R.

C. Selwyn, the proposal that he be allowed to lead a small party by canoe into the north to search out the new river and follow it to its mouth. The expedition, he assured Selwyn, would be inexpensive. The party would consist only of Tyrrell, a white assistant, three Indian canoemen and three métis bearers. It would take, Tyrrell reckoned, three or four months. At the end of that time a whole new corner of Canada would be known and the work of the Survey would take a giant leap forward. Tyrrell was persuasive and Selwyn, swayed particularly by the assurance that the expedition would be inexpensive, gave his approval.

Tyrrell at once set about preparing for the journey. As with every task he tackled, he went about it with painstaking thoroughness. First the journals of Samuel Hearne were obtained. Hearne's travels in the Barren Lands may have been incidental to his main purpose of finding a route to the Arctic, but his records of those travels were still the only information available. Similarly all the maps and accounts of travels around the perimeter that could be obtained were scoured for information. Next came the search for a suitable assistant which ended with Tyrrell's selection of his own younger brother, James. His choice was undoubtedly influenced by a characteristically paternal approach to his own family. But that was not the only consideration. James Tyrrell also had some invaluable practical experience to his credit as a member of other expeditions. For two seasons, some ten years before, he had assisted the Survey's Robert Bell in a survey of the Lake of the Woods area. Even more important than having been introduced to the work of exploration by so eminent a tutor, James also had first-hand experience of the Arctic. In 1885 he had been a member of the Gordon expedition on Hudson Bay and as part of that work had spent the following winter holed up on Ashe Island. There, on that isolated spot of land in Hudson Strait, he had learned the techniques of Arctic survival and had learned as well something of the language and customs of the Eskimo people. If that was not enough to acquit J. B. of any charge of nepotism there was also the fact that James, like his elder brother, was an able marksman, an undoubted advantage on an expedition where it would be essential to supplement supplies with what could be hunted along the way. In all an excellent choice for an assistant. As J. B. put it, "James was an earnest, diligent, indomitable man, not to be moved by hardship from the task at hand . . . I had cause to bless his loyalty and devotion to duty."

With a qualified assistant arranged, Tyrrell then turned his attention to acquiring the best canoemen he could find. J. B.'s own words best describe his choice and his reasons for it.

I planned to cross the portage from Black Lake in search of the north-bound river of which the Indians had told me, and to follow the stream to its mouth, wherever that mouth might be. Since we were likely to have a rigorous trip through unknown waters I wanted reliable and experienced men to handle the canoe. I turned naturally to the Iroquois Reserve at Caughnawaga. The Indians living beside Lachine Rapids have always been experts in whitewater. I was fortunate in engaging Pierre, Louis and Michel French. Louis had been one of the Canadian voyageurs on Lord Wolseley's expedition up the Nile. Pierre had run the Lachine Rapids in a canoe on a Christmas Day, merely for fun, so he had no weakness of nerves, and Michel was fully as strong, agile and resolute as his brothers.

Next came the hiring of three bearers. For these he turned his attention to the métis of western Canada amongst whom he would find experts in portaging and in northern travel. He found what he was looking for in John Flett, Jim Corrigal and François Maurice. Flett was from Prince Albert and was already known to J. B. Tyrrell. The other two were from Ile a la Crosse, "strong and ready for anything." Tyrrell (a hard judge of men) rated these six who would cross the Barren Lands with him and his brother facing death and mutilation "Grade AA." They were the right men for the job each with the assurance of competence. "I don't say they were saints," Tyrrell wrote years later, "but they knew the meaning of team-work." In the inhospitable Arctic wastes, team-work is not a Boy Scout ideal to be inculcated at leisure in the hope of building character. It is of the essence of survival. Tyrrell knew that in the months ahead the old adage of the chain being as strong as its weakest link would apply – and eight lives would hang suspended from that chain.

Setting out from Edmonton with his men, Tyrrell was the perfect image of the Arctic explorer. At thirty-four years old he was at the very peak of his manhood. He stood six feet tall and weighed a solid 190 pounds. His massive hands were ideally suited for wrestling with nature. Even at the end of a Canadian winter his face still wore the weather-beaten tan of years spent in the outdoors. Nordic blue eyes complemented his fair hair and beard to suggest a Viking war-lord among his Irish ancestors. Only the incongruous thick glasses he had to wear belied him as the perfect physical specimen.

While their supplies and equipment headed overland by buckboard and wagon from Edmonton to Athabasca Landing to be shipped on the Hudson's Bay Company steamer *Grahame* to Fort Chippewyan, the group went ahead by canoe toning their muscles for the long months of paddling that lay ahead. When the steamer caught up with them their baggage was loaded into the three canoes "almost to the gunwales" and the eight men, the brothers Tyrrell, the three Iroquois and the three westerners, set off for the unknown. But they were not alone. A ninth member more or less accompanied the party as they set out from Fort Chippewyan. He was Moberly, a Chippewyan Indian "guide." Tyrrell had written ahead to Dr. McKay, the local Hudson's Bay Company officer, asking him to arrange for the best guide in the country to lead the party as far into the unknown land as possible. Moberly was the result and he agreed to take them by the best route from Lake Athabasca to Black Lake and then north for about one hundred miles over the height of land that separated the two water systems. Unfortunately Moberly didn't quite live up to their expectations. Had he accompanied them into the Barren Lands where team-work was the prerequisite of survival, the results could have been disastrous. As it was they were more comic.

Before the party even set out Moberly was in conflict with the Tyrrell brothers. Riding at anchor at Fort Chippewyan was the sailboat which J. B. had used during part of the previous year's exploration of Lake Athabasca. Moberly, whose home was at the east end of the lake where the group was heading, wanted Tyrrell to take the sailboat so that he, Moberly, could transport his own belongings and his wife and two daughters to his log cabin home. Tyrrell refused and in response to Moberly's threat to abandon the party, told the guide the choice was his since his services were not really necessary. At this Moberly backed off and contented himself with bringing his wife and daughters in his own bark canoe and collecting a month's wages in advance.

When they set out from Fort Chippewyan on the morning of a midsummer's day, Moberly's pestering tactics shrank to insignificance. Nothing could mar the perfection of that day for Joe Tyrrell. Before him lay everything his romantic heart could ever hope for. Out there lay sights that no "civilized" men had ever seen. The land and its rocks would contain clues to intrigue his enquiring mind for decades. The unknown river with its unknown destination promised to satisfy his longing for adventure. Even the weather conspired to make his spirit soar. It was, in James's words, so "beautifully calm and fair" that "all nature seemed to be smiling." Soon, however, romance was forced to give way to the hard realities of northern exploration. First, the weather changed and "the smile became a frown." A strong easterly wind sprang up bringing with it mist and fog, rain and rough waters. The combination of the bad weather and strong headwinds slowed the party's progress to the extent that on one day they were totally confined to their camp. In all it took them ten days to travel 210 miles. A bad beginning for the 3,000 mile expedition they were embarked upon.

Nor was the travel made any easier by their "guide." Whether, if Moberly had had his way about taking the sailboat, he would have proved an adequate guide is a moot point. As it was, he consistently lagged behind by several miles, leaving the party to fend for itself and find its own campsites. Moberly and his family travelled at a more leisurely pace arriving each night after the camp had been pitched but before dinner was served.

At last, on June 30, the weather broke. Wind and lake were calm once more and for a whole day the sun shone bright and warm. When they stopped at noon the party indulged in the luxury of one of the few baths they were to have in the whole seven months of their journey. Refreshed, they set about preparing lunch and were joined, on schedule, by Moberly just as they were ready to eat. By this time, Moberly had picked up an aged companion to help him with the exertions of paddling the canoe. Beauvier, according to James Tyrrell, was not much more energetic than Moberly, using his paddle like a spoon in the water, with one arm all the time resting on the side of the canoe for support.

That night, by the campfire, Tyrrell had it out with Moberly and Beauvier. If they were going to continue with the expedition they would have to go ahead and lead the way. In addition, they were told, when they left Lake Athabasca behind, they would be expected to help with the portaging. James wrote afterwards, "This arrangement was accepted as being satisfactory to them." The next morning, July 1, the party set off on the last lap of their journey on Athabasca. Moberly and Beauvier, true to their word, took the lead. James, in a gesture of patriotic fervour appropriate to the day, flew a small Union Jack from the bow of his canoe. All went well until late in the morning when the party reached a cluster of cabins at the east end of the lake. Moberly and Beauvier immediately went ashore. Moberly was home and from here refused to go any further unless the bacon, flour, tea and tobacco was divided on the spot. Tyrrell refused and the guide stayed home.

Writing about it years later J. B. Tyrrell put it charitably – "he resigned." James was less generous.

> From the first his quibbling unreliable manner, characteristic of the tribe to which he belonged, had been most unsatisfactory, and now having received board for himself and his family in journeying homeward, besides a month's pay in advance, he had resolved to desert us. There was no use in trying to force him to continue with us against his inclinations, nor could we gain anything by punishing him for his deception, though punishment he richly deserved.

The contrast in the attitude of the two brothers is marked. Undoubtedly Moberly, especially after his failure to get agreement to transport his belongings from Fort Chippewyan to his home, was a "most unsatisfactory" companion and certainly not an asset to any group whose survival would depend on team-work. Indeed, even at this early stage in the endeavour, he was a liability. For one thing he was consuming precious food supplies. For another there was his role at the evening campfire. The good story-teller is a boon in any camp. As night falls and the evening meal is finished the man who can entertain in the flickering firelight can command the rapt attention of his companions. Moberly had that ability. Unfortunately his stories were all of the dangers and difficulties that lay ahead. Had Moberly sped their travel by guiding them from one good campsite to another and then led them to the least difficult portages and hastened the transport of gear over these portages, his consumption of food and tales of doom could have been accepted as a reasonable price to pay. But given Moberly's failure as a guide and helper, his other characteristics made him a distinct liability. Supplies were scarce and would be scarcer, and the unknown was fearful enough without being embellished by Moberly's imagination. Even so, for J. B. Tyrrell that was it. Moberly was an unsatisfactory companion, an unsavoury character, whose presence they could do without. It was the judgment of one man on another.

For James it was a different story. Typical of the attitude of his time Moberly's actions were expanded to be characteristic of all Chippewyans. It mattered not to him that in the very next paragraph of his account of the trip, right after he writes off the whole tribe, he describes a party of four Chippewyans who "willingly assisted" them on a portage and offered to return the next day to help again. But that did nothing to soften his judgment. Nor does he consider that perhaps he and his brother had mishandled the relationship with Moberly. Yet that was probably Moberly's point of view. It is borne out by the fact that the four Indians who helped them on their first portage did not return as they had offered. In the meantime, they had descended the river to Moberly's encampment. It is probable that his account of his experience with the expedition (and perhaps also of James's opinion of Chippewyans in general) decided them against returning. To James that was undoubtedly just another proof of the "characteristic" unreliability of their people.

Shortly after the Tyrrells and their six canoemen bade farewell to Moberly on July 1, they also bade farewell to Lake Athabasca. The journey along the lake had been hard going because of the weight of their relatively undiminished supplies and the roughness of the weather. Even so, as long as they remained on the lake they were still within the embrace of their own society. At Fond du Lac they took advantage of their last opportunity to leave letters that might find their way to the outside. These letters were the last that was heard from the party for six months. Leaving Lake Athabasca they also left behind the last vestiges of their civilization. The country to the north of Athabasca is not conducive to habitation. It is composed almost as much of water as it is of land. Myriad lakes and streams weave an intricate lace cover for the flat table of land.

Without benefit of guide, Tyrrell would lead his party through this maze in search of an easy way to cross from one water system into another. Only the first part of their route was familiar to him. From the eastern extremity of Athabasca they would ascend the Stone River, portaging past the Stony Rapids and the Elizabeth Falls to Black Lake. After that all they had was the crude map he had acquired the year before to help them identify the height of land that was the watershed between the Dubawnt system and the rivers draining into the Arctic.

In the days that lay ahead they would be carrying the canoes and their contents more often than the canoes would be carrying them. Fortunately on their first portage they had the help of four of Moberly's tribesmen whom they met on the Stone River. Twelve pairs of hands soon had the work done and at day's end, having mastered their first portage and continued upstream, they pitched camp at the foot of the "wild and beautiful cataract" that is

Woodcock Rapids. The next day, instead of immediately beginning the portage around the rapids, Tyrrell called a halt to their labours. It was Sunday and after a week of paddling a day of rest was in order. Sabbath observance was a principle of late Victorian society and Tyrrell was not about to lay it aside lightly. Later, when their expedition became a race against time and the onset of winter began to overtake them, all days would be treated alike and only raging storms would keep them from their travels. There was, however, also another principle involved at this early stage – a principle of all wilderness travel in those days. At the outset, when the men could quit and find their own way home they were treated well. Later when the point of no return had been passed and the survival of each depended on the survival of all, such niceties were put aside. The stop at the foot of Woodcock Rapids served this purpose well. Not only were they able to soak up the sylvan beauty of their surroundings but the group were also able to handsomely replenish their larder from the rich store of the river. In short order they took two magnificent salmon trout, each over three feet in length, and an abundance of whitefish weighing from six to ten pounds. For one day at least the drain on their supplies was halted and their diet received a welcome variation.

But if their resting place was attractive to the eye and the stomach, it also had its drawbacks. From old Moberly and others they had learned of the Indian legend which maintained that here, between Athabasca and Black Lakes, was the exact spot where the Great Spirit had first created the blackfly. At camp that Sunday and during the portages of the day before and the next day, the group discovered anew that this legend, like most mythology, was solidly based on fact. As they revelled in the beauty of their surroundings and replenished their supplies from the water they, at the same time, offered themselves as human sacrifices to the swarms of blackflies which, with the help of almost as many mosquitoes, sought to end the expedition by devouring the travellers. Burning green fuel to create dense clouds of smoke and covering their bodies with tar oil did nothing to deter the attacking insects; indeed as James noted "the flies only appeared to revel in it."

Nonetheless the day of rest served them well. It provided a much needed respite after a full week of paddling and before a heavy week of portaging. In all, during the six days that followed the party was to portage a total of eight miles around waterfalls and rapids and between bodies of water. Each portage had to be crossed and recrossed as many as eight times as the baggage and canoes were carried to the next portion of navigable water. James Tyrrell estimated that in the course of the following week each man walked for a total of 104 miles. Early Monday morning, the party began the task of carrying their canoes and gear around the "wild and beautiful cataract." This, the first portage that they were to tackle without outside help, was one of the worst of the whole trip. Two and a quarter miles long it included climbing a 200 foot high rocky hill and wading knee-deep through muskeg as swarms of blackflies bit pieces from their bodies and mosquitoes drank freely of their blood. All day long the men toiled at the task. As night fell they tumbled back into camp, their feet blistered and their bones aching only to discover that although they had made the round trip six times, each time laden with a hundred pounds of supplies and equipment, they had moved only about three-quarters of their load.

On the next morning, besieged once again by blackfly and mosquito, two more back-breaking trips up the long portage had to be made to finish the task. It was noon before the job was done, the canoes reloaded and the party pushed off from the shore of Middle Lake, in search of the river's entrance. The opening was not hard to find. It was identified by the foaming entrance and the roar of tumbling waters. Another portage lay immediately ahead. The obstacle in their path included a set of waterfalls that saw the water tumble a total of eighty feet from top to bottom. The next day being his younger sister's birthday, Tyrrell named them the Elizabeth Falls in her honour, the first of the names that he would leave behind as an enduring mark of his journey.

The portage ahead of them was three and a half miles long though fortunately "more level and less rocky" than the previous one. More important, it took them to the shore of Black Lake and the furthest point of J. B.'s explorations of the previous summer. From here they would search the shoreline for the beginning of the hunting route of which the Chippewyans had spoken. Then, armed with only the barest description for the first hundred miles, they would seek out the mighty river that would carry them – where? Either into the Arctic and possible death or into Hudson Bay and possible survival.

It was here between Black Lake and the Dubawnt River that Moberly would have proven his worth. Instead, the Tyrrells found their route alone – and then more portages. Six days of almost constant portaging except when crossing Black Lake, another day of rest, two more days of portaging between six small lakes and then, on July 11, Wolverine or Chipman Lake only three miles wide by six miles long but so indented by deep bays that its shore-line amounts to almost fifty miles. The Tyrrells, both of whom had a fine eye for the aesthetic in nature, were struck by the beauty of that small northern lake, its surface "studded with islands" and its banks "heavily and beautifully wooded" with spruce and birch. They were also struck by the difficulty of finding their way out. They knew that the exit from the lake would be by a large river flowing out of the north. Then, paddling against the stream, they would come to Birch Lake. From there another river would take them to what the Indians called "Big Lake" and then, across a height of land to yet another lake, the Dubawnt River and the Barren Lands.

For two days they paddled in and out of the deep bays of Chipman Lake searching for an exit. The multitude of islands blending with the mainland only made their search more difficult as they scoured the deepest recesses of the convoluted shoreline without success. Then, near the end of the second day, soaked by a cold drizzling rain whose one advantage was in reducing the number of mosquitoes and blackflies, they found their river, its current almost imperceptible, hidden by islands. The lack of current on the river had made it difficult to find but, once found, it was a distinct advantage. By dark, the group were able to paddle upstream for about seven miles before pitching camp on the low lying, wet shoreline. The next day to Birch Lake and, after another major portage, to "Big" Lake.

From here on J. B. and his party were in virgin territory. Their path can be traced across a map of the Barren Lands by the names he left behind. Big Lake became Selwyn Lake after the director of the Survey. Along the way came Carey Lake after his fiancée's father, Markham Lake after Admiral Markham, Marjorie Lake after the daughter of Lord Aberdeen, Aberdeen Lake after the Governor-General himself, and dozens more. Only Wholdaia Lake, across the height of land from Selwyn, did not keep the name that Tyrrell bestowed upon it. He named it Daly Lake after the Minister of the Interior, but he also recognized it as "Samuel Hearne's Wholdaia Lake," and that earlier more historic name was later re-adopted.

July 16 was another Sunday and, blissfully, another day of deserved rest, this time on the shores of Selwyn Lake. If God had made all the majesty of this northern wilderness, with its rugged beauty, inhospitable climate and myriad blackflies in six days and rested, then six days of exploring it, of searching out its hidden highways, of paddling its streams and portaging the rapids, were also enough to warrant a day of rest. Fortunately the day was summery and part of it was used up bathing in the lake. As James put it, "This pleasure was highly prized. After one has been subjected to the continual lacerations and stings of flies and mosquitos, and the liberal application of tar oil for a week or two, a bath is not a luxury, but a necessity."

The day of rest passed; Monday saw the travellers resume the search for the way out of Selwyn Lake and the path onward. Descending a river, there is no difficulty in finding a lake. You follow the stream and there it is. Finding a river exit from a lake without a map is another thing. From a hundred yards out on the water, its mouth may be indistinguishable from a bay. If it has a reasonably strong current it can be detected by floating some device in the water. But, as the Tyrrells found on Chipman Lake, if the river has little current there is no choice but to trace every indentation in the shoreline until the exit is found. Even that, however, was a simple task compared with the search for an exit from Selwyn Lake. Here they were looking, not for a waterway, but for a trail leading off from the shore that would carry them overland onto a completely different water system.

All day long they searched the margin of the lake without success. Then late in the day they spotted a group of Indians camped on one of the islands. To everyone's surprise it was the same group that had assisted them on their first portage after they left Lake Athabasca. As suspected, Moberly's tales of his treatment had decided them against returning for more work and instead, in going back to "Big" Lake, they had skirted past the explorers. Their reappearance could not have been more timely. With a little persuasion they agreed to show the explorers the trail over the height of land that separated Selwyn from Wholdaia Lake, and also to assist with the portage.

The trail was near at hand, but the day was well worn and camp was set. Once more, however, around the campfire the party was treated to stories of the dangers that lay ahead. The waters that roared through great impassable canyons would probably sweep them to their death and if, by some miracle they got through them safely, they would undoubtedly be eaten alive by cannibalistic Eskimos. It took considerable effort from the Tyrrell brothers to calm the men down. Only François "who cared for nothing" was undisturbed by the tales. But James saved the day by reminding the others what "miserable liars" these Indians were and holding up Moberly as a "sample of their tribe."

21

The following morning they arrived at the foot of the trail that would lead them onto the waterway that crossed the Barren Lands. The portage was only a mile and a quarter in length but it carried them across a major continental watershed or, as James put it, "a summit of the continent." James, ever the patriot, decided that some fitting memento of their crossing should be left behind. Armed with flag and hatchet he climbed a tall tamarack tree and nailed the flag to the top and then on the way down chopped off the branches to create an instant flagpole.

Once on Wholdaia Lake the nature of the trip changed. In one sense it became easier; from here on it would be downhill all the way. Until now they had been travelling upstream, portaging from one body of water to the next. Now they were heading downstream on a continuous water route, with portages around rapids, to Hudson Bay. Although travelling with the current had distinct advantages, in every other sense the difficulties were just beginning. For one thing they were constantly heading farther north into ever more inhospitable weather. With each passing day they were becoming more dependent on finding food as their supplies dwindled and at the same time the possibility of turning back diminished until, finally, it was no longer an option. For Tyrrell the pressures constantly increased. In the beginning it was enough that he was a competent and experienced explorer, well-versed in the ways of the wild. With each day that they put between themselves and Wholdaia Lake he had to find within himself new qualities of leadership that he had never before tested. The men had to be kept paddling when their bellies were empty and their destiny seemed black. Fears that they would end up frozen in the Arctic ice-pack had to be allayed. Spirits that flagged into despondency had to be raised again to push on yet another mile when it seemed hopeless to move another yard. In an account of their progress from Wholdaia Lake to Hudson Bay which he wrote himself, Tyrrell gives little hint of these difficulties.

> Here [on Wholdaia Lake] the forest was thin and intermittent and poplar was seen for the last time on our northward way. The outlet of the lake which we found after a good deal of searching is the Telzoa [Dubawnt] River, a wide, shallow stream which either rushed down heavy rapids or widened into lakes thickly studded with islands. In these lakes it was

necessary to follow the crooked, winding shore in order to find the outlet, while it was always essential to land at the head of a rapid in order to decide on the proper channel down which to run the canoes, or to determine where to make the portage.

Five weeks had now passed since leaving Fort Chippewayan [sic], and our provisions were disappearing rapidly, for we had seen no game. But on the morning of July 29th while paddling across a small lake we saw moving objects on the farther shore. Drawing nearer we made out a great herd of caribou, not to be reckoned in hundreds but in scores of thousands. The coast was a forest of antlers. Having shot a number of bucks we paused for three days while the meat was being dried and baled for easy transport, and then continued down the river freed of one anxiety; the possibility of our starving to death in the wilderness.

The river emptied into a great lake almost completely covered with ice – in midsummer! But close to shore was a lane of open water which we were able to follow for 117 miles. It took us two weeks, half of which we lay in camps, hindered by heavy storms of icy rain, to reach the outlet of this lake which roughly is about the size of Georgian Bay. I marked with growing interest from day to day the similarity of the rocky shores to the copper-bearing series of rocks to the north of Lake Superior, and I recognized from the latitude and longitude observations that this must be the Lake Dubawnt which Samuel Hearne visited while on his way to the Coppermine River in 1771-1773. The name is a corruption of the Indian word for a watery shore, *Tobot*.

The lake discharges into a river of the same name which Hearne or anyone else had never followed. It flows swiftly through a narrow gorge two-and-a-half miles long, too dangerous for canoes; then onward expanding from time to time into lakes, or narrowing to minor or major rapids. In quiet water floating ice was often jammed against the shore by the wind, and short portages were frequently necessary.

There was no wood; even the scrub willows at last we left behind and the reindeer moss was invariably wet. The almost invisible flame of a spirit-lamp which cooked our evening meals was a poor substitute for a rousing camp-fire, especially when we had been paddling against a head wind and had been slashed all day with rain or wet snow.

On the evening of August 19th we saw a solitary Eskimo

deerskin tent above the river bank. Soon we saw people running about in alarm for were we not coming from the land of the Chippewayans, the hereditary enemies of the Eskimos? The call *Chimo* (Peace) and a sentence that we were white men and glad to see the Eskimos eased their fears. A tall, fine-looking man, still trembling with nervousness, came out to meet us. A present of a plug of tobacco restored his cheerfulness and he sent his two wives and six children into the tent for a pipe. When the pipe had gone the round and some trifling presents had been given to all the members of this dual family we obtained a rude sketch of the course of the river, which, we were told, led to the sea on the east.

At two other encampments on the lower river we were hospitably received, then on September 2nd we came to a broad body of water which I recognized as Baker Lake; in the outflow of this lake leading to Chesterfield Inlet we met the salt tide. Down this great fjord enclosed in high, rocky coasts we continued our survey until the open Bay was before us.

J. B.'s account makes it all sound so simple in the retelling that it is hard to imagine how greatly the road had been fraught with danger and challenge. Always, until near the end, there was the nagging doubt about where the waterway would lead them. In general their course lay north by northeast which held out some prospect, though no certainty, that they would emerge into Hudson Bay. But on August 23, leaving Marjorie Lake, the river carried them north and west beyond the latitude of Baker Lake and Chesterfield Inlet. For three days they travelled on with growing fear that they were in fact on a tributary of the Back River which would empty them into the Arctic Ocean where death would be certain. Only where the waters of the Dubawnt meet those of the Thelon River as it flows out of Beverly Lake did their prospects brighten. There, where the two great northern rivers merge before pouring their combined waters into Aberdeen Lake, the party found loads of driftwood that the new river had brought with it from the west. From this evidence they conjectured that the river had its roots somewhere behind the treeline, probably in the vicinity of Great Slave Lake. They also deduced that, having carried the wood to this far corner of the Barren Lands, there had been few rapids and lakes along its course. They still did not know where they were nor could they be certain where they were headed. But at least they knew that they had not met the Back River – and the chances of their doing so now had been diminished. On that night, August 25, 1893, the explorers cared less about the source of the Thelon than about its harvest. For the first time in weeks they were able to replace their spirit-lamp with a blazing campfire and to luxuriate in its warmth.

The next day brought yet further comfort to them. When they set out the river still carried them toward the Arctic. The driftwood on the Thelon had offered them hope that they would emerge into Hudson Bay. Soon that hope would be confirmed. Five miles downstream the river swung sharply to the right, carrying them to the east. Then, swinging to the right again, it carried them into the "magnificent body of water" which J. B. named Aberdeen Lake after the Governor-General. Mixed with the relief from the anxiety which they had experienced, the beauty of the scene was overwhelming. James Tyrrell eloquently described it,

It was a lovely calm evening when the track of our canoes first rippled the waters of this lake, and as we landed at a bluff point on the north shore and from it gazed to the eastward over the solitary but beautiful scene, a feeling of awe crept over us. We were undoubtedly the first white men who had ever viewed it, and in the knowledge of the fact there was inspiration.

The fear which had gripped them that they were being carried into the Arctic Ocean had not been their only problem. It was not even their biggest problem. Much more important was the question of food. J. B. Tyrrell in his account of the journey mentions the great herd of caribou that they came upon on the shore of Carey Lake on July 29. In fact by that time supplies had become so low that he was considering the possibility of turning back. To retrace their steps at that point would have been a miserable task; despondent, hungry men do not paddle well. For Joe Tyrrell himself the admission of failure would have been so alien to his personality he would probably have sunk into a deep depression. The alternative, however, was even less appealing. Without a new supply of food he and his men would surely die of starvation, their strength failing until they could paddle no more and the will to live slowly dissipating. Faced with that prospect he would have no choice but to turn back. It was while he contemplated how long he could delay that decision that they spotted the caribou.

The party spread out and quickly replenished their larder with at least eighteen head of caribou. So huge were the herds that even the noisy carnage of the hunters, far from causing a stampede, did little more than send a ripple through them. And during the next four days while the meat was being dried and packed (and eaten fresh) J. B. and James toured the surrounding country and moved through the massive herds photographing them for posterity. Sitting on a rock they looked out over a sea of animals that stretched as far as the eye could see. In the meantime the caribou calves, equally as inquisitive, wandered through the camp tripping over guy ropes, upsetting equipment and generally impeding the work at hand.

Their food supply secure for the time being, the party journeyed on still facing the problems of rapids and wintry storms. On one occasion, shooting the rapids almost led to disaster. Pierre French, the most expert of the canoemen, was in the lead as usual. From the banks he had surveyed the white water and chosen his route. In midstream the water pelted between two huge rocks through an opening hardly wider than the canoe. Louis returned to the lead canoe, paddled it to midstream and pointed it straight for the tiny opening. While the others held their breath the first canoe shot through the seething hole. James's canoe came second. The men in it were less fortunate. As the others on the bank watched, the canoe got caught in an eddy just before it reached the gap. By a stroke of luck the furious water turned the craft a full 180 degrees before it reached the rocks which would have smashed it into match wood. As it was they got through safely, though backwards. Having witnessed this near disaster, the men in the third canoe were a little more cautious and decided to stay closer to shore. But Pierre French was not only a daring canoeist, he was also a wise one. Dangerous as his chosen route had been, it had the advantage of being a clear path. Not so the shore waters. Halfway through the third canoe was dashed against a big flat rock and capsized as the men dived into the frothing water. Desperately they struggled and only barely managed to grab hold of the canoe until the others could come to their rescue. No one was hurt and the damage to the canoe was minor; still it delayed their travel until repairs could be made and served as a chilling reminder of the danger they faced.

On another occasion the threat to their safety came in the form of a pack of wolves. They had just landed after a day's paddling when the onslaught began. As they hauled the canoes ashore the pack attacked. They were grey wolves, large and fierce, with a daring leader that James described as "A great gaunt, hungry-looking brute." The men were frozen into inaction, their hands glued to the gunwales of the canoes as the howling beasts charged

26

Looking over a fragment of the caribou herd towards Carey Lake. (GSC)

Drying the caribou meat for the next stage of the journey. (PAC)

27

towards them. Only Joe Tyrrell moved. With one motion he reached into the canoe suspended between land and water, seized his rifle and turned firing as he dropped to his knees. There was only time for one shot and one shot was all he needed. The great grey leader of the pack stopped in mid stride as the bullet ripped through him from end to end. As he hit the ground the others turned tail and fled. Only their howls would disturb the travellers for the rest of that night. It had been no lucky shot. From earliest childhood Tyrrell had been used to the feel of a gun. Despite his poor eyesight he had persevered until his aim was deadly accurate. In the west during his other expeditions and later in the rough mining towns of the Klondike and northern Ontario he was known to ward off trouble by putting on a display of his marksmanship. Here in the Barrens he had turned his skill to more deadly purpose and in doing so saved the lives of his seven companions.

Some of the weather they endured was only slightly less welcome than the pack of grey wolves. In his account of the journey Joe Tyrrell briefly described the ice conditions of Lake Dubawnt. He did not mention the storm which began on August 6 and confined them to camp for four days. On the first night the winds reached gale force, and the rain flooded into their tents soaking everything. For three days they lay soaked in their quarters as the storm continued unabated. Then on the fourth day (August 10) the temperature dropped below freezing and the rain turned to snow. Through all of this they were without wood for fire. Their only warmth was that generated by their own bodies as they used up their replenished food stock at an alarming rate. Worst of all each day that passed added to the growing doubt that they could make their way out of this northern wilderness before winter returned to stay.

Despite the difficulties, they had continued, journeying over 800 miles across unexplored territory until finally they reached Chesterfield Inlet and the salt water of Hudson Bay. Recognizing the inlet from accounts he had read of earlier sea going explorers, Tyrrell was elated. They had emerged on Hudson Bay after all. Recalling his joy, Tyrrell wrote "It seemed to us that our work was done; nothing remained but to paddle down the coast of Hudson Bay to Fort Churchill and then to strike for Lake Winnipeg through a land of well-marked trails."

The optimism was an understandable reaction. It arose from a keen sense of accomplishment. Every man of them was aware of the magnitude of the feat they had accomplished. The last great void on the North American continent had been pierced. Their optimism was nevertheless ill-founded, though that did not become apparent for several days. From Chesterfield Inlet to Fort Churchill was just something over 400 miles. On September 13 they left the mouth of the Inlet and struck out along the shore. In three days they travelled a hundred miles, successfully cutting across the mouth of Rankin Inlet. If they could keep that rate of travel they could expect to be in Churchill by September 26 or 27. But they could not keep up the pace. Instead, during the next twenty days, they managed to travel only 120 miles as the weather once again turned against them. On the night of September 15 a series of wild northern storms blew in on them. They were camped on a sand-bar in the middle of Corbett Inlet when the first storm broke. They were trapped. As the snow whirled and the sea raged around them, all they could do was huddle together for warmth. They could not set out for shore. The frail cedar canoes would be no match for the tossing waves. Nor could they stay where they were for any length of time. To do so would be to court disaster of another sort for the sandy island was devoid of fresh water for drinking.

As Tyrrell pondered on their predicament the elation he had felt on reaching Chesterfield Inlet vanished. He was faced now with a problem he had not foreseen. No longer did their route take them along relatively protected inland waterways. Now their frail craft had to endure the battering of an open sea, one whose shallow waters were easily churned into a seething froth. For a day and a half, as the storm continued unabated he had no choice but to sit it out. Then on the second afternoon as it subsided he had to make the awful decision of whether to order his men out onto the still heaving waters or wait in the hope that they would soon be calm. Had he been sure the storm was ending he could have waited until the seas were quiet. But this might be no more than a lull before the gale resumed with renewed violence.

Faced with that prospect he decided to shove out for shore. It was a wise choice. Soon the storm returned with a new energy that would have pinned them down for two more days. Unfortunately the onset did not wait until they had reached the shore. When they were about halfway between the sand bar and safety, in the middle of the Inlet, the wind changed direction and gathered force. Again the sea was whipped into foam. The canoes were tossed unmercifully as the men battled to keep their bows into the waves while constantly baling out the water that half filled their flimsy cedar craft. At length their sheer determination and endurance paid off and they brought the shore within their grasp – only to discover that it was lined with rocks against which the waves would dash them if they approached too close. Desperately they struggled to keep their distance as they moved along the coast searching for a break in the rocks large enough to get through. Once more the fates intervened in their favour. Up ahead a large rock jutted out further than the others. To a man they bent over the paddles and exerted every ounce of energy to reach the natural breakwater. With perfect timing they seized the opportunity and thrust their three canoes into the miniature harbour. With only seconds available they all jumped into the shoulder-deep cold water to drag the canoes ashore.

For two more days the storm continued, confining them to land. They could not, however, stay in camp. It was six weeks since they had crammed their canoes with as much caribou meat as they could get in. In six weeks eight men consume a lot of food. Once more their supply was almost exhausted. During the two days that they could not push out into the Bay they sought to replenish it with little success. As the storm raged they hunted but all they managed was a small duck and two gulls among the eight of them – not enough for a single full meal. When they left Chesterfield Inlet, J. B. had reckoned that with careful rationing he could keep the men fed for five or six days. For the remainder of what he thought would be a two-week journey he knew they could survive with nothing to eat if they had to. Now the situation had changed. Six days after they had left the mouth of Chesterfield Inlet they were still trapped on the shore at Corbett Inlet – about a quarter way to Fort Churchill – with no sign to indicate that the raging storm would soon end. The very real prospect of death by starvation now loomed before them.

On the twentieth the wind fell and for two days, their food supply reduced to a small amount of dried caribou meat which they chewed as they paddled, they travelled on as fast as they could. Then the storms struck again. Gale-force winds and snow bound them to the shore where once more they scavenged for food, this time having a bit more success with several rabbits, marmots and birds.

For days on end this pattern continued. Travelling when they could, hunting for food and lying stranded on the shore while the storms raged. On one occasion they spotted some deer on the shore and beached the canoes while they tried to bag them. The "vast and dreary plain" of the landscape offered the hunters no cover, however, and they had to try shooting from over 400 yards. At that distance their shotguns were useless, and Tyrrell's rifle, the only one they had, was of such low velocity that the wind veered the bullet from its course. Even Joe's expert marksmanship was not enough. Empty handed they returned to the canoes only to discover that in the meantime the tide had gone out and the waters of the Bay were barely visible on the horizon.

With no choice but to await the return of the tide, the search for food was renewed. Tyrrell gave Louis French the rifle and, with his brother Pierre he set off in pursuit of the deer that had fled. After searching for a couple of hours, the two Iroquois decided to split up. The remainder of Pierre's search was as futile as the first part. Louis, however, had more success, though he never did catch sight of the deer. Instead he met a polar bear. Completely disguised by his white coat, the huge animal suddenly reared out of the snow about fifty yards ahead of the hunter. As the animal charged towards him the Indian fired. The bullet found its mark and brought the white giant to its knees. Before he could get off another shot the bear was on its feet and after him. Running for his life Louis took to the shore ice hoping that the even surface would give him an advantage over the lumbering bear. Instead the bear had the advantage. The fur on its feet gave it a sure grip on the smooth ice. With the gap between them rapidly closing Louis turned and fired at short range. Again the bullet hit home and the animal was brought to the ground. While the bear roared and staggered to its feet the man clambered back onto the shore. As he did the reeling animal charged again. With only a few feet remaining between them this would be the last encounter. As the enraged bear loomed over him, its white coat stained bright red by the blood pouring from its wounds, the hunter got off one last shot. The white giant reared under the impact of the bullet and fell dead at the hunter's feet.

On the side of Hudson Bay, as winter set in, the battle between Louis French and the polar bear had been more than the conclusion of a successful hunt. Rather it was a test of which animal, the bear or the human, was best fitted to survive. Had they not met, both man and beast faced the prospect of starving to death. Having met, they joined battle, the victor to continue life by consuming the flesh of the vanquished. In the contest that had ensued, nature was reduced to its starkest reality. Having won the battle Louis French, and his compatriots, would eat and live.

When he had regained his breath Louis next had to consider

the task of getting the animal back to camp, some six miles away. Knowing that he could not handle it alone he contented himself with cutting off one of its paws as a gruesome token of the meal that lay ahead and started back to camp. The sight of the hunter waving his goary trophy in the air as he approached them sent the spirits soaring. With hardly a pause for Louis to catch his breath they were off to feast on the fallen bear. Once they had tramped the six miles to the scene of the battle they set to work with the zeal that only half starved men can muster. While some skinned the carcass, others combed the surrounding hills for moss to start a fire. Even before the skinning was finished they were cooking the meat and eating it. Nothing could have tasted better. As James Tyrrell put it, "Though the flesh of the polar bear is famed for its rankness, we would not have exchanged it at that time for its weight in silver."

In the course of the days that followed, stranded by yet another storm that blew non-stop for five days, the bear's flesh kept the group alive. It also came close to killing James Tyrrell. He, unfortunately, partook of that delicacy – polar bear liver – only to discover first-hand its highly toxic properties. As a result he was so violently ill that he felt close to death. Only by draining the last of the brandy that they had carried with them did he find relief. It is a mark of how ill he was that he even drank the brandy. According to J. B. up until this incident his brother had been a teetotaller who had never tasted liquor.

By the time the storm subsided, James had recovered. The waters of Hudson Bay, however, would not recover so quickly. Ice had set along the coastal waters of the enclosed sea. For two days they struggled on but only managed twelve or thirteen miles. It became clear to Tyrrell that if there was to be any hope of them reaching Fort Churchill he would have to abandon every non-essential for the sake of speed. On the highest convenient ground they cached two of the canoes and all but the instruments of survival. With everyone in one canoe they launched out on the heavy seas of the Bay. Within minutes they came close to swamping their tiny craft. After a hasty retreat for the recovery of another canoe, they set forth again this time with four men in each boat. The delay had cost them some valuable time but it was worth it. The men had been determined that they could all travel safely in one canoe and make better time. Despite his own misgivings, Tyrrell had agreed to the attempt being made. Once the experiment had been tried and had failed, the others were satisfied that two canoes were needed. Instead of being disgruntled the men set to the

Icebound camp on the flat shore of Hudson Bay. (PAC)

Eskimos on the edge of Baker Lake, September 2, 1893. (GSC)

33

paddles with all the strength they had left in them.

In writing about their experiences of the two weeks that followed James Tyrrell entitled the chapter *Life or Death?* He was not exaggerating. Snow covered everything. Ice was forming along the shore. And they were only halfway to Churchill. For ten days they struggled on against increasing odds that they would fail. On October 13 thinking they could go no farther, Tyrrell sent John Flett to try to reach Fort Churchill by land. Flett was in the best condition of any of the men and might have made it if the way had been clear. Unfortunately the Seal River lay across his path. Its flowing waters not yet frozen presented an unpassable barrier. When Flett returned to camp Tyrrell was left with no choice. The next day they launched their two canoes on the icy water once more. With aching limbs they forced their way south along the edge of the ever-increasing shore ice. Each stroke of the paddle racked their bodies with pain until at last, as night fell and they thought they could endure no more, they turned their flimsy craft toward the shore. But the shore was out of sight and between them and it was the heaving ice pack that they could not mount. They would have to await the returning tide!

From somewhere deep within each man they summoned up enough strength to keep going. At last the high tide flowed, only to ebb again leaving them still no closer to shore. Around the clock they battled on, the spray freezing their clothes into stiff boards. "The hours of that night," wrote James "were the longest I have ever experienced."

For seventeen hours of that vigil Joe Tyrrell sat in the icy water which inundated his canoe baling it out. His arms moved of their own accord. Dysentery had struck Louis French. His brother Michel had frozen his feet. Still they fought on amongst the icy floes in constant danger of being smashed on the rocks which pierced the surface of the water.

Finally, before they succumbed, but not much before, the returning tide carried them against solid ice as yet another storm set in. Those who could crawled out onto the ice and hauled their three stricken companions, J. B., Michel and Louis, after them. Then they dragged and carried the canoes and men to the shore where camp was pitched. One thing brought them cheer. They were back under the tree line. Enough wood was quickly gathered to build a roaring fire and on this, as they warmed themselves, they cooked a small seal that they had managed to kill the day before.

Some thirty miles (though they thought it was fifty) still

separated them from Fort Churchill. Tyrrell knew that to go back into the sea in the canoes, even if they could make it over the ice to the water line, would be certain death. Two of his men, and he himself, were totally unable to work anymore. The third French brother, their expert canoeist, Pierre, was on the verge of collapse from exhaustion. His own brother, James, was not in much better shape. The five of them would perish on the way. Only the three westerners James Corrigal, John Flett and François Maurice, were at all fit to travel. Once more he decided to try splitting the party in the hope that they could reach the trading post and come back with help. This time he would send two men – John Flett and Jim Corrigal. François Maurice would stay behind to keep the fire going in the camp which they had set in a spruce clump a couple of miles from shore. In between time he would take a gun and their dwindling supply of ammunition and try desperately to bring down a white-feathered ptarmigan with every shot.

It was October 16 when Flett and Corrigal struck out overland for Churchill. Everything depended on their success. Fortunately, life at the camp, for the first time in weeks was reasonably comfortable. Only the growing fear that their two compatriots would not reach Churchill gave cause for unease. For these men, men of action, that unease must have been great. Waiting can seem interminable. The minutes and hours of October 16 slipped past. The minutes and hours of October 17 passed even more slowly relieved only by Maurice's success in hunting. Another long night gave way to the morning of October 18 when dreams of "sweet currant cake" were replaced by the reality of "unseasoned boiled ptarmigan" for breakfast. The morning passed into afternoon. As lunch was prepared the first hour of the afternoon dragged its heavy minutes into the second. Then, as they ate, Corrigal and Flett appeared accompanied by a guide, four dog teams and drivers.

All afternoon and evening things were made ready for the journey. At sunrise they struck out for Fort Churchill and that evening, sometime after 5 o'clock, from the crest of a hill they caught sight of their destination. "It was not an imposing place," James wrote, "but even though consisting of only four or five frame buildings, the sight to us was one of deep satisfaction." It was not much of a fort but it would do.

CHAPTER 2

Walking home

A more unlikely group of conquering heroes than those who arrived at Fort Churchill on October 19, 1893, is hard to imagine. The dogsleds which carried them served not so much as state coaches as they did ambulances. The deprivations of the last month had sapped the energy of every member of the group to the point of exhaustion and collapse. Half a century later they might have been mistaken for refugees from a badly run concentration camp. When Joe Tyrrell left Ottawa the previous spring, his six foot frame had carried 190 pounds. He had the lean look of a man in excellent physical condition. Arriving in Churchill he weighed 140 pounds. His clothing hung in rags on his emaciated body. When he pulled back the hood of his parka, greasy hair formed a matted frame for his grimy sunken face. There was no strength left in his body but with his first glimpse of Fort Churchill he felt it begin to return. He could feel his pulse quicken. Their journey through the wilderness was over. Fort Churchill may not have been much of a fort but its cluster of houses and stores, and the tiny steeple on the church of the Anglican mission meant they were home.

Their last contact with western civilization had been on June 24 on Lake Athabasca when they met traders from Fond du Lac en route to Fort Chippewyan. Now, almost four months and more than 1,200 miles later, they were at another outpost of that civilization. In the meantime they had passed through the lands of two other cultures, that of the Chippewyans (one of the Athapascan Indian tribes) and that of the Eskimo. For centuries these two peoples had lived side by side yet isolated from one another. They had shared the caribou as a source of food and clothing but the Barrens had acted as a barrier into which both peoples might enter, but which neither would venture to cross. J. B. Tyrrell's expedition pin-points the separation of the Chippewyan and the Eskimo. He drew on the knowledge of the Indian to find his way into the Barren Lands. On the few occasions when he had come across Eskimo settlements he had drawn on their knowledge to find his way out.

If the ages had imposed their differences on the two peoples, the white man's advance into their territories was imposing even greater differences. While the Eskimo, occupying the most inhospitable part of the continent, was as yet relatively untouched in his lifestyle, the Chippewyan Indian, like so many of his brothers, had fallen under the sway of western man, much to his detriment. From the thousands who had once drawn their sustenance from the caribou herds of the northern plains, there remained only a few hundred by the time Tyrrell followed their route into the Barren Lands. A century before a plague (probably smallpox) had swept through the population leaving only a remnant to carry on. Of what remained of the tribe Moberly was perhaps, after all, typical – not in being a lying, unreliable scoundrel – but in having forsaken the traditional nomadic life of his people for the western-style log cabin on Lake Athabasca and in having exchanged the pursuit of the caribou for the slim pickings that might be had from the white man who had commandeered his ancient bailiwick.

Fort Churchill might represent the encroachment of the white man on both the Indian and Eskimo. Its population that winter was just over 300. Of these 49 were permanent residents. The remainder were transient natives – about 100 Chippewyans, 150 Eskimos and a few Cree. Here at Churchill the ancient separation of Chippewyan and Eskimo broke down. These were not the thoughts that occupied Joe Tyrrell's mind on October 19, 1893. The collection of dwellings that housed the oddly assorted population of Fort Churchill represented safety, shelter and nourishment for him and his men. He soon found out, however, that these benefits were not to be as warmly extended as he had expected.

Sitting on the west bank of the Churchill River opposite the site of the present-day town, the fort was the most northerly major post of the Hudson's Bay Company. The senior official at the post when Tyrrell arrived was a tall Scot named Matheson. A dour young man in his early twenties, Matheson was not exactly delighted to see the new-comers. Charged with supplying the townsfolk, he was facing a food shortage and the responsibility weighed heavy on him. Until the river froze and permitted him to journey to Stony River to pick up supplies which had been cached for him earlier in the season, things were going to be tight at the trading post. Eight more mouths to feed was hardly the answer to his prayers. Tyrrell, having just led his men through the Barrens and having faced the prospect of starvation, however, had little sympathy for the problems of the company clerk. He made a record of their reception in his notes:

> After washing we asked for a new clean set of underclothes but were told that there were none for sale in the store. We immediately set to work to attend to Michel's feet and soon had him washed and doctored with burnt alum, sulphate of zinc and sweet oil. It will be a long time before he is able to walk. We are all in rags and I tried to get a few clothes from the store, but even what was necessary to keep us warm was furnished with the utmost reluctance. I was unable to get food for the men, only a few rations of canned beef, pork four years old, flour and a little tea . . . I went out to see the men and told them to get out and shoot what ptarmigan they could, to help us on our way home. I asked Mr. Matheson to sell us some of his traps, but was refused them, unless the men would sell him any furs that they might catch at his price. I was told that everything we ate would be charged to our bill.

Even in the straitened circumstances of the fort's food shortage it is to be suspected that Matheson might have been more generous. James Tyrrell thought that he was trying to live up to the other meaning of the Company's initials. The letters H.B.C., James said, did not only stand for Hudson's Bay Company. Throughout the north they also stood for Here Before Christ. Fortunately for the travellers there was also at Fort Churchill a representative of the Anglican Church – an organization that came after Christ. The Reverend Joseph Lofthouse (later Bishop of Kenora) and his wife had built a mission house and church in the community a few years before. James had met them earlier, during his travels in Hudson Bay with the Gordon expedition. In fact he had been at the Lofthouse's wedding, which had been performed by the captain of the *Alert*, the federal government steamer whose patrols were part of the program of establishing Canadian sovereignty in the north.

Whatever Matheson lacked in hospitality, the Lofthouses made up. Joe noted, "At the mission Mr. Lofthouse had been able to grow turnips, lettuce, radishes, onions, carrots, cress, rhubarb, thyme, sage, parsley and brussels sprouts." These the couple were willing to share to ease the plight of the explorers. Unfortunately, the weeks of privation had left the hungry men unable to digest the rich fare of the missionary table. On more than one occasion, having eaten well, the contents of their stomachs were soon emptied again. Their diet of ptarmigan and water had, as Joe put it, left them suffering from "inflammation of the stomach and bowels."

It took a full week before their digestive systems began to accept a fuller diet without rebellion and their bodies were again strong enough to function without prolonged periods of rest. In the meantime the others in the party, although invited to the Lofthouse's for an evening were not such regular guests at their table. In response to Joe's instructions they continued to hunt ptarmigan to supplement the limited supply of flour and four year old pork that Joe had managed to wheedle out of the company store. Fortunately the game was plentiful and they managed to shoot over a hundred birds between them. It was more than they needed and Joe was able to give the Lofthouses some of them in return for their hospitality. It may not have been a very adequate response, but it was all he had to offer.

"Mr. Matheson" Tyrrell recognized "is very anxious to get us away." He might have added that he himself, was equally anxious to be away. The sight of the community of Fort Churchill huddled on the coast of Hudson Bay may have marked the completion of their exploration. It did not mark the end of their travels. Ottawa was still more than 2,000 miles away. Winnipeg lay some 900 miles to the south and Ottawa some 1,300 miles east of that. Getting from Winnipeg to Ottawa was no problem – the CPR would take care of that. Unfortunately there was no railway line from Churchill to Winnipeg. To get there, they would have to walk. Their departure, however, had to await the freezing over of the Churchill River. Tyrrell had managed to scrounge a dog team from Matheson to replace the canoes in carrying their gear. Until the river was frozen the dog team could not cross over to begin the first lap of their journey which would take them down the coast of the Bay and across the mouth of the Nelson River to York Factory on the mouth of the Hayes River.

It was not until November 6 that he was able to lead his men out of Churchill on the final stage of their long northern sojourn. In the meantime he prepared them for their new mode of travel. All summer long they had sat in canoes. Paddling had undoubtedly strengthened their arms. Unfortunately it was their legs that they would now have to rely on. As their strength recovered from the

39

hardships they had endured, Tyrrell set to work correcting the imbalance by taking them out on snow-shoeing expeditions. On several occasions they walked to Sloop's Cove where for over 150 years ships trading into the Bay had lain anchored. There with typical curiosity he examined the carvings which generations of sailors had scored into the smooth rock face of the cove. One among them caught Tyrrell's eye. It read simply "Sl. Hearne July ye 1 1767." Having crossed Samuel Hearne's path at Lakes Wholdaia and Dubawnt, that name touched the romantic streak in Tyrrell's personality. He readily identified with Hearne's sense of adventure and discovery. Years later, when affluence freed him from the worry of making a living, Tyrrell would serve Canadian history and the memory of Samuel Hearne well by editing the earlier explorer's journals for publication by the Champlain Society. It was a labour of love which had its roots in the simple act of having stood where Hearne stood and having run his fingers over the stark engraving in the frozen rock of this remote corner of Canada.

On another day, November 3, when their legs were stronger, he snow-shoed with his men to Eskimo Point, the narrow neck of land that juts out into Hudson Bay on the west side of the mouth of the Churchill River. There they wandered through the sturdy ruins of Fort Prince of Wales. Of all the "forts" built in pursuit of the fur trade, Prince of Wales was almost alone in deserving the title. Where the others at the most were surrounded by a wooden stockade, Prince of Wales had massive walls of granite, forty feet thick at the base. Without doubt one of the greatest stone forts ever built in North America, it has been variously labelled "an oddity" and "the preposterous fortress of the North." Sixteen years in the building, the massive structure that commanded the mouth of the Churchill was the scene of only one military action and on that occasion it was surrendered without a shot being fired.

Again the memory of Samuel Hearne lingered everywhere. It was here within these great walls of granite that Hearne had made his home between his searches for an overland route to the Coppermine and during much of his time as an employee of the Hudson's Bay Company. It was here also in August, 1782, during the American War of Independence that Hearne, had been captured and carried with all his furs to France. The surrender of Fort Prince of Wales is perhaps as inglorious as any in the annals of military history. Following the defeat of their fleet in the West

Part of Tyrrell's table of astronomical observations on the way north from Black Lake.

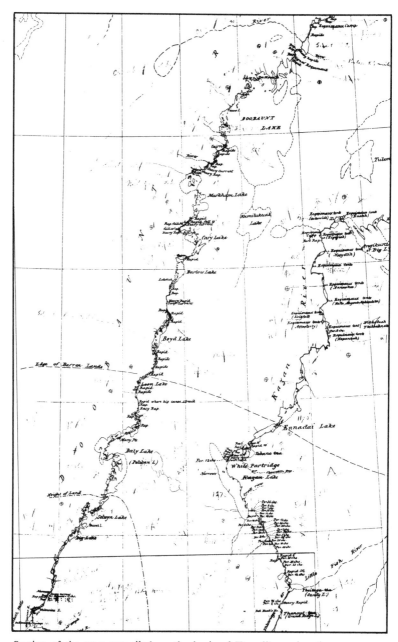

Section of the map compiled on the basis of Tyrrell's exploration.

Indies in April of that year by the British, the French had changed their strategy. Breaking up into small squadrons the remaining ships had set out to raid British commerce along the eastern seaboard. One of these squadrons, consisting of three ships under the command of Comte la Pérouse, had made its way north and became the first French ships in forty years to enter Hudson Bay.

From behind the forty foot walls of his castle, bristling with forty-two cannon, Hearne watched as the French ships landed field guns and prepared to do battle. The determined explorer was something less than an intrepid fighter. Hearne quickly appraised the situation and, by one account, ran for a white table cloth to wave from the battlements. He knew the weaknesses of his own position. With most of the fort's residents off in the interior engaged in the fur trade, he only had a garrison of thirty-nine. At the same time he had no way of knowing that la Pérouse's crews were scurvy-smitten. Nonetheless, he must also have known of the fort's strengths. The three French ships had obviously just completed a long voyage and their crews were, at best, weary. The walls behind which he sat were virtually impregnable. Even after the fort had been surrendered la Pérouse's attempt to blow up the walls met with failure. Only the gates had to be defended and they were protected from cannon fire by the V-shaped ravelin that jutted out in front of them. Finally, time was on his side. Although it was still only early August, it would not be long until the northern weather made life inside the fort much more bearable than life outside. A long seige was out of the question for la Pérouse. Somewhere in these calculations, however, Hearne decided to surrender without a fight and a surprised French admiral seized him and his furs and tried to lay waste to the fort.

When Tyrrell saw it in 1893 it stood as la Pérouse had left it, a deserted monument to a long concluded battle for empire – and to the memory of Samuel Hearne. The mortar between the huge blocks of granite was now crumbling. The unfired cannon that la Pérouse had spiked and dismantled lay where he left them among the scattered cannon balls. Only the rust that was eating the iron was new. In the midst of that devastated remnant of a bygone age, the romantic Tyrrell was once more drawn in empathy to the long-dead Hearne. That Hearne's surrender of the fort can best be described as inglorious, did not seem to affect Tyrrell. There is no indication that he ever asked himself why the noble Hearne, without a battle, surrendered Fort Prince of Wales with its forty foot walls, forty-two cannon and thirty-nine man garrison to the "scurvy-smitten crews" of la Pérouse's three ships. Hearne the explorer understandably loomed larger in Tyrrell's mind than Hearne the military failure.

In any event Tyrrell's editing of the journals of Samuel Hearne was a deed for the future. In the meantime there was a 900 mile hike to occupy Tyrrell's mind. By November 6, winter's grip was sufficiently strong to have frozen the river. The time had come to move on to Winnipeg. To get there he would zig-zag through what is now northern Manitoba from one Hudson's Bay Company post to another: from Fort Churchill to York Factory to Oxford House; Oxford House to Norway House; and then south on frozen Lake Winnipeg to Selkirk, Winnipeg and the blessed CPR.

Matheson was not only relieved to be rid of his unforeseen guests he also was able to move on with them to Stony River to pick up the rest of his winter's supplies. For five days the two parties travelled together like "a long serpentine train." Tyrrell had managed to procure six dogs, a sled laden with nine days' supplies, an Eskimo driver and an Indian guide to travel with them. The guide, James Westasecot, was "the most famous hunter and traveller in all that country." He had also acquired snow-shoes for all except Michel, whose frozen feet prohibited him from walking. He rode at first on one of Matheson's sleds; then after November 11, on their own sled once supplies were sufficiently used up to make room for him.

All went well during the first part of the journey as they skirted the edge of Hudson Bay. Jimmy Westasecot lived up to his reputation, supplementing their supplies with deer shot along the way and leading them without error through the unmarked country-side. Jimmy had another distinct advantage; he was a member of a large Cree family that more or less operated as a courier service or travel agency for the party. Unfalteringly he led them to his brother's camp, still to the north of the Nelson River. There his nephew took over to guide them to the Nelson and across it to York Factory at the mouth of the Hayes River where they would be turned over to another member of the family and so on. With such expert and professional guidance there was no problem finding good campsites where relatively comfortable evenings could be spent. James Tyrrell, in his book *Across the Sub-Arctics of Canada* waxed eloquent as he described a typical night's abode,

> a wall of brush [was] built crescent shaped, to a height of three or four feet, and in such a position as to best afford shelter from the cutting wind. The two main elements of a

good winter camp-ground are shelter and dry wood, both of which are indispensable. The snow was cleared away from the inside of the wind-break, and in its stead spruce boughs were strewn to a depth of several inches, and in front of this a big fire kindled – and camp was complete. These tasks ended, the preparation of supper was commenced. Bacon and biscuits were hauled out, while frying-pans and tea-kettles were brought and placed with their contents upon the fire. Fresh water had been found by cutting through the ice of a creek close by, so nothing was lacking.

Tin plates and cups, knives and forks were provided, but as we took hold of them they froze to our fingers, and before we could use them they had to be heated. After supper preparations were made for the night and for the morrow's tramp. Socks, duffles and moccasins, wet with perspiration from the day's march, were hung up before the fire to dry; robes and blankets were spread about the camp, and upon them our tired party assembled to enjoy a rest and smoke beside the fire before turning in for the night. Though cold, the night was beautifully calm and clear, and when from time to time the big dry sticks of wood were thrown upon the fire, showers of sparks ascended until they found hiding-places among the dark branches of the overhanging spruce trees.

Camp-fire stories and gossip were indulged in for an hour, then several logs were thrown upon the fire, and each man, rolled up in his blanket and with feet toward the fire, lay down to sleep.

Of another night's camp he wrote "about sunset made camp on the south bank of a stream known as Sam's Creek, in a lovely snow-laden evergreen forest – an ideal Canadian winter woodland picture. . . . beautiful but chilling."

During the first stage of their journey the biggest problem was precisely the one J. B. had foreseen. After four months of sitting in canoes their leg muscles were out of condition. The short preparatory sorties to Sloop's Cove and Fort Prince of Wales had done little to ease the transition. By the end of the first day's travel they were all limping badly from the toil of snow-shoeing.

Despite the leg pains and lameness, however, the party made fair progress and reached the mouth of the Nelson River without major delay or mishap. Then the problems began. A few miles upstream, still within tidewater, they found a sailboat which

Jimmy's brother had told them they could use to cross the river – another service of the Westasecot Travel Bureau. Unfortunately the boat was frozen into the sand on which it sat and had to be chopped out. Had they been able to use it as soon as they arrived at the Nelson they might have crossed the river without delay.

By the time the boat had been chopped free, however, night had fallen and, more important, the weather which until now had been fine, began to change. James writes:

> During the night the wind, which had been blowing pretty strongly for two days past, increased to a gale from the north-west. This unwelcome guest did not come by himself, but brought with him his friend the snow-storm, and they two held high carnival all night, vying with each other as to which should cause the strange intruders in the grove the more discomfort. The gale shrieked through the trees and threatened to level our shelter, nor was he contented with this, but also entered the camp and played pranks with our fire and blankets. The more stealthy snow-storm, making less noise than his blustering friend, before daylight had filled the ravine with white drifts and almost buried us.

Despite the gale and the dense fog that arose from the water into the colder air above it, the loosened boat was dragged to the edge of the shore ice and loaded in preparation for setting sail for the other shore when the tide returned to lift them into the water. All went as planned and they sailed upstream about three miles along the north bank before turning into the dense fog to cross the two miles of river that separated them from the south shore. Ice floating down the river was successfully avoided until "suddenly there loomed out of the mist right ahead a dense field of ice, broken and rafted and hurrying down with the current." Only quick action at the helm and sail saved them from being smashed against the ice and tossed into the chilling waters where in a matter of minutes they would have sunk into the oblivion of a coma and certain death. It seemed the elements were again conspiring to defeat their mission. Foiled by the field of ice they brought the craft about and pointed it back to the north shore only to discover that the strong headwind made it impossible to return under sail. Instead they manned the oars and forlornly rowed back to where they started.

Back on the north side of the river, still unable to see the far shore through the fog, they again pitched camp. The next morning when they did manage to catch a glimpse of the other side of the river, the sight left them even further disheartened. On the south bank, which was their destination, ice had formed for about a mile into the water making the shore inaccessible by boat. Even worse in the centre of the river heavy ice floes were being carried to the Bay by the mighty stream. From the south shore of the Nelson, York Factory was only a day's journey. For Tyrrell, on the north shore, it was twelve days away. On top of that the small food supply which he had managed to secure in Churchill was now virtually gone and once more storms were raging frequently. Joseph Tyrrell put it succinctly, "For ten days we lay in furious inactivity subsisting on the few rabbits, foxes and other game that we were able to catch."

Then, on November 23, Tyrrell says that "a slant of extreme good fortune" enabled them to cross the river. His brother James, ever more graphic, tells a different story in which "good fortune" exists only to the extent that they were not dashed against the ice or carried by the inexorable stream out into the open Bay and certain death. On the 22nd, noticing that about two miles upstream the ice seemed less thick than previously Tyrrell decided to move the boat to that area and try again to cross over. All but Michel, still suffering from frozen feet, set to the task. For the first half mile they towed the boat through the water by means of a long line to the shore and then, when the thickness of the ice in the river made it impossible to go further, they hauled it onto the shore ice and dragged it the other mile and a half to the chosen launching site. At last, when their exertions succeeded, they returned downstream to begin portaging their camp over the two miles of shore ice, to await the new day. All was ready for the supreme effort.

From early the next morning until long after dark they fought the river and its ice. All the time, as they struggled on, the unyielding flow of the Nelson carried them down towards the open sea. By the time the day was done the river's current had carried them more than twenty miles downstream. They started out with oars to propel themselves through the water. When the closeness of the ice floes made the oars inoperable, they used poles to push against the ice. And when the ice took hold of them and both oars and poles were as useless as match sticks, they used axes to hack their way through. Almost as soon as they left the river bank the ice pack seized them in its firm grasp and carried them unrelentingly towards the sea.

"We pushed and we pulled, we pounded and hacked" wrote

James. In time their dogged stubbornness paid off. They made it to open water, but only to be seized immediately in the grip of another floe. Once more they obstinately fought their way through to open water. Once more they freed themselves. This time they succeeded in reaching what appeared to be shore ice where they could safely gain access to the southern bank of the river. But the day's work had just begun.

Instead of shore ice they were standing on an island of ice caught in a jam in midstream. The shore, inaccessible, lay across yet another open stream liberally dotted with ice floating to the sea. At any moment, Tyrrell knew, the jam that held their island in place could break and they, with or without their boat, would be carried out to the open waters of Hudson Bay. A quick tour of inspection showed that there was no way to get the boat around the floating ice. The only choice he had was to move across the island. Once more the men unloaded the boat this time to portage its contents across the ice. But when they tried to drag the boat across the task proved too much for them. They were strong men and each of them pulled and shoved with all their might but the heavy boat on the rough ice was more than they could handle. Tyrrell called a halt to the effort and then set them to another task. The last chance of survival lay in their ability to cut a canal through the icy island before it broke loose from its moorings.

Long hours of hacking and hauling met with success. Once more they launched out into the stream only to be caught again and again in the ice floes that unmercifully threatened to carry them to the sea. Finally, only ten yards from the shore ice they were caught up in yet another floe that refused to loose them from its grip. Try as they might they could not free themselves from its icy hand. In the end it was not their exertions that set them free. Rather it was the elements, those very elements that so often threatened extinction, that came to their aid. James Tyrrell put it well, "civil war among the floes caused a split and brought deliverance." As the pressure from one floe against another released them, they returned to the oars and rowed desperately for shore.

The boat briefly touched the shore ice before being caught up once again in the floes. As it did François Maurice jumped from the bow with a line. The force of the ice and water was almost too much for the stalwart métis from Ile a la Crosse and he was dragged over the surface before finally managing to dig in his heels and hold the boat till the others could clamber to his aid. Quickly they emptied the boat and crossed the treacherous mile of ice that lay between them and the river bank. Then, after thawing out by a fire, in the clear moonlit night they set off for Hayes River and York Factory. The first leg of their homeward journey had been completed safely.

The day of the York boats plying the waterways of what is now Manitoba were pretty well over by 1893. York Factory had seen its greatest day when it had been one of the most important centres of the fur trade and a principal supply depot of the Hudson's Bay Company. From here the York boats had gone up the Hayes River and fanned out into the interior loaded with supplies and returned laden with furs. Those days were gone forever. Not only had the fur trade diminished both in absolute and in relative terms, but the westward expansion of the railroads had opened more efficient lines of communication. James Tyrrell recalled that when he had visited the post in 1886 it had a population of about thirty white men. But by the time he arrived with his brother in November 1893 there were only three. Fortunately for Michel French one of the three was a doctor. For Michel the expedition was finished. He had no need to travel further for help for his frozen feet.

Even though York Factory was no longer the central distributing point for Hudson's Bay Company posts that it had once been, supplies were plentiful and readily available. So four days after they arrived the group was ready to move on this time with three dog teams and yet another Westasecot brother, Charlie, as guide. The travellers were in better shape for this stage of their journey which would take them up the Hayes River from York Factory to Oxford House. James wrote:

> The condition of our party on leaving York was vastly different from what it had been on leaving Churchill. The two hundred mile tramp, although crippling some of us and causing all plenty of exertion, had hardened our muscles so much that, with the ten days' 'lie up' on the bank of the Nelson River, and a four days' rest at York, we were now in first-class walking trim, and started up the Hayes River at a brisk pace.

Despite temperatures of 40° below and the necessity of the Tyrrell brothers travelling part of the last night on their hands and knees to find the trail of the rest of the party who had gone ahead, the journey to Oxford House was relatively uneventful.

A few days' rest, the acquisition of more supplies and fresh dog teams, and the group set out on the next lap of their journey. Norway House was approximately 150 miles southwest of Oxford House lying on the banks of Playgreen Lake, a northern extension of Lake Winnipeg. Once more although temperatures again dipped to 40° below, the travellers met no serious obstacles. The biggest problem was the dogs they had acquired.

> Two of the dog-teams procured at Oxford had been intended to haul my brother and myself, and for a time they did so, but the poor animals were in such a wretched condition from the effects of former hard work that we preferred to walk most of the time, and before we reached our destination considered ourselves fortunate that we escaped without having to haul the dogs.

In a sense Norway House was the end of the journey. At least it was the end of the group that had set out from Athabasca Landing almost seven months before. Only the Tyrrell brothers and the remaining two French brothers would descend Lake Winnipeg to Selkirk. John Flett, Jim Corrigal and François Maurice would strike out on their own for Grand Rapids on the west side of the lake to follow the Saskatchewan River system for home.

Dogs were plentiful at Norway House and in better condition than those at Oxford House. J. B. therefore had no trouble in acquiring four good new teams for his half of the party. Thus mobilized they struck out down the lake on the 400 mile last lap of their great expedition. With so many dog teams the Tyrrell brothers no longer had to walk. Instead, "warmly rolled up in robes and blankets" they each rode on a sled, less considerate of the men during this last stage of their journey than at any time during the two thousand mile trek. While the Tyrrells rode in comfort, if not in splendour, Louis and Pierre French were left to walk and, since the new dogs were "fine, powerful animals," often to run to keep up. The strain, on top of all they had undergone, proved too much. Halfway to Selkirk, Pierre's legs gave out. Three days later the same fate befell Louis. A few years later, J. B. Tyrrell, in reference to dog trains noted that the secret to getting good mileage from your dogs was the pace you set for them, not the distance you made them cover. During the last stage of his first Barren Lands trip he allowed the dogs to set the pace for his men. Fortunately Lake Winnipeg was more heavily populated than the Barren Lands. As each man gave out, arrangements were made for him to follow to Winnipeg by other means. For Pierre it was with a load of fish being hauled from the Berens

River. For Louis it was by horse and sleigh. In the meantime the Tyrrells pushed on.

"Expedition very successful" read one of the telegrams Joe sent from Selkirk on New Year's Day 1894, "All well." The news was picked up in the press. Tyrrell was three months overdue and his fate had become a matter of public speculation. Newspapers across Canada, in the United States and Britain, hailed him as a hero. The romance of his northern odyssey caught hold of the public imagination and Tyrrell revelled in his new-found fame. His brother James wrote a book about their adventure, *Across the Sub-Arctics of Canada*. A decade later when Jack London was writing *Call of the Wild* he needed to create a suitably fierce enemy for his canine hero, Buck, to do battle with. The result was Spitz and to make sure his readers knew just how tough and fierce Spitz was London described him as having been part of a Geological Survey expedition through the Barren Lands. Since only Tyrrell had been there and he had travelled by canoe, London's poetic licence was showing but, as always, it showed to good effect. Any dog that could have survived with Tyrrell in the Barrens was immediately recognizable as a remarkably tough creature. To overcome such an enemy Buck would indeed have to be something special. Unwittingly the great chronicler of the Klondike was also recording the fame that Joe Tyrrell had achieved by his exploration. For a time his name was synonymous with the Canadian north.

Of all the Canadian newspapers that recorded his exploits only one, the *Mining Review*, sounded a sour note. Its readership was in the ranks of the speculators and promoters as well as the more substantial investors and businessmen of the mining community. Those segments of the Canadian population in the 1890s were already highly critical of the work of the Geological Survey. As far as they were concerned the Survey should have been directing all its attention to the business of discovering new deposits of readily exploitable resources. Mapping out water routes, tracing geological formations or the course of ancient glaciers were all nonsense unless they related directly to the identification of resource deposits which could be immediately extracted. With a strong mining lobby in Ottawa, the Survey was under considerable pressure to conform to the demands of the industry. The *Mining Review* was not going to miss an opportunity to drive home once more the demands of its constituents. The achievement of "this modern Gulliver" it trumpeted, was of "utter insignificance" in what it added to the economic well-being of the country.

Tyrrell's trip had not been a particular success in identifying new mineral deposits. But to thereby adjudge it a failure was to demonstrate acute tunnel vision. Tyrrell's journey was never intended to find new ore bodies. His task was to make a first survey of the area, gleaning what geological and biological data he could in the process. A good gauge of his success in the assigned task was the map he produced when it was all over. As with all his scientific work it was as deadly accurate as the instruments at his disposal allowed. The scale was two miles to the inch. Today, almost a century later, there are many much more detailed maps of various parts of Canada. The most detailed of the whole country, however, is still only on a scale of 1:250,000, or four miles to the inch – half as detailed as Tyrrell's original map. Much more information has been added to the map of the area in the intervening years but that does nothing to detract from his accomplishment in first opening up the country – the *Mining Review* notwithstanding.

Perhaps nothing demonstrates the magnitude of Tyrrell's endeavour more than the disastrous story of the first group which tried to retrace his route of 1893. Certainly nothing could more clearly illustrate the qualities of mind and character which had been required to bring the endeavour to its successful conclusion. Tyrrell himself could never understand why anyone would want to repeat his journey. Once in conversation, late in life, a companion commented that he would like to travel the Dubawnt to Chesterfield Inlet by canoe. "Why on earth would you want to do that?" Tyrrell asked. "You can go there by plane you know." The challenge of the 1893 expedition had not been to travel the Dubawnt. It had been to discover where it went, and thus to increase our knowledge of the world. To undergo such hardship for pleasure, made no sense at all.

Others see the world differently, however, and sooner or later, it was inevitable that someone would try to repeat the voyage. In fact it was more than sixty years before anyone made the attempt. The group of six who set out on the Dubawnt in 1955 was under the leadership of Arthur Moffatt. Described by the *New York Times* as "a veteran woodsman" from Norwich, Vermont, Moffatt was certainly an experienced canoeman. In 1937, when only seventeen years old, he had travelled alone down the 700 miles of northern Ontario's Albany River from its source near Sioux Lookout to its mouth in James Bay. In the seventeen years that

J. B. Tyrrell in posed shot after the Barren Lands expedition. (TFRBL)

followed he repeated that journey several times. Between 1950 and 1954 he led groups of like-minded adventurers down the Albany annually. But with each passing year Moffatt himself longed for more adventure and challenge than the Albany afforded.

How Moffatt first settled on a repetition of Tyrrell's expedition to fulfil his search for adventure is not clear. But as he paddled down the Albany in the early 'fifties a plan hatched in his mind to retrace Tyrrell's course. J. B.'s report and James's book were scoured for information. J. B. himself, by then in his nineties, was contacted for his advice and in the summer of 1955, with five other men, Moffatt set out for the Dubawnt. The expedition would not be an exact duplicate of Tyrrell's. Where Tyrrell had started out by canoe from Athabasca Landing to harden his men, Moffatt and his party travelled by train, plane and truck to Black Lake. Where Tyrrell on reaching Chesterfield Inlet still had to make his way to Fort Churchill and then walk to Winnipeg, Moffatt and his party arranged to be flown out from Baker Lake. When Tyrrell was overdue by three months reports of his possible death were carried in the newspapers; when Moffatt was overdue by five days planes went out in search of his party.

But the biggest differences between the expeditions are revealed in the diaries of the two men. From the first J. B. Tyrrell was in command of his party. There was no question of democracy or equality. The party in 1893 was like a ship at sea where the law of the captain is supreme. Only after they had been out for almost a month did Moffatt assume the leadership of his party; even then he described himself not as a captain but as a sergeant. Never during the Tyrrell expedition were depression and anxiety allowed to dominate. There were anxious moments and days on end when life hung in the balance, but the luxury of self-pity was never permitted. From the first Moffatt's diary has words like "apprehensive" and "gloomy." Then it degenerates into "worrying," "edgy" and "angry." At the outset paddles were left behind. In the middle, arguments raged. And in the end, on September 14, 1955, misjudging Tyrrell's descriptions of the rapids they would encounter before entering Marjorie Lake, the Moffatt diary is silent. Arthur Moffatt had died of exposure after his canoe tipped.

The Tyrrell route of 1893 has since been successfully negotiated by several parties, but the disaster that befell Moffatt stands as a testament to the magnitude of Tyrrell's achievement and as a warning to all who come after.

CHAPTER 3

The making of the man

The story of J. B. Tyrrell's crossing the Barren Lands is the stuff of which legends are made. In other cultures, both ancient and modern, exploits such as his would have entered into the mythology of the people. To the ancient Greeks he would have been a Hercules performing great feats, or at the very least a Jason setting out in a cedar strip Argo in search of the golden fleece. There are enough anecdotes about him that could have been woven into the legend to make it a fascinating tapestry. There was, for instance, the time when he was giving a first time visitor to the foothills of the Rockies a tour of the majestic.

"Where would you find bears in this country?" the visitor asked.

Tyrrell replied by kicking a nearby bush.

"In places like this," he said.

As he spoke a roar sounded from the bush. The visitor was only slightly more amazed than his host when a great black bear rose out of the brush.

On another occasion while riding across the prairies a companion who had heard of his reputation of being able to put out a candle at twenty paces with a six gun bet him that he could not shoot a dozen rabbits in succession from the back of his horse. The rabbits were plentiful enough and Tyrrell drew his Colt revolvers and killed twelve rabbits in a row. Then, for good measure he reloaded the gun and shot a thirteenth. At that point his companion spotted a hawk perched on a tree about sixty yards away.

"I bet you couldn't hit the bird" he said and increased the wager.

In reply, Tyrrell simply aimed the revolver and fired. The bird tumbled from the tree.

In his own day the stories of Joe Tyrrell's adventures were well known. Today, however, he is all but forgotten. Of the man himself and his exploits most Canadians remain blissfully ignorant. Perhaps it is the diversity of the Canadian culture that creates a fear of heroes lest some element of the community be offended. In Tyrrell's crossing of the Barren Lands that fear should be easily stilled. So many of the elements of the Canadian mosaic are gathered into a unity. The celtic Tyrrells venturing into the unknown; the French-speaking Quebec Indian Louis French fighting for survival with a bear; the Indian guides with their folklore; the métis packers, still unhappy with the surveying of the arable plains but sure enough of their way through the wilds of the north that in the end one of them keeps the group alive while the other two go to raise a relief party. The "ethnic" groups are missing – the Ukrainians and Poles, the Germans and Greeks – but by and large they had not yet arrived in the new northern world. Soon they would flood in when Laurier's Minister of the Interior Clifford Sifton opened up the land to settlement. When they came to complete the mosaic they settled in areas that Tyrrell on other expeditions had explored for them. Colossus-like he strode across the Canadian scene at the turn of the century. He was the first native born and trained explorer to carry a major piece of exploration from its inception to a successful conclusion. Yet in his later life and since his death he has been allowed to sink into obscurity.

His life straddled the second half of the nineteenth and the first half of the twentieth century. In many ways he stood at the cross-roads of the two centuries. This was certainly true of his work as an explorer. Twentieth century exploration for the most part has been a process of providing in ever-increasing detail the data on geological formations, plant growth, soil capabilities and mineral resources of areas where the basic exploration of the terrain has already been done. Much of Tyrrell's work was of this type. He led expeditions into central Alberta and the lake region of Manitoba with these objectives. In carrying them out Tyrrell fulfilled his function with admirable thoroughness identifying the extensive coal deposits at Drumheller, confirming that the Athabasca tar sands were worthy of further investigation, finding new sandstone deposits suitable for building in Manitoba, surveying the rich farm land of the Dauphin area. In these endeavours he was a twentieth century geologist and surveyor confirming and correcting the readings of the first generation of explorers who had sketched the outlines of the map. His work was never definitive. It was not meant to be. Like the geological formations which are examined so too the work of knowing the country through exploration is built strata upon strata, layer after layer.

But if Tyrrell added to the layers of technical information on the structure of the Canadian land, he was also amongst the last of that earlier great breed of explorers who ventured into the interior wilderness to sketch the rough outline of the land. Like those who had gone before, he followed the river wherever it might lead never sure that it might not lead to disaster. He set off with a fraction of the food he needed knowing that the remainder would have to be taken from nature. He ran a swift race with the brief Canadian summer trying, not always successfully, to reach the end of the journey before the strong hand of winter seized the land in its grip.

Exploration, however, was only his first career. From that he went on to distinction in the world of mining. Here again he stood at the cross-roads of the centuries. He started off by taking part in the Klondike gold rush with a pan in his hand and ended up sinking a deeper shaft than anyone thought possible in the mines of northern Ontario. In taking part in opening up the mineral resources which he had helped identify, he hoped to create a stable Canadian resource extraction industry that his young country might benefit from the riches which she held in her bosom. By this route he sought to provide a firm base for Canada's growth so that she might claim her place in the twentieth century family of nations. "The further strength and greatness of Canada," he once told the editor of *Fortune* magazine, "depends on the existence and development of her mineral resources."

Two major influences shaped the course of Joseph Burr Tyrrell's life. The second of them, however, did not come into play until he was nearing middle age. During his fortieth year he joined the gold rush to the Klondike and the experience changed him as it changed everyone who took part. By that time, however, his great explorations were behind him and the Klondike influence had no effect on that aspect of his life. Rather it was his Upper Canada childhood which moulded his work as an explorer.

At the time of his birth the idea of a federal union of the British North American colonies had only recently been broached by Governor Head in the legislature of the old Province of Canada which had been established in the wake of the Durham Report. John A. Macdonald and George-Etienne Cartier were already co-operating in the political alliance by which they governed the two peoples of what became Ontario and Quebec. And George Brown was frothing with righteous indignation at Macdonald's latest skulduggery. Three months before Tyrrell's birth, Brown had defeated Macdonald in the legislature and gained power, only to lose it again within two days and have to sit helplessly on the sidelines as Macdonald outmanoeuvred him with the famous "double shuffle" of cabinet positions. That was taking place in Toronto (no longer York but still very much Hogtown) the temporary seat of government of the united colony of Upper and Lower Canada. In the meantime Queen Victoria had already named Ottawa as her choice for a new capital.

Tyrrell was eight years old before Confederation came about and he was an old man by the time the status of "Canadian citizen" was introduced. Having been born before his country existed, his family tells of how he had to pay a dollar to have his citizenship confirmed. It was only a matter of form. He was a Canadian long before that, not only by birth but by inclination and action. He was part of the dream of a great north, strong and free, and the dream was part of him. He recalled "I was ten years old before the Union Pacific Railway was completed and my first Geography text-book marked everything west of the Mississippi 'The Great American Desert.' In like manner, eight hundred miles of prairie between the Red River and the Bow Valley were only a buffalo-run." For the first part of his working life he immersed himself in the task of discovering what lay within that buffalo-run.

His boyhood in Weston, Ontario prepared him well for the task. The village of Weston that was his boyhood home has since been engulfed by the urban sprawl of Metropolitan Toronto. In 1858 though, and throughout his early life, it was a separate, thriving centre of local agriculture. Growing up in that thinly populated rural community developed in him a love of the outdoors that never left him throughout the ninety-nine years of his long life. For most of his adulthood he made his home in one or other of Toronto or Ottawa. The city, however, was for him merely a fixed address from which he could venture into the wilds. He grew up close to nature and he always retained his communion with the world of living things. Even the rocks of his native land had life. Underneath them were the firmly fixed foundations of the earth, but the surface was a living, moving organism which he sought to know and whose mysteries he worked to unravel.

As a child he was free to roam the open fields and explore the banks of the Humber River. Looking back he could claim "Every square foot of the countryside within walking distance of my home was known to me." Nearby were stands of forests that had not yet fallen before the axe. Wildlife abounded and he early developed an intense interest in it. His boyhood bedroom was a miniature zoo and his fascination with animal life stayed with him throughout his life. There was, however, no sanctity to animal life. From early childhood he was taught to handle guns. His first shotgun was a family heirloom used in battle by his Irish grandfather. Through time he progressed to the rifle and revolver. In future days, crossing the unknown wilderness his marksmanship was invaluable and guaranteed a food supply; but he never hunted for pleasure though occasionally he would to provide a bear rug or deer head for a friend.

Just as important as the physical environment in which he grew up was the society. From it he took his system of values. Experience modified his ideals and the Klondike shook some loose but on the whole they were so deeply embedded in his personality that they guided him throughout his lifetime. Some of his values may seem quaint by today's standards; they were, nonetheless, the necessary accoutrements of the type of life he lived. There was the sense of Victorian integrity that a man's word was his bond. In the backwater of the frontier where sources of supplies were few and payment was by promissory note, a man could pass once breaking his word. In every year, from 1882 to 1898, Joe Tyrrell went west. He sometimes had difficulty in having his needs fulfilled, but never because his dependability was questioned. On one occasion, when the factor of a Hudson's Bay Company post was under orders from his superior not to sell anything to Tyrrell as a representative of the Geological Survey, Tyrrell arranged to have everything he wanted charged to his own account. On another occasion, ill with typhoid, he was fed a bottle of brandy by those who nursed him back to health. The next summer he returned with two bottles to replace it. During his 1893 expedition into the Barren Lands his men unwittingly started to break up the frame of a cached Eskimo kayak. He left a plug of tobacco to reimburse the unknown owners for the damage done. The following year, back in the Barrens, he met up with the owners of the kayak who lavishly bestowed their hospitality on him.

Deeper even than the integrity of his word was the sense of duty that ruled his life. His mother was a staunch Methodist, a religious denomination that has inspired not a few of its sons with a deep sense of obligation to serve well their fellow men. Tyrrell described his mother. "She was of Puritan temperament, self disciplined, extremely devout, attentive to every good and pious cause and incessant in her advice to all her children to seek first the highest gifts of the spirit." His father was a different sort – "rather of the Cavalier type – proud of his good name though not self satisfied." A junior son of a family of landed Irish gentry, he had come to Canada in 1836 to seek his fortune. He was a stonemason by trade and had worked his way along the north shore of Lake Ontario building houses as he went. When he reached Weston he met Elizabeth Burr whose Loyalist ancestors had arrived in North America in 1682 and in Canada in 1787. The two married and by the time Joseph was born the elder Tyrrell had established himself as the "Squire of Weston." He built a huge, twenty-four room stone mansion for his family. He raised his children to remember that they were a cut above the ordinary. They were, after all, descendants of the Tyrrells of Castle Grange whose history went back a thousand years. The family motto was *Veritas via vitae* – Truth is the path of life – and it was impressed on each member of the family. They were expected to take it seriously.

It was a childhood of rigorous discipline imposed by a strong-willed matriarchal mother of firm religious conviction and little compassion and a father of proud ancestry, who for the sake of peace gave his wife complete authority within the home, while he found his freedom in the outdoors and alleviated her severity with a gentle humour. It was an environment that inculcated a deep sense of duty and obligation – duty to family and country and, lastly, to self. It created an imperative to serve in the public good, to devote one's energies to worthwhile action; a duty to perfect and improve one's own position and capacities, to excel in the manly arts, to face hazard and danger and never complain. One was expected to be modest and to understate achievements in pretending to others, and perhaps to one's self, that everything which came to pass was by coincidence or an act of Providence, and never by one's own doing, or intervention.

Tyrrell's sense of duty to family was demonstrated as a young man giving over a half of a year's income to bail his father out of troubled financial times, sending his sister to Ireland to meet a cousin and future husband thereby continuing the tradition of living at Castle Grange, buying another sister a typewriter and helping to put a brother through medical school. The pattern continued into later life. As an adult, looking for partners for his endeavours in the Klondike, he turned to his brother and cousin. Looking for an assistant for his venture into the Barren Lands he turned to his brother James and thirty years later he is to be found financing James's venture into poultry farming, and baling him out when the venture failed. He even wrote to Mackenzie King on one occasion to try to get his brother a job. For a life-long Tory who hated King with a burning ferocity that act reveals how deeply the sense of duty was ingrained.

There were bad effects from his background too. For one thing it created in him a social snobbery which called for a standard of life that was difficult to maintain. Even the "Squire of Weston" had had difficulty in maintaining the twenty-four room mansion that he had built for his family and had to depend on his sons to help him with his debt. Similarly for Joe Tyrrell as a young married man in his thirties, there were expectations of a standard and way of life that he could not afford on his salary. That in turn spurred him on in his search for wealth and when he attained it he resumed the family tradition of squirearchy and tried to pass on to his children and grandchildren that they were not as other people.

At the same time the tradition did create in him an understanding that with position goes responsibility. He had an obligation to offer leadership and, in his expeditions, in his scientific work, in his mining endeavours and in a thousand other ways, he took that obligation seriously. There is a myth that Canada has no aristocracy. In fact, since the first arrival of the white man, the social hierarchy has been clearly visible whether as the seigneurie in Quebec or the gentry in Ontario. Nor has it been merely a hierarchy of wealth. Though that is often a part of it, the real aristocracy has been one of birth, education, position and connection – a self-proclaimed elite superstructure presiding over an appearance of equality.

Born into that upper crust of Upper Canada, nothing would do but that his education should be rounded out at Upper Canada College and the University of Toronto. The element of conscious elitism was an unpleasant side of Tyrrell's personality. He could be heavy-handed, imperious and ambitious. It also brought out in him a name-dropping snobbishness and a self-righteousness which mixed with his vanity made him a difficult man to like. His later experience in the Klondike ameliorated these aspects of his personality. There a man's worth was measured by the weight of the poke he carried, not by his birth or education. Yet he never quite got over his elitist upbringing and in later years, after he had made his own fortune, it returned to blunt his enjoyment of life.

Yet these negative aspects of the man played an important part in driving him towards his goals. They set in motion the restless energy that could never be content with mediocrity. His childhood had prepared him well for what lay ahead. Even an early bout of scarlet fever which left him forever hard of hearing and with poor eyesight, did not go amiss. The deaf have around them a wall of solitude. For those who must live and work in close contact with others, to be so afflicted presents a terrible ordeal. For those who would venture onto the vast tundra, traverse thick forests with thin populations, or paddle the empty lakes and rivers of the wilds, the sureness of being able to do with little communication with one's fellows can be a tangible asset. Perhaps the loneliness of deafness can even drive a person on to search for greatness. Even so, his affliction, which worsened with time, was a great burden. Late in life, when the technological advances spurred on by World War II made it possible for him to replace his ungainly and only partially effective ear trumpet with an effective hearing aid of manageable size, Tyrrell once again was able to hear the sounds he had missed since boyhood. Wearing his new hearing aid for the first time, he came in from his garden with tears in his eyes. After fifty years he had heard the birds sing again.

His poor eyesight taught him, from early childhood, to examine things closely. Throughout his life he carried this habit with him. His observations on field trips and surveys were remarkable for their accuracy. As a member of the staff of the Geological Survey, it was part of his job to search out new plant forms and evidence of ancient life forms. Long after he had left the Survey, however, he was still finding fossils, bones, plants and rock specimens to send to museums and institutions for identification and evaluation. In no small measure the extensiveness of his contribution to the advance of these branches of science lay in his ingrained habit of looking closely at everything he saw.

Fortunately effective glasses for the hard of seeing preceded effective hearing aids by a long time. Without a hearing aid Tyrrell could function unimpaired in the wilderness. Without glasses he could not have functioned at all. During one of his explorations the extent of his infirmity was driven home to him. His normal method of operation was to send the men who assisted him in his work on ahead with the dog teams, pack-horses or buck-boards loaded with their supplies and equipment. While they pushed on he followed in the rear examining the country they were passing through, collecting his samples and recording his astronomical and atmospheric readings. On this occasion he accidentally knocked his glasses off his face. Unable to see them, terrified lest he step on them, and afraid to try to catch up with his men lest he be unable to lead them back to the spot, he decided that all he could do was stand where he was until the men ahead concluded that he was overdue and returned to search for him. For long hours he waited, before help came and his vision was restored.

Looking back on his long life at the age of ninety-six, Tyrrell summed up his childhood and youth.

It is a fashion nowadays to assume that the Puritan way of life was gloomy, that young people groaned under its harsh restrictions and longed for a way of escape. I did not find it so. My home was a happy one, Sundays and week-days alike, a place where affection, unselfishness and mutual trust prevailed.

But 'time and tide wait for no man' and it is hardly necessary for me to say that tremendous changes and advances have been made during my ninety-six years. . . .

The march through this era of development has been for me a thrilling adventure. It has been a time of difficulties faced and conquered, a time of poverty and wealth, of weakness and strength, of depression and recovery. Economic troubles have appeared from time to time. Are they worse than those of 1873 or of 1890? Many say YES, with a confidence which I believe lacks the foundation of knowledge. I remember two distinct periods in Canada when young men had no future and when the pessimists wailed like guests at a prolonged wake. I myself, was a young man during the worst of these bad times and after a creditable College course, gave thanks for a job at Ten Dollars a week.

I believe that any young man who has taken the trouble to equip himself with definite, accurate and modern knowledge of some sort, who has the temperament to endure disappointment and injustice, and the will to do honest and unremitting work, will find a place in this fruitful Country for his talent and will be on the way to success.

If his background prepared him for the challenging tasks that lay ahead that was not the whole recipe for his success. There was another factor. He was lucky. At several points during his life, when he seemed to be in a blind alley, doors opened that allowed his escape from the prison of drudgery. Opportunities arose, over which he had little control, that permitted him to use his talents and to expand and grow. If they had not he would never have accomplished so much, even in such a long lifetime. The story of his life, however, is not simply a tale of one lucky break after another. There were periods when his well seemed to have run dry and fortune to have deserted him. This was so on the small time frame of individual projects. During an expedition there could be days and weeks when weather conditions made travel all but impossible. Several times bouts of serious illness threatened his very life. It was also true in the larger framework of time. For years on end, at least twice in his life, Providence seemed to have deserted him and he was given over to a dreary existence of dull routine.

These times were, however, the exception for J. B. Tyrrell. For the most part he seemed to bask in the sunshine of fortune's smile. At times this was an illusion, though one which he was happy to foster. He liked to portray himself as a man to whom good things came uninvited and unexpected – a man without ambition and without guile. He was anything but. On many occasions when Lady Luck's butler answered the door it was in response to his persistent knocking. Had the door not been opened he might have smashed his way through it. On more than one occasion he thought nothing of prying the door open by using his father's political connections. William Tyrrell, like J. B. after him, was a life-long Conservative. Unlike his son however, William was willing to enter the fray of the political arena. Successful in becoming reeve of Weston, he tried four times to be elected to higher office. Before Confederation he made one unsuccessful bid for election to the Legislative Assembly. After Confederation he tried twice to be elected to the Legislature of Ontario and once, to the Parliament of Canada. He was defeated in all four attempts, though J. B. Tyrrell always maintained that his father had in fact won the election to the federal House. By his account his brother, Robert, who was a doctor, had years later been called to the deathbed of the man who had acted as returning officer in the constituency in 1872. It seems that before dying, the man wanted to clear his conscience of a number of things and confessed to Robert that William Tyrrell had in fact won the seat in 1872 but that the results had been rigged to show a Liberal win. The important thing in Joseph's life, however, was not whether his father had won or lost (although he liked to think that he had won) but that he had run at all. By his years of prominent activity for the Conservative party William Tyrrell was thereby entitled to join the grasping throng who plagued John A. Macdonald and his ministers for a share of the spoils of office. Joseph never hesitated to influence fortune by using his father's political credit.

Even so, at a number of important junctions in his life, it was luck – the happy coincidence of circumstances – that opened the way. The same ingredient runs through the story of most successful lives. As does another common denominator – the will to seize hold of the opportunities that are presented and move through the open door to follow an unknown path wherever it might lead. That path for Joe Tyrrell, on a number of occasions sharply changed the direction of his life. In all of these changes he had a hand. Whatever else J. B. Tyrrell may have been he was not a man to be buffeted by chance or nature. Had he been he would never have survived his expeditions and his ventures into challenging new careers. Nonetheless, there was a fortuitous conjunction of his will and his fate. The ancient Greeks would have called it his *moira* – today we call it his luck.

The first of these lucky breaks came in 1881, a year after he had graduated from the University of Toronto. The career chosen for him had been the law. To that end he had been enrolled in the Arts course and on graduation was articled to a Toronto law firm. But throughout his university training he had continued his early interest in the natural sciences. In addition to his optional courses in those areas, he also pursued them in every minute of his spare time. He bought a microscope and with it conducted research into a type of mite that causes illness to cats. Shortly after graduation he wrote up a paper on the subject and had it accepted for publication by the *Ottawa Field Naturalist*. Such enthusiasm naturally attracted the attention of the science faculty which was just beginning to establish itself at the University of Toronto. Among these new professors was Edward Chapman, who taught geology. He and Tyrrell became life-long friends and, in the early days, it was he who introduced Tyrrell to the work of the Geological Survey of Canada. While still an undergraduate Tyrrell, at Chapman's urging, started reading the annual reports of the Survey with their accounts of the work of the Survey's exploring geologists. At the time it seemed a worthy activity that would further satisfy the demands of Tyrrell's questioning mind. In retrospect, it was much more important. It led to the first major change in the direction of Tyrrell's life.

Reading the law can be dull and boring. The roster of sons of middle class families of Tyrrell's generation who were enrolled in the law only to leave at the first opportunity is legend. They went out from their fathers' frustrated dreams of careers at the bar into every conceivable line of work. Many of them, like Tyrrell, left a mark on the world such as they could never have done dressed in wig and gown. For Tyrrell the break with his father's wishes for his future was a difficult one. The deep sense of duty with which he had been raised demanded that he subjugate his own wishes to those of his parents – "Honour thy Father and thy Mother." He never wrote the word "Father" with a small "f." It always had a capital, as did "Mother." Looking back on his life he was never able to explain his abandonment of the law as a career in terms of his own desires and inclinations – or even in terms of his "duty" to himself. Instead he continued to explain it in terms of medical need. He suffered from pneumonia when he was sixteen years old. Six years later, in search for an excuse to change his job, he found his doctor in agreement that he would have fewer chest and respiratory problems if he had a job that was less confining.

Armed with this medical opinion and the knowledge that the Geological Survey was hiring additional assistants to help complete its move from Montreal to Ottawa, Tyrrell persuaded his father that he should take a year away from the law to work for the Survey. He also persuaded his father to intervene with John A. Macdonald and their own Conservative M.P., Clark Wallace, whom the older Tyrrell had helped elect for the first time in 1878. That the medical problem was a ruse is borne out by the fact that the job he applied for, and got, with the Survey was a temporary one which, if anything was even more confining than reading law would have been. In its move from Montreal the Survey had packed its collection of specimens of all the known rocks in Canada into some 2,000 boxes, barrels and crates. Tyrrell's job as a third-class clerk, was to help the Survey's palaeontologist, J. F. Whiteaves unpack and identify the collection that had been gathered over the organization's forty year history. Many had carried labels when they were put into the boxes; some had not. When they were unpacked in Ottawa few labels were still attached. Tyrrell had never formally studied geology, but here in the basement of the Survey's new home in a converted hotel on Sussex Drive in Ottawa, identifying, describing and labelling the collection of rocks and fossils under the able supervision of Whiteaves, Tyrrell had what he described as "a practical post-graduate course in Geology and Mineralogy, which lasted for a full year and a half."

Of all the chance occurrences that shaped the course of Tyrrell's life none was more far-reaching than the first. He had used his own ingenuity to escape the career chosen for him. He had used his father's political connections to get the low-grade job. Yet these would have counted for nothing if it had not been for the earlier decision of the government to move the headquarters of the Geological Survey of Canada from Montreal to Ottawa. Without that happy circumstance there would have been no room for him. Had Tyrrell applied to the Survey at a time when it was settled in either its old location or its new, he would undoubtedly have been rejected. A Bachelor of Arts degree from Toronto was hardly the best qualification for a job with an organization whose task it was to explore the geography and geology of the country. The Survey was always hard pressed for funds and it is doubtful if, had it not been for the move, it would have been hiring anyone at all. In addition, although it had relied on enthusiastic amateurs in the past, it was already moving into a policy of only recruiting people with a background in related disciplines as the universities began to produce graduates in these fields. Tyrrell in fact was one of the last of the self-trained geologists to make an important contribution to the work of the Survey. The first of the great coincidences in his life had made it all possible. Once it had done so, however, he left nothing to chance. From the first day he delved into the contents of those boxes with a rare enthusiasm, his quick intelligence readily grasping at all that could be learned about his new field.

Never had the Geological Survey received better value for $500.00 a year. Before 1881 was out the director of the Survey, Dr. A. R. C. Selwyn, had recognized the young man's quality and had recommended him for a permanent position on the staff. It was a good choice. Tyrrell stayed with the Survey for almost eighteen years. During that time his accomplishments mounted impressively and it was only when he felt that there was no longer room for his growth within the organization that he, in the end, resigned.

CHAPTER 4

Discovering dinosaurs

The unsung heroes of Canadian history are the men of the Geological Survey. In keeping with the long-standing national preference for "little grey men" they have been allowed to sink into the anonymity of their civil service. There, shielded from the glare of public acclaim by their political masters and the mandarinate of the bureaucracy, they have dwelt in obscurity. Tyrrell was a member of that band of able men who risked life and limb, enduring privation and starvation to explore this land of Canada. They were a collection of unique individuals, strong and free, who preferred the vast outdoors, with all its hazards, to being cooped up behind a desk or in a dank laboratory. The whole realm of nature was their laboratory. They were primarily geologists, but they worked also as botanists and biologists and, on occasion as medical doctors, hunters, and beasts of burden. They were the personification of the concept of the true north. Collectively and individually, by the knowledge of the land that their work made available, they opened up Canada to Canadians. In all respects except one J. B. Tyrrell was typical of the breed. From very early in his career, he had difficulty accepting the faceless anonymity of his compatriots. Indeed, he refused to accept it, and even during his employment with the Survey he broke out of that prison of obscurity.

The Geological Survey of Canada had been around for twenty-five years before Confederation. The "Canada" that created it, and to whose territory it was at first limited, was the old Province of Canada consisting of the southern portions of present-day Ontario and Quebec. As the country expanded, by Confederation in 1867 and its additions, by the acquisition of Rupert's Land and the North Western Territory from the Hudson's Bay Company in 1869, and by the later acquisition of the Arctic islands, so too did the Survey's area of exploration. Founded first in response to the demands of the industrial revolution for the identification of new world mineral resources, the huge acquisition of territory in 1869 placed on the Survey an urgent need to concentrate on the exploration and discovery of what lay within the new territories and unknown regions of the country. In the years that followed these twin objectives of uncovering the minerals and exploring the half continent put the Survey's leadership under tremendous pressure. It was frequently the focus of public criticism which rose to a howl whenever it appeared to be paying too much attention to exploration and not enough to the immediate needs of the mining industry.

In the first half century of its history the Survey had only two directors. The first, the Scotsman Sir William Logan, stayed with the job from 1842 through Confederation to 1869. The second director and the man who hired Tyrrell, was A. R. C. Selwyn, an Englishman as able in his work as he was abrasive in his personality. There can be no greater testimony to the ability of these two men than the accomplishments of the Survey under their leadership. Manpower was in short supply and money was extremely scarce, but the quality of work was excellent and its handful of men (there were only about twenty when Tyrrell joined them) were to be found each summer in the farthest corners of the kingdom. Systematically, area after area was added to the map of Canada. First, long track surveys around the perimeter or through the middle of the territory would be made, often retracing the steps of earlier fur trade explorers checking their frequently inaccurate data and correcting the maps that had resulted. Then the secondary routes of the area would be travelled. Finally, interesting specific sections would be scoured thoroughly for information on their origins and composition to be added to that gleaned during the earlier phases of the work.

From the first day unpacking boxes in the basement of the former hotel that had become the Survey's new headquarters, Joe Tyrrell longed to join that annual summer exodus. Even before his permanent appointment to the staff was confirmed he was cajoling Selwyn to send him out into the field. Nor did he stop there. His father's political friends were again summoned up and, daringly, he even went so far as to threaten resignation. Later in life, when his experience as an explorer made him much more valuable to the Survey, a similar threat to quit produced no results and he actually did leave at great loss to the Survey. In 1882, however, when his departure would hardly have been noticed, his constant badgering paid off. Selwyn, whatever his faults, and he had many, had a keen eye for spotting talent. In many ways that single attribute did more for the Survey than all his others put together. With the severe restrictions on manpower and money with which he had to operate, the Survey's accomplishments depended entirely on the calibre of the men he was able to send into the field each year. In the young and ambitious J. B. Tyrrell, Selwyn recognized the potential of a good explorer and a keen observer. He also recognized an abundance of the enthusiasm that was the Survey's life-blood. So early in 1883 Selwyn, having confirmed Tyrrell's permanent appointment, gave him his first assignment to the great outdoors that he loved and longed for. His job was to assist G. M. Dawson in his expedition to the foothills of the Rockies and through the passes into the mountains.

Tyrrell was ecstatic. George Mercer Dawson was the son of Canada's greatest geologist. His father, Sir John William Dawson, was principal of McGill University and a constant friend of the Survey. Prior to the 1881 move to its new headquarters in Ottawa, Dawson had been in constant and close touch with Selwyn in shaping the organization's policies. Perhaps there is no more telling evidence of the older Dawson's influence than a memorandum written by Selwyn when he was trying to dissuade his political masters from forcing him to move away from Montreal. If the Survey left that city, wrote Selwyn, he would lose the close and valued relationship with Dawson.

The younger Dawson, like so many sons who follow in a great father's footsteps, was forever overshadowed in his chosen career. Yet George Dawson had no superior amongst exploring Canadian geologists. His immense contribution to the knowledge of the land is without measure. If the young Tyrrell could have had no fuller introduction to the science of geology than his work of unpacking the Survey's specimens under Whiteaves's guidance, he could also have had no more complete introduction to the art of exploration than he received under Dawson's tutelage. The diminutive, hunchbacked figure of Dawson on horseback or crawling over the face of a rock was perhaps a comical sight. But there was nothing comical about his explorations. They were serious operations in the course of which he taxed his own body to the limit and demanded the same of all around him. Tyrrell says of his expedition with Dawson, "I was twenty-five years old and had learned already one of the most important principles of the trail – that when one feels so exhausted that another step seems impossible, one can always go five miles farther before making camp." Tyrrell cherished the memory of the experience with his hard taskmaster who "had every consideration for his horses but no great sentiment about his men." He was, however, willing to share his vast knowledge of the earth with his assistants, and was untiring in answering probing questions and explaining phenomena.

When Tyrrell joined him as his assistant, Dawson had already been exploring the area of southern Alberta for a couple of years. The Survey was anxious, in advance of the construction of the CPR rail line through the area, to explore the territory and identify its coal deposits. To get to Winnipeg by rail in 1883 the route was still via Chicago and Minneapolis-St. Paul. From Winnipeg the railway line had been completed as far as Maple Creek near what became the western border of Saskatchewan. Dawson and his party rode the line to the end of steel, with a stop off at Brandon to buy horses and wagons with which they would complete their journey to the foot of the Rockies.

Beyond Maple Creek was the open range criss-crossed with the rutted trails of prairie schooners. From here they would travel to Fort Macleod on horseback or buck-board while their supplies were hauled in the wagons. A whole new world was unfolding before Tyrrell's eyes. At twenty-four years old he had never been west of Manitoulin Island. Now he was crossing the seemingly boundless ocean of the prairie. It was not the prairie of today with its rippling waves of golden grain. It was an earlier prairie, unfenced and covered with its rough native grasses. He described it as a "trackless wilderness."

If the land in its vastness was new to him, so too was the social order or rather the lack of it. His entire life to date had been spent in the settled communities of Ontario. Now he was on the frontier with all its dangers where a man had to be constantly alert and ready to defend himself. Both at Brandon where they picked up their supplies and at Maple Creek where they left the railroad, they were warned of the danger ahead. Bandits and horse thieves were marauding on the trail. Whiskey traders were doing a roaring business with the railway construction men. Everyone was advising Dawson to turn back. Instead he bought a few extra guns and some more ammunition. As the party wound its way from Maple Creek to Fort Macleod its members took turns as outriders, checking out coulees and other hiding spots for possible ambushers. At night they took turns standing guard against possible attackers.

The Canadian west could be as wild and woolly as the land to the south. The job done by the North-West Mounted Police in bringing law and order to the west in advance of his settlement has long been a source of national pride. Even so lawlessness was rampant. The new police force was barely adequate to the task and at times had its own problems with the outlaws. Tyrrell heard of one such incident where horse thieves from across the border had stampeded the Mounties' horses "leaving the detachment distinctly unmounted – their scarlet tunics matched by their faces." For the young Upper Canadian it was a fine introduction to the west and to the hazards of exploration. He was also being introduced to the rigours of exploration. Working for the Geological Survey of Canada was not an easy route to tourism. Each day's travel began early. Awake before the sun rose, they had usually eaten breakfast and were on the trail by 5.30 AM. Dawson's policy of mounting a guard through the night meant that some nights there was little or no sleep at all. Whatever the compensation of such long hours of work, it was not the haute cuisine. Their diet, except when they reinforced it by hunting or occasional purchase, consisted of salt pork, flour made into bannocks, and tea.

Fort Macleod brought welcome relief from their spartan diet. Here, for the first time since leaving Brandon, they enjoyed fresh meat and "yeast bread." Maple Creek had only yielded some sugar, dried apples and baking powder. The fort itself, however, was something of a disappointment to Tyrrell. In his mind's eye he had built the NWMP base into a thing of heroic proportions. On arriving there reality quickly replaced the young adventurer's illusions. The party made their camp on the opposite side of the Oldman River within earshot of the Mounties' bugle calls. The next day they took the ferry over to the "great city." It took them seven minutes to pass from one end of the higgledy-piggledy town to the other, even allowing for the necessity of picking their way through the piles of garbage that lay everywhere. The town itself, Tyrrell noted, had "a good deal of individuality for everyone appeared to have built his house just where he liked."

In the course of the next week they travelled along the banks of the Oldman River upstream into the foothills. One of the early ranches in the area, the Garnett ranch, would be the base of operations for the summer's work. The wagons and all the equipment and supplies they would not need during the first part of their exploration, together with the specimens they had already collected along the way, were left at the ranch under the care of the four Garnett brothers. From this base they would twice strike

72

Dawson's photograph of the Garnett Ranch – his base of operations in 1883. (GSC)

G. M. Dawson's photograph of one of his campsites in the Rockies in 1881. (GSC)

out westward into the mountains and, in between, into the southern country, with one night over the border in Montana. On all three sorties their travel into the mountainous regions would be on horseback or on foot. The real work of the expedition had begun.

Dawson gave his freshman assistant his first assignment. As they worked their way over the Crow's Nest Pass, 4,450 feet above sea level, Tyrrell was told to make a pace survey of their journey. Each morning, early, he set out walking at a regulated pace counting his steps to measure the distance. Using a compass he would point himself straight for a point up ahead and count the number of steps he took to get there. Then he would take another reading on the compass and so on all through the day. After Tyrrell left each morning Dawson supervised the dismantling of camp before he and the others set out on horseback, Dawson making side trips or stopping to examine interesting formations and gather specimens. Somewhere around mid-morning they would pass Tyrrell. Later they would stop to prepare lunch while Tyrrell had a chance to catch up. After lunch the pattern was repeated and at night, often after dark, he would arrive at their chosen campsite. The first time he set out on his own, Tyrrell did not think there would be any chance of keeping the rendezvous twenty miles ahead. They were in an unknown country and he felt sure he would never see his companions again. But his fears were groundless and when he met the others twenty miles on, a new confidence surged through him. His first day as an explorer had ended successfully.

The assigned task was not an easy one. There was the obvious difficulty of walking all day long counting his steps along the way. In rough country, where the field of vision was limited, the difficulties were compounded by the necessity of moving along in short segments. It was also made more difficult by the necessity, in rough country, of adjusting his count to make up for the variations in the length of his steps as a result of climbing over rocks and other obstacles. For many, the biggest problem would have been in the loneliness of being in the mountains all day long without companionship. A day of it might be relished, but day after day required tremendous inner resources. In this, after the uncertainty of the first day, Tyrrell was fortunate in two ways. First, his partial deafness had already forced him in large measure to reconcile himself to his own company. He was able to be alone; indeed, he was content with his own company. Secondly, he was engrossed by everything around him. Nature knew no bounds for J. B. Tyrrell. Everything was a mystery to be unfolded by his enquiring mind. On this expedition, the work was Dawson's and so was all the credit. Yet, when it was over Selwyn acknowledged in his report, that Tyrrell's own efforts had been responsible for producing "a large collection of plants." Dawson had given his assistant a couple of boards and a bundle of blotting paper and told him to collect whatever he could. It was the least important aspect of the expedition but Tyrrell tackled it with such enthusiasm that it merited special notice.

Occasionally, and only occasionally, Dawson would accompany him on foot part of the way. On the other days, whenever he wanted, Tyrrell was free to go off to one side or the other to examine anything of interest – provided always he returned to the point in the path that he had left to resume his pacing. On one of these side trips he made his first mineral discovery – a three foot thick coal seam. Coal was the major object of their search and Tyrrell's discovery helped guarantee the success of the mission – it also provided the economic basis for the existence of the future town of Fernie, B.C.

From the Crow's Nest Pass they returned to the Garnett ranch, made a short run south during the first two weeks in August and then went back into the western mountains once again via the Kootenay Passes. By September they were heading north on the Columbia River for the Kicking Horse Pass. In the next year the railway would push its way through the pass entering the mountains from the east. With it would come the first elements of the population of the interior. Until the railway arrived, however, a more deserted piece of real estate than that which lay behind the mountain barriers is hard to imagine. Even in 1883, though, it was strange who you could bump into amidst the towering 12,000 foot peaks. On September 21 they were camped on the banks of the Columbia River near the present-day site of Golden, where the Kicking Horse River joins the parent stream, when Major A. B. Rogers walked in. The doughty surveyor of the CPR had spent the summer searching out an alternate route for the railway in order that it might avoid having to follow the great hairpin bend of the Columbia. Scouring around the Selkirk Mountains he had finally found the pass that has borne his name ever since. Now he was heading east to inform the engineers who were pushing the railroad up towards the Kicking Horse Pass. Dawson and Tyrrell were the first to learn of his discovery. That night they sat around the campfire until midnight listening to Rogers's stories of his adventures in locating the route for the railway to follow through the mountains. Later Tyrrell wrote in his notebook:

Among his stories I distinctly remember one about an assistant he had had when exploring for a favourable location for a Railway through the Rocky Mountains. He, the assistant, explored one cross valley which was found unsuitable for a Railway, but which had a lake in it which he named *'Louise'* after Princess Louise, the wife of the Marquis of Lorne, the Governor-General of Canada. Rogers here remarked, 'as this was outside of his duties I discharged him for dragging her Excellency's name into obscurity.'

By the time they reached Kicking Horse Pass in late September their work, fortunately, was more or less over. The pass was not easy to cross; at times it consisted of a narrow ledge high above the river where one foot or hoof out of place would have meant certain death. At other times they were crossing masses or rocks where a horse could hardly find a footing. At night, unable to pitch their tents on the steep mountainsides, they slept with the stars for a roof and the towering trees for walls. "But all the way" wrote J. B. Tyrrell, "we had a series of glorious pictures before us." The world, however, was changing. At Kicking Horse Pass they were amidst the advance parties of railwaymen, the engineers whom Rogers had been hurrying to see. Their job was to decide on the location of the track that was pursuing them. During the course of the summer the rails had been extended to Morley completing the prairie section of the track. From there Dawson was able to secure passage to Calgary for himself and his men aboard one of the construction trains that carried materials to the end of steel.

Calgary itself was crowded, though barely in existence. Its site at the juncture of the Bow and Elbow Rivers had been decided upon and a cable car had been thrown across the Bow. But the town itself consisted of a handful of buildings and the inevitable Calgary House Hotel, already overflowing and having to put its guests (including Dawson and Tyrrell) into annexes – or more precisely – tents.

On October 13, the main work of the summer behind them, Dawson headed home. Tyrrell, however, was left behind to return to the Garnetts' ranch to take care of the materials left behind. Since the next stage coach for Fort Macleod would not leave Calgary for almost a week, Tyrrell decided to set out on horseback. As a result he added further contact with the early ranchers of the area to the experience he had during the summer's work. For the most part he found the tradition of western hospitality already firmly established in that sparsely populated land. There was one exception, however. Arriving in a storm at the Oxley Ranch, two days out of Calgary, Tyrrell sought out the manager of the spread to arrange accommodation for the night. The manager, however, told him that he had better keep on moving along. The bunkhouses and stables were full and he would not be able to spend the night there. In response Tyrrell simply led his horse to the stable and tied it in an empty stall. When he had finished looking after his animal, he went back to the bunkhouse just as the chow was being ladeled out, sat down and ate with the ranch hands. At night he found an empty corner where he slept, curled up in his saddle blanket. The next morning he again joined the men for breakfast, paid the cook for his meals, saddled up his horse and rode off. He had learned another lesson in his new career. Overbearing official-dom whether in government or private enterprise should simply be ignored.

For the most part, though, he did not have to resort to such tactics. The stranger riding up to a western ranch house was welcomed. He brought with him news of the outside and usually repaid his hosts by helping out with the work at hand. On one occasion during this journey Tyrrell repaid the rancher's hospitality in strange coin. Returning to Fort Macleod en route for Calgary from the Garnett ranch he stopped over at the Geddes's spread on Pincher Creek. In the course of the conversation, his host learned that part of the expedition's work that summer had been to search for coal. Geddes, perhaps jokingly, said he wished Tyrrell would find some for him. Taking him at his word, Tyrrell stayed on an extra day to explore some of the valleys in the area and sure enough found evidence of coal in one of them. Some time later, when he ran into Geddes again, Tyrrell asked him about his ranch. In reply Geddes told him he was no longer in the business. Instead he was mining coal.

Back in Calgary once more, Tyrrell's work for the summer was finished. With the prairie section of the railroad completed, he was able to take a CPR train all the way to Winnipeg. Although he would complain about the condition of the second-class coach in which he rode, the summer of 1883 had brought a major advance in the speed with which one could cross the continent from the foothills of the Rockies to the banks of the Ottawa. The trip still required a journey through the United States around the southern shores of the Great Lakes. Two years before, however, when Tyrrell went to Ottawa to join the Survey, it had not even been possible to journey by rail from Toronto to Ottawa. The construction of the railroad was quickly changing the face of the land and Tyrrell was among the first to experience its effects.

Of more importance to the apprentice explorer, however, was the change which the summer of 1883 had wrought in him. There was a new confidence in his step. He had had to cajole Selwyn to send him on his first mission, but now his work had justified his demands. Dawson was a hard taskmaster with little patience with mediocrity but he had nothing but praise for Tyrrell. The Geological Survey had recruited an able apprentice. Tyrrell himself knew that he had found his niche and in doing so his life had changed. Looking back on it, he wrote "I went out a boy and came back a man."

Tyrrell's luck held. In the normal course of things he could have expected to go out on a half dozen more field trips as an assistant before he was entrusted with his own mission. In 1884, however, the Survey was under intense pressure to prove its worth. A select committee of the House of Commons had been appointed to look into its operations and as part of his effort to head off criticism Selwyn decided to put every available man into the field.

The timing could not have been better. Dawson had been well pleased with his assistant's work the year before. He might also have been well pleased with his own success for he had taken an untried youth and, in one short season, turned him into a field geologist. Selwyn decided to risk quickly taking him one step further by giving him an area of his own to investigate in 1884.

The territory assigned was a huge square of some 45,000 square miles in the centre of what became the province of Alberta. It ran more or less from the Bow River and Calgary in the south to the Saskatchewan River and Edmonton in the north and from the future Saskatchewan border in the east to the Rocky Mountains in the west. Here, in the heartland of Alberta, was the job that would make or break Joseph Tyrrell as an explorer with the Geological Survey. Tyrrell was willing to take the chance. If he handled himself competently he could expect to move on to ever more challenging assignments. He never lacked in self-confidence and had no doubt in his own mind that he would succeed. He also knew the other side of the coin. With a tight budget Selwyn could not afford deadwood on the Survey's staff and was ruthless in chopping it out. If he failed, Tyrrell knew he would be looking for another job. Not even his father's political influence would be able to save him.

In all it was to take Tyrrell three years to complete his investigation of the area. The success of the enterprise, however, was assured long before that. If his luck had held in being appointed to lead his own expedition, it had continued into the dramatic findings of his first trip. The territory assigned to Tyrrell was not virgin country in the sense of being unexplored. Along the southern extremity was the newly laid railway track. At the northern extremity of the area, all along the Saskatchewan River, were the sites of existing and former posts of the fur trade. Other explorers had gone ahead of him. Anthony Hendry had run a great swath through the middle of it in 1754-55 and had been followed by numerous others, amongst them William Pink, John Palliser, Peter Fidler, David Thompson and George Simpson. Of all these explorers and traders the one that interested Tyrrell most was David Thompson. In preparing for the expedition and during it Tyrrell used a base map prepared by Thompson in 1813 after his journeys on behalf of the North West Company. The map had been updated by Palliser in the 1850s but had been untouched ever since. Thompson fascinated Tyrrell. At that time he was an almost forgotten figure and yet, as Tyrrell was to discover, his work was far-ranging and extremely accurate.

If the country under investigation was not new in the sense of being unexplored, it was new in the sense of being virtually unpopulated. With the arrival of the railroad in Calgary the previous summer that was beginning to change. It would be only a short time before settlers began pushing north into the region. Indeed that was the *raison d'être* for his being there, to search out the mineral deposits of the area, especially, the coal that would help sustain the new population. Tyrrell's expedition was part of a three-pronged attack on the problem of filling in the details of the country before the settlers arrived. The work was under the general supervision of G. M. Dawson, who was leading a party of his own farther to the south. Tyrrell and his friend, R. G. McConnell, another junior member of the Survey's staff, spearheaded the other two excursions. The three parties operated with the same methods that Dawson had used the previous year. Supplies and equipment were carried by buck-board and wagon while the geologists travelled mainly on horseback – earning for themselves the nickname, "the Geological Cavalry." Tyrrell, however, once credited his success as an explorer to his refusal to be rigid about the methods he used. This was demonstrated during his first solo expedition when he dismounted and with one of his two native helpers decided to canoe down the Red Deer River. His use of the canoe that summer was his first experience with what would become his most common vehicle during his years with the Survey. It was perhaps appropriate that the major discoveries of the summer came during that part of the expedition.

The base point for the operations was Calgary, its population only beginning to grow. The town itself had changed little from the previous year. It still consisted of but a few houses, stores and stables and a lot of tents gathered around the railway station with a cable ferry across the Bow River. From this base Tyrrell's 45,000 square mile territory stretched to the north and east. It was a deserted corner of the globe which he described as a vast solitude where a man could travel for weeks at a time without meeting any other human being. Setting out from the cluster of buildings that were the roots of Calgary, Tyrrell said he could "realize something of the feeling of the younger mariner who wishes to sail his ship within sight of shore rather than strike out across the boundless ocean."

But this young prairie mariner did not hesitate long before he struck out onto the boundless ocean. Nor, for that matter, did he wait long to dive beneath the prairie waves. The best way for a geologist to find out what lies under the ground, he deduced, was to travel through its valleys. There, where water had sliced through the earth's surface, he would be able to detect on the valley walls the layers of geological formations left behind by earlier ages. It was to this end that he decided early in the expedition that since the Red Deer River flowed more or less through the centre of his territory he would begin his work by canoeing along the river course. The decision was fortuitous for in one week he guaranteed the success of his summer's work.

June 9 was a warm, sunny, early summer day. Just before noon Tyrrell and his canoeman pulled up on the bank of the river to prepare lunch. He had already established the work pattern that he intended following. Up for breakfast before dawn and then in the early light packing their gear into the canoe in preparation for shoving off into the stream. All morning they would follow the river's course stopping here and there so that Tyrrell could clamber up the bank to inspect an interesting formation or check out a possible coal seam. A rest and a good meal around noon followed by a walk along the bank before returning to the canoe to repeat the morning pattern. Here and there he would meet up with the wagon that was hauling most of his supplies.

Until lunch June 9 was a day like the others. After lunch it was like no other. Tyrrell set off as usual to examine the nearby banks of the stream in more detail on foot while his canoeman cleaned up the cooking equipment. After he had walked three-quarters of a mile he spotted a strange brownish substance sticking out from the side of the valley about 200 feet above the water level. He quickly climbed up the steep slope. When he reached the brown rock-like substance he stood staring at it. Slowly he fell to his knees and with his hands began clearing the dirt from around it. His big clumsy looking Irish hands were as gentle as a surgeon's as he carefully exposed his find. There is no record of the precise moment Tyrrell realized what he had stumbled upon. But as he cleared away the dirt excitement mounted in him. He had uncovered the fossilized skeleton of a dinosaur. Tyrrell was engrossed by his discovery. All afternoon he continued to dig carefully using either his hands or his little geologist's hammer. For tens of millions of years these bones had lain undisturbed where the prehistoric monster had died. Now he was bringing them to light. A sense of awe gripped him and time stood still. Before Tyrrell's find there had been no indication that so ancient a graveyard existed in the Bad Lands of Alberta. So rare was the find, in fact, that there was no one in Canada capable of evaluating it and the Survey had to ship the bones to Philadelphia for appraisal. He had read of the ancient animals and he had seen the bones that Dawson had uncovered in southern Saskatchewan ten years before. Now he had found another and greater burial place. Although by the end of the day his careful delving into the valleyside had yielded an adequate collection of bones to take back to Ottawa, he still could only guess how extensive the find was. The next day, however, when further downstream, he discovered yet more bones and added them to the collection, he began to realize the magnitude of the deposit. A month later when he looked up the valleyside and saw a great ugly face with rows of "sharp, spikelike teeth" grinning down at him he knew for certain that nothing like this had ever been found before.

The discovery of the dinosaur remains alone would have been sufficient to justify the expense of the trip ten thousand times over. At least it would have been in the eyes of humanity, and perhaps even in the eyes of Selwyn and Dawson. It would not have been looked upon so kindly by the majority of the mining community and a good number of parliamentarians. Fortunately the Red Deer valley had something for everyone. Three days after he had first uncovered the prehistoric remains, and having noted as much as he could about their location and frequency, Tyrrell made another major discovery. As he continued downstream, elated by his find but remembering his instructions, he continued to pay close attention to the evidence of coal seams. On June 12 his investigation paid off. He satisfied the Survey's critics by locating the outcroppings of one of the greatest coal deposits in all of Canada. From this initial discovery grew the extensive coal-mining industry centred in the town of Drumheller. There could never be another week quite like it during the rest of Tyrrell's career. Though he went on to great accomplishments, it is difficult to imagine a single week in which more information could be uncovered than the largest deposit of prehistoric bones in the whole of Canada and the greatest deposit of workable coal.

The week also provided good lessons for Tyrrell on the nature and difficulties of exploration. In his excitement he had been more than diligent in making a collection of the dinosaur bones. Having collected them, however, he now ran head-on into the problem of transportation. With only a wagon and canoe at his disposal, he found it impossible to carry them all and was forced to stockpile most of them to be picked up later. Even so he loaded the wagon so heavily that its axle soon gave out. From then on he was constantly replacing it with new axles made from freshly cut spruce trees which broke easily under the weight of the bones. In exploration specimens should be few and light.

There were other lessons in store for him during this first summer on his own. One was the danger of fire. The mid-1880s were a period of extreme drought in the west. Conditions of dryness were at least as bad as in the dirty 'thirties. The difference was that the land was more or less unpopulated and the dislocations that resulted from the lack of moisture were minimal. It was not, however, minimal for those who were in the territory in those years, though its effects were not felt so much in the form of crop failures as in the form of fires.

In the mountains with Dawson the previous summer, Tyrrell had seen the charred remains of once magnificent forest stands. For days on end they had travelled through the ashes and stumps of pine and spruce. "It is frightful" Tyrrell wrote in his journal "to see so much fine timber gone, rampikes standing in millions all over the country." They themselves were in no danger for, as Tyrrell noted, the territory they were passing through had been "burned over dozens of times" and there was nothing left to burn. In the distance, though, they could see the fires raging and by mid-July the air everywhere in the mountains was getting smoky.

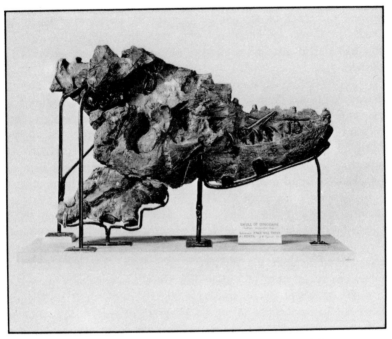

One of the dinosaur heads uncovered by Tyrrell in 1884. (GSC)

During his work on the plains in 1884, fire came dangerously close. This time it was a prairie fire which had been touched off by their own campfire. They had an instant lesson on how quickly the prairie grass can carry flames. A puff of wind turned a smouldering ember into a spreading inferno. Fortunately one of the men was in the camp. His quick action saved them from losing everything. They were camped close by a creek and the man worked feverishly to get everything across the natural barrier beyond the reach of the flames. Despite the speed with which he worked, however, he could not save everything. Tyrrell's own tent was badly damaged and a number of small items were completely burned.

At the end of the summer as he rode home on the train, Tyrrell discovered how extensive the fires were. From Calgary to Winnipeg on both sides of the tracks fires were burning everywhere. The railway might have been a blessing to the country but the sparks from its steam locomotives were a curse to the dry prairies. At one stop the point was underlined as he watched the gory sight of two badly burned men being carried on to the train on stretchers.

Another constant of his expeditions of 1884-86 was the restlessness of the Indians and métis. The Riel Rebellion of 1885 jeopardized most of the western trips of the Surveys. Although they all took place, they were delayed for weeks. Tyrrell himself volunteered to join the military forces being sent to crush the rebellion. A member of the militia since his university days, he thought he might be of some use as a scout or guide. Selwyn, however, had no desire to see his program of work thrown out of kilter any more than necessary and intervened to see that Tyrrell stayed with the Survey. Aside from the delay in starting out, and the disturbing knowledge that they were being kept under surveillance by Indian scouts, the Rebellion had little effect on their work. Crowfoot was in command of the Blackfeet and was determined that his people would not be dragged into the conflict.

Tyrrell only met the famous Indian chief once. In September 1885, having forgotten the lesson of his first expedition with Dawson, Tyrrell awakened one morning to find all but two of his horses had disappeared. After a futile attempt to pay an Indian boy $2.00 to secure the return of the horses (the boy and the $2.00 disappeared as surely as the horses) Tyrrell arranged a meeting with Crowfoot. Their horses had been gone for three days by the time he saw the Chief and a $2.00 reward would obviously no longer be enough to secure their return. Instead Tyrrell upped the amount to $10.00. As Tyrrell put it, Crowfoot "listened with

An earlier west. Dawson's photograph of Fort Calgary in 1881 before the railroad came. (GSC)

Edmonton as Tyrrell saw it from the south side of the Saskatchewan River in 1886. (GSC)

dignity" to the offer. The next day they had their horses back. The meeting with Crowfoot was brief, to the point and all business. An encounter with another Indian in that summer of 1885 touched Tyrrell much more deeply. From it he emerged with a friend whom he would remember for the rest of his life. From it he also derived an understanding of the native people that marked his dealings with them thereafter.

The man's name was William, a Stony Indian from around Morley about forty miles west of Calgary, whom Tyrrell hired as a guide for a side trip to Rocky Mountain House. Together they left the main party and set out to the north. William – young and intelligent – was an ideal travelling companion for Joe Tyrrell. Beginning to pick up a smattering of Indian languages, he learned much more from William who could speak Stony, Cree and a little English. The young guide was also imbued with the love of his people and knew well the heritage of the land they were passing through. These he shared freely with Tyrrell as the relationship between them warmed into friendship. As they passed the battle-grounds of the Cree and Blackfeet from the old days of tribal warfare, the "trackless wilderness" took on a new dimension. It was an enriching experience for J. B. Tyrrell.

Tyrrell in turn tried to impart something of his culture to the young brave. Leaving Morley, Tyrrell presented William with a full set of clothing. William appreciated the gift but, nonetheless, after the first day refused to wear the alien trousers though he continued to wear the shirt. Tyrrell was amused at William's absorption of the Christian faith from the missionaries. Asked to chop wood for the fire on a Sunday, William refused. He was, however, willing to break the wood by hand. Later in the same day huge clouds of snow geese darkened the fall sky as they passed overhead on their annual migration to the south. It was the greatest flock of geese that Tyrrell saw in all his long years in the north and west and he immediately reached for his gun to replenish the larder. William, however, refused to shoot at them. The missionary had told him it was wrong to hunt on a Sunday.

Most of all, however, it was the state of William's health that drew them together. It was this which imprinted William forever in Tyrrell's memory. There would be hundreds of Indian people popping in and out of Tyrrell's life during his travels for the Survey. The memory of most of them blurred into a confusion of names and faces over the years that followed. But the poignancy of William's short life stayed with him. At times as they rode the trails together the young man complained of pains in his chest.

Tyrrell gave him doses of the only "pain killer" he had with him. He knew, however, that his medicine would be to no avail. He had rightly diagnosed William as having "consumption." When they parted that summer Tyrrell feared it would be forever. The following spring his fears were confirmed. William had died during the intervening winter.

During the summer of 1885 and 1886 Tyrrell completed his survey and exploration of the area assigned to him. The spectacular dinosaur and coal finds of 1884 had no doubt increased his stature within the Survey. In the first year, he had been sent out on his own to hire two local men to assist him in his work. In the next two years, however, in addition to a full complement of local men, he also had the help of assistants from the Survey under his command. His rise from third-class clerk to top-rate explorer had truly been meteoric. Despite the upgrading of his work, however, there was never again to be a week like that first one. As Tyrrell put it, "there were no startling discoveries to balance the discomfort."

The discomforts remained, however. Not least of them were bugs. He made a note in his journal about their schedule. "Black flies without number from six a.m. till noon. At eight o'clock the bull-dog flies came to their assistance and made the horses' lives a burden to them until evening. There was a short respite, then the mosquitoes arrived to prevent any rest for the night." Later he would visit the region where Indian legend maintained the Great Spirit had created the blackfly and the mosquito. Later still he would boast that he had developed an immunity to insect bites. But in the summers of 1884, 1885 and 1886 he knew what it felt like to be eaten by them.

These were, however, minor irritants in the larger scheme of things. Far outweighing them was the fact that he had found the kind of life he wanted. He could ask for nothing more. In summer he had before him the outdoors he loved. In winter he had the discipline of long, painful but strangely satisfying hours of writing to produce reports of his summers in the field. Most of all there was the assurance that he had gained his competence. He was moving towards a high degree of professional ability and this was recognized by his compatriots and his superiors as well as by a small though widely scattered public.

CHAPTER 5

Journeyman explorer

Mrs. Buchanan's boarding-house was hardly the ideal accommodation for a young man intent on enjoying the pleasures of life. At ten minutes after midnight on a Saturday night the landlady would wander through the halls of her Rideau Street home in Ottawa's lower town. If there was the least noise coming from any of the rooms she knocked sharply on the door and in her booming Scottish voice reminded her high-spirited boarders that the Sabbath had begun. On the other hand Ottawa was hardly the ideal field in which to sow wild oats. Ottawa society was as tightly corseted as Queen Victoria herself. A man who did not recognize that fact and accept its limitations would soon find himself branded a roué and ostracized in the community. Joe Tyrrell and his compatriots in the Survey had little trouble accepting these limitations. They were, after all, seasonal. For six months of each year a different set of rules applied. In the free society of the unsettled country he explored, there was an easy acceptance of the idea that the woman a man slept with on a regular basis was his "wife." There was, however, no implication that the relationship should last until death parted them. The Hudson's Bay factor transferred from one post to another would leave his native "wife" behind when he moved. The explorer abandoning his base camp, it can be assumed, did likewise.

Within the confines of the well-defined Ottawa social *milieu*, however, Mrs. Buchanan with her strict rules of decorum and no-nonsense approach to life, ran a fine boarding-house. Her main floor suite was occupied by Senator and Mrs. Boyd. That in itself guaranteed the other respectable boarders an introduction into the city's best drawing rooms. Most of the other rooms were occupied by younger members of the Survey. Mrs. Buchanan might almost have put up a sign reading "geological lodgings." In addition to Joe Tyrrell there was his brother James, R. G. McConnell, who was also assigned to the western plains, W. McInnes, A. P. Low and F. D. Adams.

Tyrrell had moved into Mrs. Buchanan's house in 1884. From then until he married in 1894 he returned every winter. Even when she moved from her convenient house on Rideau Street to a less convenient one on Metcalfe Street below Parliament Hill, he and the others were undaunted. They moved with her.

For her part Mrs. Buchanan took good care of her youthful explorers. In the winter they had good food and clean accommodation. In the summer, when they were out on their annual field trips, they did not have to put all their belongings into storage or pay rent on their rooms. She might rent the rooms in the meantime but when they returned from the field the same rooms would be waiting as they had left them. As bachelors their possessions were reasonably limited, although some had particular bulky belongings which would have been awkward to hold on to without Mrs. Buchanan's help. Tyrrell, for example, had as his prized possession a huge leather armchair. Fortunately for Mrs. Buchanan he had not yet begun to indulge his penchant for grandfather clocks. His first of these was not acquired until his colleagues in the Survey presented him with one as a wedding gift. By the time he died he had a dozen or more ticking and chiming in every corner of the house. Whether Mrs. Buchanan's good offices would have extended that far is a little doubtful.

Ottawa before the turn of the century was still very much a small lumbering town. As the country's seat of government it obviously had an enhanced political and social life that it would not otherwise have enjoyed. Even so it hardly equated with life in even the smallest national capital today. The civil service was small and there was absolutely no diplomatic corps. Parliament itself was rarely in session for more than three months each year. In 1881, the year Tyrrell arrived in Ottawa, Parliament had risen in March and did not resume its sitting until the following February. The constant enlivener of the capital scene which distinguished it from any other small town in Canada was the presence of the Governor-General for most of the year. The Marquess of Lorne was a close friend of George Dawson and a frequent visitor in the winter months to the Survey's headquarters. The young officers of the Survey thus had an automatic introduction to the dances and teas at Government House which was the social centre of the capital. These were the highlights of the winter calendar and Tyrrell enjoyed them to the fullest. Later, he would treat his close association with Government House (by then occupied by Lord Aberdeen) with considerable snobbishness. In the 1880s he was less troubled with that weakness. In those years he could still enjoy the events for themselves with a light heart and little concern about who he met or talked with. On one occasion he decided to apply some of his field expertise to a Rideau Hall dance. Before setting out he attached a pedometer to his pants. By the end of the evening he discovered he had danced for twenty-two miles – though admittedly the floor of the ball-room at Government House was somewhat smoother than that of the Red Deer valley.

If the dances at Rideau Hall were the highlights of the social year, a more regular diet was provided for Tyrrell and his friends by their membership in the Ottawa Field Naturalists Club which ran a mixture of social programs and minor excursions into the surrounding area. To fill in the blanks there was the Ottawa Curling, Fencing and Snowshoes Club, whose name speaks for itself; and to further enliven life the snowbound wanderers occasionally managed to escape the confines of Ottawa for larger, and sometimes warmer, centres. Usually these occasions had a business element attached to them as in 1889, for example, when Tyrrell, Dr. Robert Bell, A. C. Lawson and McConnell descended on New York for the annual meeting of the Geological Society of America and in 1893 when, on his way to the Barren Lands he spent a week with Selwyn, Low and McConnell at the World's Columbian Exposition in Chicago. The one purely social jaunt of those years was in 1885 when he and McConnell, his closest friend, went to New Orleans to partake of the pleasures of Mardi Gras – he kept no very full account of that expedition.

For the most part, though, Tyrrell's life in winter was as absorbed by his work as it was in summer. One of the criticisms that had been directed at the Survey by the 1884 Commons' Committee was its delay in recent years in publishing information about the work carried out. To correct this situation Selwyn was pressing his staff to write up an interim account of each summer's exploration for publication in summary form in the Survey's annual report. When an investigation was concluded the entire work had to be weighed, analysed and written up for similar publication. In addition maps had to be prepared to accompany the verbal report. Tyrrell knew nothing of the art and science of cartography when he first arrived in Ottawa, but he soon learned. At the end of his first season in 1883 Dawson presented him with a copy of Chauvenet's *Manual of Spherical and Practical Astronomy* and set him to work making a map based on the pace survey he had conducted.

Even if Selwyn had not been standing over his staff, it is likely that Tyrrell at least would have worked just as hard at producing accounts of his work. He was always anxious, once a task was completed, to see the results published as soon as possible. Tyrrell, therefore, happily devoted long hours to the preparation of his reports, often returning to the office in the evenings and working through until the early hours of the morning.

His official accounts of his explorations, like everything else he wrote, were prepared with painstaking attention to detail. He found writing them laborious, and it often shows. He spoke enviously of Dawson who could produce 4,000 words of a scientific paper in one day with hardly any need for revision, while he, Tyrrell, was lucky if he managed 1,000 words all of which needed painful revision.

Even devoting most of his time to his work, he found that there were simply not enough hours in each day to accomplish all he would have liked. During the first six years in Ottawa he had maintained a professional interest in three fields: botany, zoology and geology. By 1887 he had recognized that if he were to continue in this way he would be spreading himself too thin and would end up accomplishing little in any field. With quiet deliberateness he therefore decided to abandon the study of animal and plant life in favour of developing his expertise on the rocks. He cancelled his subscriptions to all the journals and magazines he had been receiving except those on geology. That decision was a momentous one. On it rested much of his future life not only with the Geological Survey but afterwards as a mining consultant and executive.

That same year had been momentous in another way. His assignment in Alberta had been completed in 1886. In the four years he had spent in the area Tyrrell had earned his spurs as an explorer. Each year had brought an increase in responsibility. At first, under the direct supervision of G. M. Dawson, he had established his powers of observation and his ready ability to grasp the significance of what he found. In his second year he had demonstrated that he could work, and work well, without supervision. Finally in the last two years he had proven his capacity to handle a larger operation by heading up a group in which he was assisted by other experts. Dawson, however, had remained in charge of the general direction of the work on the western plains and in the foothills. On his next assignment the full responsibility for the success or failure of the operation would rest on Tyrrell's own shoulders.

His assignment was to explore what was then northern Manitoba. When the province of Manitoba was created in 1870 following the acquisition of the territories from the Hudson's Bay Company, it had acquired the nickname "the postage-stamp province" from its size and shape – a small square measuring about half its present length along the 49th parallel and extending roughly to the southern extremities of Lakes Winnipeg and Manitoba. In 1881 the province had received its first of two enlargements. Its southern border with the United States was extended to its present length, while to the north it now included all of Lake Manitoba and most of Lakes Winnipeg and Winnipegosis. It still retained its square postage stamp shape but it was now of a larger denomination. With the increase in size and the later completion of the railway, the need to determine the geography and geology of the area was greatly heightened.

The great surge of immigration engineered by Clifford Sifton that would populate the west was still a decade in the future, but already there was a steady if small stream of settlers moving into the territory. The fur traders had been in the area for a century and a half and yet the land and its composition were still almost completely unknown. Once again Tyrrell was to fall back on the maps and journals of David Thompson as the most complete and accurate left by any of his predecessors. In all it would take Tyrrell five years to complete his exploration of the area. During the course of those years he started his work in the western end of the region and each year moved farther to the east.

Personal disaster twice threatened to end his career as an explorer prematurely and, on one of these occasions, his life hung in the balance for weeks. The first incident occurred late in the 1887 season. Chopping wood on October 23, Tyrrell swung the axe into his foot. The wound was bad enough that, after attempting to carry on, he was forced to end the season's work before he was ready to. Had the wound been much more severe or had it become infected in the difficult conditions of the field he might well have lost his foot and found it impossible to continue his annual excursions as an explorer. As it was his recovery was complete and he was able to return to Manitoba the following spring to pick up where he had left off. That next year, however, disaster of another

A lunch stop on the prairies with buck-board and Red River carts. (GSC)

Tyrrell (far left) and some of his party in 1886. D. B. Dowling is next to Tyrrell. (GSC)

sort befell him, cutting off the summer's work in mid-August and placing his life in jeopardy.

Late in July he had been joined in the west by his first teacher in the Survey, J. F. Whiteaves. Whiteaves was making one of his periodic trips into the field to examine the rocks and fossils in their natural environment and Tyrrell had agreed to join forces with him for part of the summer. In mid-August as the party, on the way back to Lake Winnipeg, were about to enter Lake St. Martin, Tyrrell was stricken with typhoid. He had just finished shooting his canoe through the last set of rapids above the lake when he suddenly felt overcome by tiredness. Telling his companions that he was going to rest for a while he lay down on the bank of the river. When next he regained his senses he was in a bed in the Winnipeg General Hospital. In between two weeks had elapsed during which his life had been at stake. On numerous occasions during the course of his explorations the price of failure would have been death. He never shirked in the face of danger. It was part of his ethos that the value of a man's life was in the way he faced difficulty and overcame it. Tyrrell was never found wanting in those hours. But the fight for life in 1887 was of a different kind. There was no matter of strength or courage. He lay unconscious while the forces of nature battled it out within him. In the end his strong body's urge to life won out.

The delirium that had overcome Tyrrell had alerted Whiteaves and their canoemen of the danger and the need to get him out of the wilderness as quickly as possible. Between them they managed to lift his heavy six foot frame into the bottom of one of the canoes and set out back upstream over the rapids to Fairford and an Anglican mission house operated by the Reverend Bruce. The missionary had two things to offer; a bottle of "fine old brandy" and a sailboat. The brandy he started administering at once, but heavy winds made it impossible to set out with the sailboat on Lake Manitoba. Instead Bruce made his charge as comfortable as possible and mounted a constant vigil until, two days later, when the wind finally subsided, they could set out under sail to transport the patient to Manitoba House, the nearest trading post and centre of population. There Tyrrell was given some Indian herbal medicine by "a wise old Indian woman" before being put in a small steamboat owned by a local lumberman and taken to Westbourne at the south end of the lake. Dr. O'Brien was sent from Portage-la-Prairie, twenty miles away.

By the time the good doctor arrived Tyrrell was almost beyond hope. Indeed, Dr. O'Brien concluded that he would only last a day or two at the most. A week later he was still alive and still lying in a tent at the south end of Lake Manitoba. Arrangements could have been made sooner for an engine and car to come up the spur line of the Manitoba and Northwestern Railway to pick him up. Back in Portage, however, Dr. O'Brien had made it clear that he thought Tyrrell would soon be dead. There seemed little point in sending out a train to pick up a corpse. When word trickled down to Portage that after a week Tyrrell was still alive, the attitude changed and an engine and car were soon puffing up the line to Westbourne to pick up the still delirious patient and start him on the way to Winnipeg and proper medical attention. Although he was unaware of what was going on during this time and his struggle for survival on the shores of Lake Winnipeg had nothing to do with any conscious will to live, the dogged determination with which he battled his bout with typhoid is typical of the man. The will to survive, which often found conscious assertion in his exploits, ran into the deepest recesses of his mind and being. Another human might well have succumbed to the banshee's call; Tyrrell could not.

It was another two months before Tyrrell was discharged from the Winnipeg General and able to head east on the CPR. By then he was well on the road to recovery. It was December before he was able to return to work and, though he led his party back into the field in the spring of 1889, he was still not fully recovered and found his work slowed by the need for frequent rest. That did not stop him from making a side trip to Fairford to thank Reverend Bruce and replace his bottle of brandy with two bottles of whiskey. It is also an interesting sidelight on Tyrrell's brush with death in his thirtieth year that, although his notes and diaries often display a mild hypochondria when he was in good health, in dealing with this serious illness he is quite matter of fact about it.

Despite Tyrrell's illness the work of the Survey in Manitoba had continued during the summer of 1888. During his last year in Alberta, Tyrrell had been assigned Donaldson Dowling as an assistant. Tyrrell had mixed feelings about Dowling and although they worked together for seven years he never quite managed to come to grips with the younger man's personality. He had great admiration for Dowling's intelligence – "positively brilliant" was the way he described him. Perhaps the greatest compliment of all was when he described Dowling as being "as keen a geologist as I was." Tyrrell had a good opinion of himself and when he ranked someone as his equal it was the highest compliment he was capable of paying.

There was, however, another side to Dowling that was alien to Tyrrell and quite beyond his comprehension. Dowling was lazy or, as Tyrrell put it, his "brilliance was clouded by physical inertia." Throughout his work for the Survey, Tyrrell found great pleasure in reaching new and unknown places and of being "the first civilized man to see this-and-that." In no small measure the satisfaction of working for the Survey, of facing hardship and deprivation, of going hungry and living under canvas when the temperatures dipped below freezing, lay in those moments when the unknown was suddenly revealed or the earth glowed in the glory of the setting sun or the borealis race. He was surprised to find that Dowling did not share that pleasure. Camped near the deep dark waters of Cree Lake in 1892 Tyrrell suggested they climb a nearby hill to get a view of the lake. After a hard day's work, Dowling's reply was "We'll see it tomorrow." Tyrrell was at a loss. "That practical viewpoint I could not regard with any measure of sympathy; I could not even understand it.. Languor in exploration seemed to me an absurdity." When it came to geology, however, Tyrrell acknowledged that Dowling "worked like a man inspired."

It was fortunate that he did, for during most of the 1888 expedition while Tyrrell fought death, Dowling was on his own. Even when Tyrrell was in the field, Dowling was often off on his own side trips and although Tyrrell could complain about his assistant's lack of romance, he could not fault him on the quality of his work. To Tyrrell's credit he never tried. He had a sufficient breadth of view to accept those who differed from himself. Given that capacity in the senior man, the two geologists were able to work well together. Between them in the course of the five years from 1887 to 1891, they covered the entire area of what was then northern Manitoba. In doing so they used the whole range of travelling devices. In 1887 they travelled north from Brandon on horseback. Their goal was Riding and Duck Mountains and the territory to the east as far as Lake Manitoba. The next year they decided to take to canoes on the waters of the lakes, in 1889 they acquired sailboats to examine the shores of Lake Winnipeg. In between they travelled the interlake district.

By the time they had finished they had acquired a good knowledge of the land and its properties. The road, if not paved, had been smoothed for the migration that would soon settle

Early Manitoba as Tyrrell saw it. Top: the village of Russell in 1887; and bottom: sailboats at Swampy, Manitoba. Tyrrell's boat, the *Pterodactyl*, is on the far left. (GSC)

Manitoba. Twenty years after his work in the area was finished Tyrrell was back in the district and saw a changed land. In 1889 there had been a solitary shack on the Vermilion River where the town of Dauphin would soon be. When he went back in 1908 the transformation had taken place. The shack "had become a town of three thousand people." Tyrrell had concluded that the land of that area was well suited for farming and events had proven him right. In later years a farm implement dealer told him that if a man had come to them in 1887 wanting to buy a baler for a farm on the Vermilion River they would have concluded he was insane and refused to sell him the machinery for anything other than spot cash. Twenty years later the area was a major centre of agricultural production.

During these years in Manitoba two of Tyrrell's primary interests outside of his immediate work as an explorer were beginning to take shape. His decision at the end of 1887 to devote all his time to the study of geology quickly began to pay dividends. Before he was finished in Manitoba he had collected a good deal of evidence and data on the massive body of ice that had covered the area during the ice age. It was the beginning of a development which would lead him in 1897 to propound some revolutionary new theories on the process of glaciation which in turn would open the door for the scientific community to reach a new understanding of where the world had been long ages before and how it had progressed since. Also in the area of theoretical geology, Tyrrell used his time in Manitoba to further advance the knowledge of Lake Agassiz, the ancient lake that had once covered much of the eastern prairie with its waves. Tyrrell was during those years the Canadian editor of the *American Geologist*. His counterpart in the United States was Warren Upham, who did more than any other man to push back the frontiers of knowledge on the ancient lake. To Upham's work, Tyrrell added the footnotes further delineating the extent of land that the lake had once covered, just as others would later add the footnotes and revise the details on his own theories of glaciation.

At the same time his interest in David Thompson was growing and developing. Thompson came to occupy in Tyrrell's estimation the position of "the greatest land geographer who ever lived." In Alberta he had used Thompson's map as a guide for his work. In Manitoba his path kept crossing and recrossing Thompson's. Even back in Ontario, recuperating from his bout with typhoid, he could not escape the earlier explorer. A neighbour of his father's in Weston told him, while he was convalescing there, that he had in his home Thompson's handwritten narrative of his travels. During that late winter of 1888 Tyrrell took the opportunity to read Thompson's manuscript. With each passing year as he checked his own findings against those of Thompson he became more and more aware of how accurate and how extensive Thompson's surveys were. A few years later Tyrrell purchased the manuscript for his own use and for years after he spent much of his spare time editing it and adding material from Thompson's notebooks. In 1916, having thus prepared the manuscript it was published by the Champlain Society. That action, added to the speeches, papers and article that Tyrrell delivered on Thompson, saw the earlier explorer restored to his rightful place in the annals of Canadian history.

The sceptic might suggest that Tyrrell's only interest in reviving the memory of Thompson (and later of Samuel Hearne) was in maintaining the reputation of those whose work most closely coincided with his own. In fact this motivation was somewhat more altruistic. He was one of the most competent men to undertake the task of making the diaries and journals available to future generations. He had walked their trails and crossed their paths and he knew the difficulties on rivers and lakes which they had encountered. He knew the land they had crossed and the long cold nights on the prairie and on the tundra which they had endured to cross it. He knew too of the challenge of setting out into the unknown.

His interest in history was deep and abiding. In an age when it is fashionable for "professional" historians to decry the work of "amateurs," Tyrrell's efforts are likely to be written off as lacking in analysis or refinement of judgment. In Tyrrell's case such criticism would be foolish. His sojourn into history was not the minor dabblings of one of the idle rich, his interest in these earlier explorers occupied more than half his lifetime and his work on them was carried out with the same thoroughness with which he mapped the contours of a river on a scale of two miles to the inch. In addition, as he travelled through the country of the fur traders, he had used every opportunity that presented itself to trace the history of the region. At each Hudson's Bay Company post, he delved into the records of the past as deeply as time permitted. He was well prepared for the task of editing the journals. As a sidelight his interest in the history of the regions has, in many cases, provided the only remaining evidence on the exact sites of some of the old trading posts and forts. Many of the Hudson's Bay Company records are vague on the locations of the posts and today the sites have often been ploughed under or built over. But in the 1880s and '90s there were still signs of where the wooden structures had once stood and Tyrrell diligently took time out to plot the location of the ruins.

There was a logical progression to Tyrrell's move into the north; indeed it seems in retrospect that there was an element of inevitability to it. Once his work on what was then the northern half of Manitoba was finished it was natural to extend the area of investigation yet further to the north into the territory that would be added to Manitoba in 1912 and the northern section of what was to become the province of Saskatchewan. In 1892 Tyrrell, with Dowling once more as his assistant, was instructed to open up this new field of exploration. The area assigned was essentially that between Lake Athabasca and the Churchill River in the north and south and between Athabasca River and Reindeer Lake to the west and east. The move into these more northerly climes was a foretaste and a fore-runner of things to come. Soon Tyrrell was to embark on the greatest expedition of his life. The Barren Lands expedition of 1893 arose directly out of his work in 1892.

In 1892, once more, only the missionaries and fur traders had gone before him and foremost among them was David Thompson. Again it was driven home to Tyrrell how extensive and accurate Thompson's travels and observations had been. Even so the fur traders and missionaries had been content to move around the perimeter of this new territory. In the middle was a vast area covering the northern half of Saskatchewan and spilling over into Alberta and Manitoba, of which nothing was known. Tyrrell's task was to open the area.

To tackle the job Tyrrell decided that he and Dowling should split into two parties. Tyrrell sent his assistant west to Edmonton and Athabasca Landing. From there Dowling was to lead one group down the Athabasca River into Lake Athabasca making a survey of the district as he went. Then, not later than August 1, he was to rendezvous with Tyrrell at Fond du Lac in the narrow eastern part of the lake and from there they would combine their forces as they moved back to the east. For his own part Tyrrell in the meantime would lead a party northward through the middle of the territory to Fond du Lac. Starting from Ile a la Crosse, which was reached via Prince Albert, Tyrrell's route would take him, with many portages, down the Churchill and then up its tributary, the fast flowing Caribou River, on which it was possible only to make seven or eight miles a day against the swift current. From the upper reaches of the Caribou River he would lead his group over the height of land to Cree Lake and then down the Cree River to Black Lake and Athabasca Lake for his meeting with Dowling.

Early in the work Tyrrell was reminded once more that in the business of exploration, the unexpected and possible tragedy were constant companions. Nature's violence was always close at hand. His party was camped in a grove of poplars on the banks of the Caribou at the time. When they turned in for the night it was a clear, starry evening. Overnight, however, a storm started brewing. As the wind grew in strength one of the old poplars, having stood in the face of storms for decades, finally gave out, its trunk snapping in the gale. The tree crashed straight into the middle of their camp, its trunk landing across one of the tents where a man lay sleeping. Two huge limbs dug into the ground on either side of the tent. The trunk stopped just inches above the canvas. Had the limbs broken, or had the tent been pitched a couple of feet to one side or the other the occupant would have been crushed.

Making note of the incident, Tyrrell remarked that it had almost destroyed his record of never having a man killed on one of his expeditions. It was a seemingly heartless comment. A man had almost been killed and all he could think about was his record. It was, however, an achievement to be proud of. In the course of his field work for the Survey he led about a hundred men out into the unknown and brought every one back alive.

By the time Tyrrell reached Black Lake in late July he was at the halfway point of the summer's work. He was also at the utmost extremity of known territory. Even David Thompson had never ventured further to the north. On his way into the region, however, he had been startled to meet another party coming out. These were, surprisingly, not fur traders or Indians or other members of the Survey on an overlapping mission. Instead they were Americans on a hunting expedition during which they had wintered near Cree Lake. Not quite the modern American tourist who flies into Canada's northern lakes to hunt and fish, they were the forerunners of that breed. The two parties stopped to exchange news and information. For good measure Tyrrell, in the way of the wilds, gave them some sugar – a commodity they had been without for months. The meeting with the Americans, however, yielded nothing but an interesting footnote in the history of exploration.

A meeting with Indian hunting parties on Black Lake a few

weeks later was a different matter. It opened up an enormous territory of the Canadian north and gave Tyrrell a claim to fame instead of a life of anonymous, though dedicated, service which was the fate of most of his colleagues. On the beach of Black Lake, beside three tiny log cabins, nine Chippewyan canoes were drawn up. Tyrrell was in a hurry to meet Dowling and could only stop briefly. What he heard of the heights of land and the great river on the other side which flowed to the north caught his imagination. At every opportunity from here on he would find out all he could about this Chippewyan hunting ground. There was plenty of opportunity. Before he had ever left Black Lake at least ten more Indian canoes had passed him on their way to the north. From each he learned a little more. Arriving at Fond du Lac ahead of Dowling he continued his quest for information.

Tyrrell was fascinated by the stories of the uncharted northern stream. Here was the explorer's dream, an unsuspected route through a vast unknown territory; an opportunity, at one fell swoop, to remove one of the last remaining veils from the face of the north. Already the plan for 1893 was hatching in his mind.

But that was next year's adventure. In the meantime there was other work to be done before winter set in. For the next three weeks the whole party travelled as a unit exploring the eastern portion of Athabasca Lake, Black Lake and the route to Wollaston Lake. Here Tyrrell again decided to split the party. He sent Dowling and the others to cross from Wollaston to Reindeer Lake and then via Ile a la Crosse to Prince Albert where they would meet again. In the meantime he and two of the Indian canoemen who had travelled with him all season set out up the Geikie River on an old, unused Chippewyan route to once again explore the interior of the region.

Paddling up the Geikie from Wollaston Lake, Tyrrell was paddling into a new and unique experience. For perhaps the only time in all his wanderings he was about to become lost. It is hard to imagine the feeling. For ten years he had been travelling through unmapped territory yet in all that time he had been reasonably sure of where he was and roughly where he was going. There were no signposts and much of the time he was making the first maps of the area. Around any bend of any river there might be new discoveries or new dangers. Yet through it all he had a fixed notion of where he was and how to get out again. In the upper reaches of the Geikie that was no longer true. The river branched out in all directions and soon they were travelling along one of the thousands of streams that drained the area. Then they started portaging between the hundreds of small lakes trying to reach the height of land. Soon they were lost with no hope of retracing their steps to Wollaston Lake. In the midst of these difficulties, serving to further disorient him, Tyrrell's watch broke and he was left to judge the time from the sun. Of one aspect of time though he had no doubt. All around him were nature's signs that the season was far gone and there were few weeks left for unplanned exploration.

Tyrrell was worried. They had not met a living soul since leaving Wollaston. Nor were the two men accompanying him of any help. Neither one of them was Chippewyan. They knew nothing of the country they were in. Tyrrell wrote:

> As no one has any idea of the course we have to follow, we have to search the shores of all the lakes for signs of portages, and these are all very old, no Indian having been here in summer for a great many years. The portages when found are all blocked up, and have to be chopped out. Now we are camped on a little lake with a stream flowing northward or north-eastward from it. We are going to follow this stream, but where it will lead us to, no one here knows.

The problem was getting serious.

For days they wandered lost amongst the hills, streams and little lakes of northern Saskatchewan. The dense forest around them offered few landmarks. For once Joe Tyrrell lost sight of the romance of exploring new territory. Each new lake was beginning to look like the one before. They were, however, different and at last they stumbled upon one which one of his companions recognized. Years before on a hunting trip he had reached this lake from his home near Ile a la Crosse.

Relief flooded Tyrrell's mind. All that remained now was to descend the waterways back to their starting point at Ile a la Crosse. There were difficulties in store. The rivers and trails always had their difficulties. But by comparison to the terrible anxiety of being cut adrift without his bearings the problems were now minor. The most annoying of these was the fact that during the delay they had used up all of their supplies and were now forced to hunt for everything they ate. In addition, on one of the portages, Tyrrell encountered a new danger that he had never experienced before. As they set out on the portage he noticed a large piece of birch bark hung on one of the trees. Guessing that it had been put there deliberately he took it down and discovered it had writing in Indian characters on it. Completely at a loss as to its meaning he handed it to one of his companions for translation. Translated it read, roughly "Danger. There are two bear traps hidden on the path of this portage."

Thus forewarned the travellers passed without harm and by early October were back in Prince Albert. After a side trip to examine some coal seams in the neighbourhood, Tyrrell was soon homeward bound though, as he put it, Ottawa and Mrs. Buchanan's boarding-house were really little more than a "diversion" during his bachelor days. His real home was in the wilderness. Looking back on those years he summed up his life as a journeyman explorer:

It seemed that hard physical and mental labour for from fourteen to sixteen hours a day was just what I needed. I slept violently, I ate with energy, when meals were available, and the untainted air of the North renewed my youth like the eagle's. . . . My ideal of peace and comfort was a tent by a clear brook anywhere north of 50 degrees of North Latitude, a ground-sheet and blankets enough, a side of salt pork and a bag of flour. For variety of diet I had the conversation of wood-wise and hard-bitten white frontiersmen and voyageurs. For glory I had the stars and the Northern Lights. For education I had the clear evidence in every mile of the Creator's genius in the building of a world. . . .

With only a few exceptions the Indians who travelled with us from time to time were good workers and amusing companions. Their close knowledge of trails and canoe-routes, old and new, was freely given and was most valuable. I had a fair command of the Cree dialect; good enough to carry on a conversation and I learned not a few of the traditions of the tribes.

CHAPTER 6

Return to the Barrens

"Talk to him if you can; but he is the hardest man to talk to I ever met." With these words of caution Eleanor Carey introduced her younger sister, Mary Edith, to Joseph Burr Tyrrell. Joe never was much of a conversationalist. The hearing impediment which was the legacy of his early bout with scarlet fever inhibited him for the rest of his life in the give and take of conversation. He was, however, a good talker, especially if steered onto the subject of his work. Edith Carey may have been young – only that day she had "put up" her hair for the first time – but she was wise in the ways of the world. Within minutes, with a few loud-voiced questions, she had him talking about himself and his explorations. From then on she was content, "Desdemona-like," to sit listening – all the while "admiring his splendid physique."

J. B. Tyrrell did present a striking figure to the impressionable daughter of a Baptist minister. Six foot tall, fair hair and beard, a handsome man of no mean accomplishment, it was little wonder the young lady was swept off her feet. She had first spotted him sitting in a pew of her father's church. All through the service on that first day she "entertained" herself by looking at him. It was love at first sight. "That night" wrote Doll "when talking to my sister Ellie, I said 'When one sees a man of that kind, all others seem so uninteresting and tame!' It was evident what had happened. I had met 'my man' and instantly had recognized him."

Their courtship proceeded in accordance with the rules of the day. Joe found excuses to visit Doll's home: at first, on Sunday evenings, to discuss the morning's sermon with the Reverend Carey; later, and more ingeniously, to discuss the Book of Ezekiel. In this, as in everything, he was meticulous. Doll described his technique. "He purchased a Commentary on Ezekiel and brought his profound geological knowledge to bear on the Valley of the Dry Bones."

The field work of the summer of 1891 intervened and passed. During the ensuing winter the courtship was resumed and bore fruit. Joe put it succinctly, "Socially I spent some evenings at the home of the Rev. Dr. Carey on Metcalfe Street, and on May 29th, 1892 I asked his youngest daughter to marry me, and she said she would." That done, J. B. set out for his 1892 expedition into the Athabasca region. Before he left, however, he made sure that his future bride would be well prepared for marriage. He set out "a course of reading" in the field of geology for her, including Archibald Geikie's *Primer of Geology* and his *Textbook of Geology* and Alexander Winchell's *Walks and Talks in the Geological Field.*

At the more mundane level, however, he was somewhat less instructive in the knowledge he passed on to Doll. Joe had one major problem facing him as he contemplated marriage. He was broke. His salary was not large and his generosity in meeting the needs of his parents in their old age had prevented him from accumulating any savings. In the late Victorian era for a man to marry penniless was not a particularly popular or acceptable action. With what was perhaps his last act of freedom from financial concern – at least until he became a millionaire from mining gold – he simply ignored the problem. Until after they were married he never mentioned to her that they might have difficulty living in the style to which they both aspired on his salary of $1,500.00 a year. He was not being deceitful. As he saw it financial matters were not a fitting subject for discussion between a man and a woman. It was a man's duty to shield a woman from such harsh realities. She was, after all, the weaker vessel – an ornament of whom little was expected except a command of the social graces. He paid dearly for his lack of candour. It contained the roots of many future conflicts between themselves and with others. In the years of financial strain that followed she nagged him over finances and finally forced him to search out another career.

In the meantime, however, no such clouds shaded them from the full light of love. The long separations caused by his work meant that much of their courtship was conducted by mail. The letters are cast in the popular romantic conceptions of the times; seemingly flowery and poetic, they are in fact rather stiff. In his letters to her he never, before their marriage, addressed her by her nickname "Doll" but always by her given name "Edith" and each letter is signed, after appropriate assurances of undying love,

"J. B. Tyrrell." Only once in all the love letters does he reveal his own self-knowledge to her. Referring back to a tiff they had had, he writes that the thought of having almost "lost" her makes him "shudder" every time he thinks of it. He goes on "But that merely arises from my own egotism which is unmercifully strong. A solitary life tends to make one egotistical." Even this accurate self-analysis, however, was tinted with the romantic notion that love would conquer. The letter continues, "in future your interests will add a higher motive to existence and a constant thought for another will develop a higher and fuller manhood in me."

"Her wedding gown was of white Irish poplin, with trimming of Limerick lace, tulle veil and orange blossoms." So read the *Ottawa Citizen* report of the wedding. The Irish poplin and Limerick lace were appropriate. They hearkened back to her Irish ancestors from whom she also inherited her swift temper and quick tongue.

Although Joe and Doll were to have a long married life it was far from a smooth relationship. In the more permissive social environment of the later twentieth century they would probably have seriously contemplated separation and divorce. But in the late nineteenth and early twentieth century that was hardly a reasonable alternative. Instead they stuck it out together along a rocky road marked by long visits home to mother and great screaming matches between the two of them. Joe's hearing problem led him to talk loudly anyway and when his voice increased in volume in the middle of a dispute he was automatically close to shouting. Doll, not to be outdone, or shouted down (or ignored on the pretext that he had not heard her) raised her voice accordingly and soon the rafters were ringing. As early as 1897, Joe was writing that they would have to try harder to avoid angering each other and was longing for a common interest that would absorb them both. Doll was paying the price for her Victorian women's guile which had snared a husband by pretending that the great thing they held in common was an insatiable interest in his life and work. J. B. was not the first man to discover that when the marriage was consummated the interest was more easily sated.

Yet there was also a tenderness between them. A grand-daughter, recalling their last years together when Doll was senile and J. B. was in his late eighties and willing to see his life end if only his strong body would give out, remembers in particular how he would run his fingers through her hair or how their hands would meet in a gentle assurance of love.

That same gentleness was also characteristic of their earlier

107

years. But in those days, faced with tight finances, it was often buried from sight. Doll was ambitious for her husband and her nagging coloured his relationship with many of his colleagues, his best friends, and even with his own brother and northern companion, James. When, a few years after they were married, it turned out that the Survey was sending both Joe and his longtime friend R. G. McConnell to the Yukon to investigate the gold deposits, Doll was urging Joe to make sure he finished writing his report on the Territory before McConnell could get his done. "You must work night and day to get it finished" she wrote, and it must be a "splendid report." That way Tyrrell's report would be published and his friend McConnell's would be left to gather dust. With James, Doll's venom also came at the time of the gold rush. She could not forgive James for publishing an account of the Barren Lands trip and when Joe was thinking of inviting his brother to join him in the Klondike in 1900, Doll wrote, "I should never consent" to James becoming a partner in the business. A year later she had relented enough that Joe did invite James to come to the Klondike, but they never became partners and after one season James returned to Ontario.

All that was in the future, however. On February 14, 1894, there was not even a cloud on the horizon as the "lovely bride" threw her "bouquet of white roses and lily of the valley" over her shoulder and left with her handsome husband for a honeymoon at Niagara Falls. Joe had changed since she first met him. For one thing he had shaved off his beard for the wedding. For another, he had gained the status of a celebrity.

The telegraph wires that had carried the "All well" message to the east on New Year's Day, 1894 and the wide publicity that had ensued alerted social Ottawa. By the time Tyrrell arrived there he found himself in great demand for soirées and dinners. And when the six foot tall "scientific vagabond" took "Dr. Carey's vivacious and lovely young daughter" as his wife on St. Valentine's Day, the invitations only increased as the romantic interest heightened. Years later Doll recalled how one Ottawa matron whom she met at Government House shook her warmly by the hand and said "Had I known how distinguished your husband was, I would certainly have called upon you, but I will do so now."

Government House was the centre of Ottawa's social life at the turn of the century. There, in the best European tradition, suitably modified to meet the exigencies of the lumber town capital at the junction of the Rideau and the Ottawa, the vice-regal couple held court. And in that court the Squire of Weston's son and the Baptist minister's daughter were now warmly welcomed. Even before they were married J. B. had been invited to dinner by the Governor-General. Then, after dinner, as the cigars were passed around and the port served, Tyrrell regaled Lord and Lady Aberdeen and their aides with stories of his exploits in the Barren Lands. The Aberdeens were new to Canada having arrived only the previous September to take up their duties. In a sense Tyrrell's monologue was therefore their introduction to the more remote corners of their vice-regal domain and to the work of exploring it. The account of his travels fascinated the Aberdeens and they and their aides sat up until the early hours of the morning listening to his tale. From that first contact Tyrrell became a firm favourite at the court of Queen Victoria's representative. Always a bit of a snob, Tyrrell bathed in the warmth of the vice-regal smile. Other invitations followed. One was to give a lecture at the Haddo Club composed of the members of the household at Rideau Hall. Here, once again Tyrrell held his audience spellbound as he recounted his adventures and evaluated the importance of the land he had gone through. On another occasion the Aberdeen's invited Joe and Doll to be the guests of honour at a dinner – the final, public seal of vice-regal approval. From then on they were much in demand as guests on the Ottawa scene.

This social prominence plus the public renown that came in the wake of the newspaper accounts of his exploits were welcome to Tyrrell. Years later he would insist that the notoriety had been "almost embarrassing." He was, after all, only "a man plugging along on $1,800.00 a year and more interested in his job than in the transitory laurels of popularity." The disclaimer is appropriately modest. It is also a little dishonest. J. B. may indeed have realized that his brief moment of fame was but a "transitory laurel." He also knew that such fame could be used to good measure. From his first interview with a reporter in Calgary on his way back from his expedition with G. M. Dawson, he had been more than willing to see his exploits placed before the attention of the public. He was his own P.R. man and he did it well. He recognized the variety of the media and tailored the accounts of his adventures accordingly. For the annual reports of the Survey his writings were detailed, meticulous and comprehensive; for the scientific community, his articles and papers were innovative and careful; for the popular press his stories were adventurous and inspiring.

If he had any doubts about the value of "transitory laurels" his experiences in the winter of 1893-94 after he returned from the Barren Lands would have laid them to rest. Tyrrell wanted to go back into the area the following summer for yet another expedition, this time crossing the tundra by a different though parallel route. From the Eskimos and Indians in 1893 Tyrrell had heard of the Kazan River lying to the south and east of the Dubawnt and draining the area of northwestern Manitoba and northeastern Saskatchewan. To travel this route seemed the logical follow-up to his work of 1893. He broached the matter with Dr. Selwyn who agreed that such an exploration would be valuable. As director of the Geological Survey, however, Selwyn had two problems to contend with in authorizing the trip. First, there was the fact that the publicity surrounding Tyrrell's achievement was causing unrest amongst the other members of his staff. Tyrrell was not the only man in the Survey to brave the elements or risk his life in unfolding the mysteries of the subcontinent. All of them, his contemporaries like Low and McConnell, his seniors like Dawson and Bell, and Selwyn himself, even his juniors the new technocrats of exploration like Dowling who could see no point in climbing a hill just to see a sunset, took similar risks. But Tyrrell's exploits had caught the public imagination. He had opened up for the average Canadian a glimpse of "the true north, strong and free." Indeed he did more than give them a glimpse, he became its personification. He, too, was strong and free. In the annals of Canadian history, whenever that image had been evoked, the response had been overwhelming. John Diefenbaker did it in 1958, John A. Macdonald did it in 1867, and Tyrrell did it in 1893. The price, however, was petty jealousy within the Geological Survey. Tyrrell wrote "it was not to be wondered at if some members of the staff who had done just as good and difficult exploratory work got tired of the stories about our work, and perhaps in good nature criticized it." The scathing remarks about "Tyrrell's polar bears" were not all that good natured. Selwyn, aware of the disgruntlement was not anxious to reinforce it by sending Tyrrell back into the Barren Lands.

On top of that there was the cost of the expedition. As always Selwyn's budget was inadequate and, comparatively, Tyrrell's 1893 expedition had been an expensive proposition, eating up over $7,000.00 of the Survey's limited funds. Already under pressure from the mining community to do more and spend less, Selwyn was not anxious to invite the *Mining Review* to renew its attack on Tyrrell and the Survey by sending him back into the same area again. Nor was he anxious to give the Opposition in Parliament any more ammunition with which to bombard him. When the $7,000.00 cost of Tyrrell's expedition came under criticism there, Sir John Thompson, then Prime Minister, had to get into the act. Even at $7,000.00 he told the House, Tyrrell's party had almost starved to death. He hated to think what might have happened had they been fed more penuriously.

Faced with both of these factors, Selwyn assured his northern vagabond that he appreciated the value of the work he had done and recognized the need to follow it up by returning to the Barren Lands. He also informed him, however, that there would be no funds available for such a trip in 1894. The vagabond would be confined to less far-reaching endeavours. It was here that Tyrrell showed that he was well aware of the fact that his "transitory laurels" had some substance to them. The social events at Rideau Hall brought him into contact with Robert Munro-Ferguson, a wealthy young Scottish adventurer who had hunted big game in Africa and who, Tyrrell was told, had been in partnership with Teddy Roosevelt in a ranching operation in the western United States. He had come to Canada the previous September with Lord Aberdeen and was now resident in Ottawa as the Governor-General's aide-de-camp. But the relatively sedate life of Canada's capital did little to quench his thirst for adventure. Listening to Tyrrell's accounts of his escapades only further aroused his desire to break out from the routine of life at Rideau Hall. The final straw was Tyrrell's description of the massive herds of caribou that roamed the northern wilderness. Munro-Ferguson decided that there was nothing for it but to go on another safari – this time to the Barren Lands of Canada as part of the next Tyrrell expedition.

Knowing Munro-Ferguson's desire and aware of the Governor-General's interest, Tyrrell knew he had powerful allies in persuading the director of the Survey to change his mind. Ferguson's role was mainly financial. He was willing to pay his own expenses. The Governor-General's role was both financial and political. He, too, was willing to pick up part of the tab out of his own pocket. More important, however, he was willing to use his influence with his advisers to persuade Selwyn to change his mind. Undoubtedly, in constitutional terms, the Governor-General relied on the prerogative of the Crown to "encourage" his ministers in a course of action. In practical terms he persuaded Selwyn's boss, T. M. Daly, the Minister of the Interior, that the director was making a bad decision and should think again. Whether the proposition was put to Selwyn in the language of political realities is unknown. What is known is that on Queen Victoria's seventy-fifth birthday (May 24, 1894) Selwyn told Tyrrell that he had been reconsidering his decision and would probably be sending him back to the Barren Lands after all – no doubt he would have been only too happy at that point to send his ambitious assistant to a much warmer place. Be that as it may, a few days later he confirmed with Tyrrell that he would be returning to the Barren Lands – though the Survey would only provide a budget of $1,300.00 for the expedition. The "transitory laurels" had proven their worth.

Once he had been given permission to go back to the Barren Lands, Tyrrell the political manoeuvrer faded into the background and Tyrrell the professional explorer took over once more. Selwyn's confirmation that he would be returning was only given on May 28. Two weeks later, on June 12, he and Munro-Ferguson were on the train to Winnipeg. In those intervening two weeks, all the preparations had to be made. Two nineteen foot cedar strip canoes were acquired from the Peterborough Canoe Company. New instruments were purchased in Toronto to replace the ones left behind on the shore of the Hudson Bay the year before. Since funds were tight the expert canoemen from Caughnawaga had to be replaced by men available in Winnipeg. The Winnipegers would be on the payroll for a shorter period and their fare would not have to be paid to travel halfway across the continent to take up their duties and to return home at the end of the season. Telegrams were sent to the Hudson's Bay Company in Winnipeg to hire the men and also to arrange for the purchase of supplies and letters of credit to be used at the company posts along the way. Finally, having learned from his experience of the preceding year, arrangements were made for the Hudson's Bay Company to ship sufficient supplies to Fort Churchill during the summer so that the party would not be a drain on the local population when they showed up in the fall. Joe figured that if they had 500 pounds of flour, 25 pounds of tea, 100 pounds of rolled bacon, 100 pounds of sugar and 50 pounds of evaporated apricots waiting for them at the fort, the welcome would be somewhat warmer than it had been the year before. While still dealing with the problem of food supply, Tyrrell also concluded an arrangement with the Militia Department to undertake what was probably the first example of testing Canadian military equipment in a northern environment. The Department was considering arming the militia with the new Lee Metford 303 rifle and J. B. undertook to take one of the guns with him to test under field conditions. The gun was reputed to have a range of three miles. If it could drop a deer at 400 yards it would make a good militia rifle – it would also make life much simpler on the coast of Hudson Bay. When it was put to the test the gun lived up to his expectations. "A magnificent rifle" Tyrrell proclaimed. The first time he tested it was at one of the trading posts on the Saskatchewan River. To a round of applause from the assembled populace the bullet ripped through two huge tree trunks. Later, on the shore of Hudson Bay he was able to kill game at distances of up to 700 yards. It was certainly an improvement over the Winchester he had used the year before. When he reported back to the Militia Department, they were sufficiently grateful that they presented him with the gun as a souvenir.

Finally, before leaving on the expedition, he had his new wife to take care of. Doll's father had by this time left his Ottawa parish to serve in a church in Saint John, New Brunswick. Since she could not reasonably be left to fend for herself in Ottawa, J. B. arranged for her to spend the summer and fall with her parents in her native Maritimes. Then, with Doll safely on the train he had to hunt up an insurance agent so that she would not be left destitute if he did not return.

With the arrangements made he and Munro-Ferguson boarded their train for the west. Their arrival in Winnipeg was replete with a welcome from the Lieutenant-Governor. Tyrrell already knew Sir John Schultz from his previous work in the area and the highlight of this visit was that Schultz swore him in as a justice of the peace for the Keewatin District. The days in Winnipeg were busy ones for Tyrrell. All the final preparations had to be made for the journey ahead. The supplies still had to be checked out with the Hudson's Bay Company as did the canoemen the company had hired for him. Because of the limited funds allocated for the expedition he had only bought two Peterborough canoes from the east. Here in Winnipeg, Governor Schultz offered to supply a third for them. Tyrrell, delighted, went off in search of a good cedar vessel only to discover that there was none to be had and that he would have to settle for a rougher, and therefore slower one made out of birch bark. In addition, at the last minute, he suddenly had to find a replacement for their cook. The one he had already hired had just seen his home destroyed by fire and had to stay in Winnipeg until he could re-establish his family. Three potential replacements were identified. To their chagrin, the first, and best of these had just been hired by another expedition. The next, a young Englishman, named Nichols was willing to accompany them. Unfortunately, he had just been married and his wife "wouldn't let him come." The search for a cook provided Munro-Ferguson with his first introduction to life on the Canadian frontier. He committed to his diary what he discovered about Nichols's search for a wife.

Apparently Nichols, who lived at Selkirk, went to Winnipeg and told "the boys" that he needed a wife and to "send him up samples." They were also told that he "would prefer a hot blooded Italian" to a cup of "ice water." The boys checked out what was available and "a good many were sent up for trial and on approval – the best apparently 'took hold.' " Once she had taken hold, the explorers discovered, Nichols's freedom of movement was over – he was no longer available as a travelling cook.

They were therefore left with their third and last prospect, an unknown quantity named Bell. Joe Tyrrell, always willing to give a man a fair trial, wrote to Doll shortly after they set out, "Our cook has been serving us excellent meals – ham, fish, bread, pie etc. The dried apricots made excellent pies. He is a young fellow with only one eye, very much given to talking, but if he can paddle and cook that will not matter much." Ferguson's description of Bell was a little less generous. He described him as "a picayune little cuss with one eye [who] went on the dead drunk for several days." As it turned out Ferguson's description was the more accurate, although undoubtedly coloured by an unexpected and unwanted swim in the Saskatchewan River. As they were leaving Lake Winnipeg and moving through the Grand Rapids at the outset of their journey by canoe, the cook at one point was on the bank hauling the canoe which held one of the men, a portion of their supplies, two carrier pigeons which Tyrrell planned on sending back with messages from the wilderness, and Munro-Ferguson. Bell (whether drunk or sober is not clear) slipped; the canoe tipped; the birds drowned; Munro-Ferguson found out how cold northern water can be in June. Munro-Ferguson was furious at the "one-eyed fraudulent, misrepresented cook." His two bags containing all his belongings were dumped into the water. Although they floated the "heavy rush of water" carried them two miles downstream before they could be retrieved. By that time everything was "properly soaked." They were not so fortunate with some of the other items. In addition to the pigeons they lost more than $200.00 worth of equipment and supplies including two guns, all of the bacon and some of the flour. Munro-Ferguson found some solace, however, in the fact that "every stitch of the one-eyed scullion's clothes and bedding" was lost. Needless to say the cook was fired at the next post.

Writing back to Doll, oblivious of any inconsistency, Tyrrell explained that he had been fired because he was unable to cook for a party in the field. Back in Winnipeg, drunk again, Bell spread word of the "disaster" that had befallen them on the Grand Rapids and Sir John Schultz had to wire Doll and assure her that the reports, which were being picked up by the press, were unfounded.

Given these early experiences, it is little wonder that in one of his first diary entries Ferguson is asking himself, "Why the devil didn't I take a rational and comfortable, if not luxurious, trip elsewhere (instead of sticking my ugly great nose into this country. It's only a desert anyway!)" His reply to himself is revealing. Not being able to afford to "winter out" like some of his colleagues his alternative was to satisfy his cravings by venturing into little known parts of Canada. Since he did not have his own steam yacht that he could sail into Chesterfield Inlet, accompanying Tyrrell was the next best thing. "It is the only portion of the Barren Grounds and everlasting bliss of me at present attainable."

On the surface the 1894 expedition was similar to that of the previous year. Both were by canoe through unexplored Barren regions. Both lasted some seven months. The routes ran parallel. In fact, however, the two undertakings were very different. Eighteen ninety-three was a venture into the unknown. Eighteen ninety-four on the other hand was merely a voyage through uncharted lands. There would be dangers enough to satisfy the adventurous spirit of Munro-Ferguson and to call forth the full skill and knowledge of J. B. Tyrrell in bringing his party back to safety. Each curve in the river could open upon rapids that would smash their feeble craft. Winter could seize them in its grip and not let go. Some lone polar bear might win the fight for survival against its human enemy or a two man party en route to Fort Churchill for help might be lost in a storm that lasted longer than their strength.

Nevertheless, the 1894 expedition was different in kind. For one thing their outlet to the sea could be predicted. If the Dubawnt River emptied into Hudson Bay then the Kazan River, rising to the south and east of the Dubawnt could not drain into the Arctic Ocean. In addition the trip would be shorter, the terrain that lay ahead reasonably predictable and the route down the shore of Hudson Bay to Fort Churchill already known. Finally they were to discover the Kazan area was more densely populated by Eskimos than the Dubawnt had been. One consequence of the increased contact with Eskimos was that Tyrrell (although less fluent in the native language than his brother James) was able to ascertain that the Kazan emptied into Baker Lake. If they followed it to its mouth the last part of the trip would be an exact duplication of the previous year's voyage. Always in search of new roads to travel, Tyrrell managed to extract directions from the Eskimos on how to portage from the Kazan to another river emptying into Hudson Bay. This new river, and the lake in which it had its origin, he named the Ferguson in honour of his companion.

Another important difference between the two expeditions was that the starting point was more easily reached in 1894 than had been the case the previous year. Instead of heading to Edmonton and then north, the party struck out from Selkirk by steamer up Lake Winnipeg to Grand Rapids where they launched their canoes. From there the route was across Cedar Lake and up the Saskatchewan River, past the modern day site of The Pas, to Cumberland House. Then, via the Sturgeon, Churchill and Reindeer Rivers, to Reindeer Lake and its northernmost trading post of the Du Brochet. From Du Brochet they travelled up the Cochrane River for a hundred miles before portaging to the Thlewiaza River which they followed downstream until they could portage into Kasba Lake.

Up to this point they were in known country some of which J. B. had explored during the preceding ten years. But from Kasba Lake as they descended the Kazan River, they were once again in virgin territory crossed only by Samuel Hearne over a century before. When the Eskimos he met told him that the river he was on emptied into Baker Lake, Tyrrell was in a quandary. This new information was contradictory to that which he had gathered the year before. The Eskimos he had met then had told him that the river emptied into the Bay. Whom would he believe? After much deliberation Tyrrell decided to listen to the men who lived in the area and instead of continuing down the Kazan struck out to the east from Tathkyed Lake, portaging over the height of land that separated the coastal river system from the interior. Then through the headwaters of the Ferguson River to the river itself and the open Bay.

Once more his arrival at Hudson Bay marked the beginning of a race against winter's onslaught. He emerged at the mouth of the Ferguson on Neville Bay on September 18, almost a week later than he had reached sea water the year before. But this time he was further south, well past Corbett Inlet, the scene of the sand-bar trials of 1893. In fact although he was a week later

116

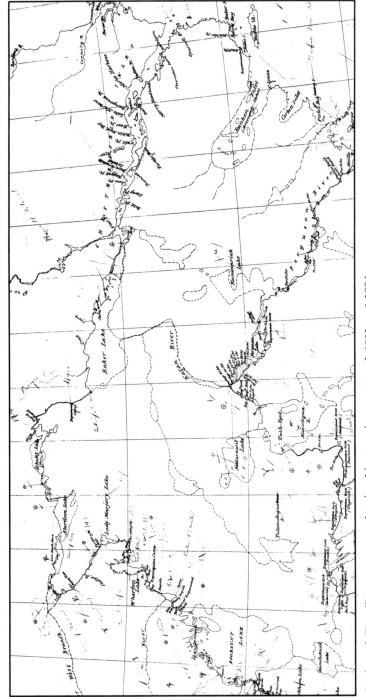

Section of Tyrrell's survey map showing his two river routes of 1893 and 1894.

117

in reaching the Bay, Tyrrell knew that they were still fully a week earlier in reaching Neville Bay. When he emerged at the mouth of the Ferguson River on September 18, Tyrrell identified it as having been passed on September 25 the previous year.

Even with a week's jump on the previous year's timetable, however, there was no time to lose. The day before he and his men reached the mouth of the Ferguson they had been unable to travel at all because of a storm with hurricane force winds. For three days before that they had pushed on through high north-easterly winds that were accompanied by sleet and snow. He remembered well that at this time the year before he had been stormbound on the shore of Corbett Inlet. Recalling this, and knowing how quickly the ice could set along the coast, Tyrrell knew they had to push on with all speed. Fortunately the weather held and although they were a week later in launching out on Hudson Bay they managed to reach Fort Churchill on October 1, a full two weeks earlier than the year before.

Once again the forbidding Barren Lands had been challenged and conquered. Once again the conquerors still had to walk home. But their early arrival and late onset of suitable winter travelling conditions meant that the expedition had to wait almost two full months at Churchill. Fortunately the supplies which Tyrrell had arranged to have forwarded by steamer were on hand and their presence caused no hardship to the regular inhabitants of the post and mission.

Safely ensconced in Fort Churchill well ahead of schedule and with an ample food supply, Tyrrell was quite content to await the onslaught of winter before setting out for Winnipeg. Never one to be idle he delved more deeply into the records of the local operations of the Hudson's Bay Company than he was usually able to do. He had also had the foresight to include a stock of plotting paper with the supplies he had forwarded to the fort. As a result he was able to start making a map out of the survey notes he had made of the area they had passed through. In between times he also managed to return to Fort Prince of Wales to drink in some more of the spirit of Samuel Hearne. Munro-Ferguson was not so enamoured of Hearne as was Tyrrell. In his estimation, Hearne "lost all claim to glory by surrendering the impregnable fort . . . to the French without firing a gun." By his estimation the French sailors were "so plague stricken with scurvy they could have done nothing but begged forgiveness for coming, and alms, and a hospital." Munro-Ferguson's estimation of Hearne, however, was not going to deter Tyrrell from enjoying another visit to the fort. In any event he also had a practical reason for going – to collect some of the cannon balls to be shipped to the museum in Ottawa.

Fruitful and enjoyable as these activities might be, however, they were really only a way of filling time as they awaited the arrival of winter. Inevitably they still had to walk to Winnipeg.

Retracing his own footsteps was never Tyrrell's idea of productive activity. He had been forced to do so coming down the side of the Bay from the mouth of the Ferguson River, and at first glance it appeared as though he was going to have to do so again in travelling from Churchill to Winnipeg. The route was Fort Churchill to York Factory to Oxford House to Norway House as it had been the year before. A map showing the Hudson's Bay posts of western and nothern Canada leaves the impression that they had been scattered liberally on the face of the land from a giant salt shaker. In fact they had grown out of more than two centuries of hard-nosed experience with the fur trade. There was nothing arbitrary about the Hayes River route from Hudson Bay to Lake Winnipeg. In the first hundred years or so of fur trade operations York Factory (operating under various names) had occupied no fewer than ten sites around the mouths of the Nelson and Hayes Rivers. It had even at one time been situated on the north bank of the Nelson just below Flamborough Head almost at the exact spot where Tyrrell and his party had been holed up for twelve days in 1893. In the second hundred years of the fur trade, however, the York Factory post had been situated where Tyrrell found it on the Hayes River. Its location was not arbitrary. It was the product of more than 200 years experience in the business of moving furs to market and moving supplies and provisions to the men of the interior. In short it was part of a well thought out response to a massive logistical problem.

J. B. Tyrrell was not in the fur business however. He was an explorer and his endeavour was not aimed at moving safely along routes that had already been tried and tested. At the same time he was not the type of man who would take a difficult road just for the sake of doing so. That being the case the two other potential water routes to the interior – the Churchill and Nelson Rivers – were ruled out automatically. They had been tested in their time by the fur traders and found wanting. There was little to be gained from following these known pathways rejected by the fur traders in favour of the less turbulent and more navigable (both by boat and dogsled) Hayes River. As Tyrrell thought about his way home, however, he came up with yet another alternative. For years past there had been sporadic interest in building a railway to Fort Churchill. In the speculation about a railway link to Hudson Bay the route most often referred to would take the railroad via Split Lake on the Nelson River. But the speculation about the route was just that – speculation. No one, neither white man nor Indian, had ever traversed the country. It was the ideal challenge for Tyrrell, made only more appealing by his calculation that it would reduce the 900 mile trip of the established route by some 200 miles.

Tyrrell broached the subject with Captain Hayes who had taken charge of Fort Churchill from Matheson. Until that point, Hayes had been everything Matheson had not been in extending the hospitality of the post. The fact that Tyrrell had arranged his own supplies made it easier to contemplate visitors who would stay on until freeze-up. Even so Tyrrell's proposal brought a flat refusal of any co-operation from Hayes.

"I have been instructed," he told Tyrrell, "to forward you to York Factory and that is what I intend doing."

Tyrrell argued and pleaded with him but to no avail. When his request that Hayes rent him sleighs and teams of dogs was turned down he asked if he could buy them. That too was rejected out of hand. Besides his instructions, Hayes said, there was also the fact that the land between Fort Churchill and Split Lake was obviously impassable, otherwise the Indians would have found a route through it and they and the company would have used it. The attitude was as typical of the conservative element of the business community then as it is now: what has been tried and tested works; and what works has been tried and tested. To the scientist and the explorer, however, the attitude is alien. Tyrrell's reaction was immediate and predictable.

"I at once decided that it was time somebody explored it."

There could be no other response from Tyrrell. He was an innovator. His whole life revolved around searching out the unknown and finding new ways of doing old tasks. The overland route to Split Lake was exactly the type of challenge he could not resist. He was going to Split Lake. The only question was, "How?"

For an answer Tyrrell turned to Jimmy Westasecot. Anyone who could operate as Jimmy had the previous year, could surely be persuaded to tackle the impossible. The choice was the right one. Jimmy had quit working for the company the previous summer and was living with his family in the woods on the opposite side of the river, hunting and fishing. Hesitant at first, Tyrrell's offer of pay, rations for his family and a government pension for his wife if he failed to survive the journey into the unknown, persuaded him to go along. Between them they agreed on a simple method of travel. For the first half of the journey they would travel generally southward through country with which Jimmy was reasonably familiar. Then they would turn to the southwest on a line for Split Lake. Each morning during the second half of their journey Tyrrell would take a bearing on the compass and point in the direction of Split Lake. Jimmy would then set off in the lead, through woods, around rocks, over hills, across streams, in the general direction. The next morning Tyrrell, who would follow in the rear pacing and surveying the country they passed through, would adjust their direction by the amount that Jimmy had varied from the course set, and off they would go again. With any other guide this method of operation would have been highly risky. You do not travel across country in a straight line. But Tyrrell had experience of Jimmy Westasecot's unerring sense of direction. He was confident that, at most, they would only be led a few degrees off the course he had set and in this he was proven right.

Jimmy's resourcefulness also proved itself in the acquisition of dogs. First he arranged with another Indian, David Dick, who had a sleigh and four dogs to go with them. He also told Tyrrell that if he waited until another band of Indians came to trade at the post he would be able to buy dogs and sleds from them. Sure enough on November 22, a group of eight Chippewyans arrived at the post. Between them they had five sleds and about twenty dogs. Moving in amongst them as they traded their furs at the store Tyrrell succeeded in persuading them to sell a sled and four dogs.

The eight dogs he had thus far acquired were not particularly fine specimens, nor were the sleighs very well built. They would be adequate though if he could do no better. Tyrrell decided, however, to try once more to get some decent animals, sleighs and men from the company. Faced with the fact that he was powerless to sway Tyrrell from his course, Hayes finally relented and agreed to rent him another sleigh with a team of six decent animals and two drivers to go with him for the first week. This was all Tyrrell needed. After six days travel their supplies would be sufficiently depleted that the two smaller sleighs would be adequate for the rest of the journey.

There were, after all, no impassable obstacles along the way. The greatest difficulty in fact came not from the land but from the snow that lay upon it in lightly packed depths of up to five feet. Sinking into the soft snow made travel so difficult that on one day, although the weather was fine, they succeeded in covering only eight miles. To meet the problem Tyrrell introduced a number of expedients. The next day, for example, he did not break camp but instead sent two of the men out ahead to snow-shoe for ten miles and back, thus creating a trail that the dogs could move over the next day. On another day Munro-Ferguson and one of the other men harnessed themselves in front of the dog teams, while Tyrrell gave up his place in the rear to walk on snow-shoes right behind Jimmy in order to pack the snow for the animals. In Tyrrell's view it was well worth the effort. They left Fort Churchill on November 28 and on December 15 arrived at Split Lake, 250 miles south and west of Fort Churchill. Another corner of the country had been opened up and he had established that the proposed railway route to Hudson Bay was a possibility, indeed when the line was built it more or less followed Tyrrell's route from Churchill though it continued further south, across the Nelson, before veering to the south west.

From Split Lake they set out up the Nelson River for Cross Lake and on to Norway House for Christmas; then by the familiar Lake Winnipeg route to Selkirk and another series of telegrams carrying the words "All well."

For Munro-Ferguson the journey had been everything he had hoped. The only thing he could have asked was a greater companionship. "I have nothing to do with Tyrrell," he complained in his diary, "he is on his usual trip under government orders!"

Tyrrell, however, was not able to ignore his guest completely. On the banks of the Saskatchewan one night they were treated to a meal of fried moose meat by a group of local Indians. Later they returned to their camp in a muskeg swamp. It was a stormy night and as the wind howled Munro-Ferguson's pleasant dreams took a turn for the worse and developed into moose-meat inspired nightmares. He dreamt that the tent was floating away just as his belongings had when the canoe capsized in the river. "I heaved

Northern "travel agent" Jimmy Westasecot outside the Hudson's Bay Company trading post at Split Lake. (TFRBL)

Joseph Tyrrell and Robert Munro-Ferguson on the steps of Government House in Winnipeg in January, 1895. (TFRBL)

piles of heavy baggage on top of Tyrrell in a furious effort to climb out and escape through the back of the tent. Loudly insisting that he should follow and escape too." Tyrrell did not much appreciate having his sleep disturbed. Even worse, the nightmare was contagious. Several times during the rest of the night Tyrrell woke up screaming at some ethereal phantom. "Nonetheless" concluded Munro-Ferguson "the moose meat was a pleasant change after a week [of] straight bacon three times a day."

Munro-Ferguson's diary of the expedition reveals the Canadian west as it appeared to a novitiate before the turn of the century. Selkirk, that crucible of western history, he described as "the toughest of holes" and nearby was an Indian reservation "said to be the most immoral corner of the country." Nor did he have much to say for Selkirk's civic officials. The Mayor was a "genuine bum." Of the country itself, however, he had nothing but praise. "It seems a sort of ideal wild north west for the young man of adventurous spirit to come to." The woods full of wild flowers caught his eye – roses, honeysuckle and crimson tiger lilies. Then there were the sunsets. In this he and Tyrrell were adequate companions. Together on a rocky ledge, overlooking a lake with the air smoke-filled from the uncontrolled bush fires, they stood speechless as the sun set in the west. In his tent that night, the diarist tried to recapture the moment. The effect of the sunset on the smoky atmosphere was "quite soul stirring and simple – merely a contrast of the dark blue water on the lake with deep violet tints and the very softest pink and grey sky." Even without the setting sun the scenery was magnificent. Climbing The Pas ridge, that ancient beach of a now vanished sea, he was reminded of the south of France "looking across the flat country towards the Pyrenees."

Travelling through this beautiful land presented its difficulties, however. On the portages Munro-Ferguson was amazed at the capacity of the hired men to "carry heavy burdens with a light heart and jump around on the roughest, ruggedest rocks in moccasins as if they were soundly shod and upon asphalt." For himself he found out that although new boots hurt, moccasins were not the answer. He tried them for one day and exclaimed, "Pity the poor tenderfoot!"

The experience with the native and métis people went deeper than his amazement at their capacity to move over rock faces. Their culture was everywhere. Pushing the canoes up a series of rapids into a small lake, he had first-hand experience of that gentle Indian humour which never bursts into laughter but can

124

emanate in "whoops and yells." As the river emerged from the lake it bent and created a strong eddy that kept forcing the travellers back downstream. The local Indians gathered on the banks to provide an appreciative audience as they fought time and again to reach the lake. Earlier at The Pas they had shared in an Indian dance that had gone on all through the night. Tyrrell and Munro-Ferguson had sensibly gone to bed at a respectable hour. The three hired men, however, had made a night of it and the next day were something less than strenuous in paddling the canoes.

The Indians of the wilderness he found continued the ageless lifestyle of their ancestors. Among these people, he wrote, "crimes of violence and diseases of depravity are few and far between in such primitive, shut off lands." They hunted and trapped in an unexplored land which was still as it had been in the era of the voyageurs. "The old voyageurs were hardy, healthy men though somewhat unrefined perhaps! They have not drawn the Indians down to the lowest depths of civilized vice – and developed the cruelty of the brute – as other outcasts of society have done on the plains and at the mines further south and west." That other scene, where the native people had been "tamely degraded," he despised. Here was the "low and lowering condition of the noble savage," which would quickly bring out the worst in any man. The priests and missionaries, with a few exceptions, did little to improve conditions. They were "not hypersensitive and do not expect much."

Whether Munro-Ferguson's passing did anything to raise the moral stature of the people is a moot point. Shortly after the moose-meat nightmare the party had met up with an Indian camp on the Saskatchewan River. The inhabitants consisted of an older man and two younger men with their wives, a grass widow, a bunch of children and two young women of marriageable age. One of the girls caught his eye. She was scraping an animal skin but, more important, she was wearing a skirt of Munro tartan. "She was a wild-looking little maiden with wonderfully delicate-looking long pointed fingers." Under her tartan skirt she wore "a pair of thick, striped woolen drawers! She was stooping to pick up a knife that had dropped behind the hide among the willows. And stretched herself out with a wonderful cat-like sinuous motion to get it. They are of course quite unimpeded by modern and much of any other dress in their movements." He found the sight "remarkably graceful in spite of the slight *exposée* that occurred." In the next sentence he goes on to complain about the mosquitoes.

"Walk away for a moment or two among the rushes" and the insects settle down all over you." He fails to mention whether his walk among the rushes was a solitary one.

He does talk, however, of the role of the women in the society. Sometimes it was difficult to persuade the Indian men to act as guides but "the squaws will take a man into unknown country." Whenever there was a question of whether a guide would be provided it was the women who decided. He noted, "It was a trait quite touching to behold. And so natural as to make one feel quite at home in these far distant wildernesses."

During the first part of the journey, the diarist was fascinated by the reminders of Louis Riel. Before setting out Schultz had pointed out the house in which he had taken refuge the night he escaped from Fort Garry after Riel had condemned him to death and the church where he had unsuccessfully harangued the men to march against Riel. Even more engrossing was the wreck of the *Northcote* which they visited at Cumberland House. The derelict of the former boat of the Winnipeg and North Western Navigation Company had run the gauntlet of Riel's men to Batôche. Examining the shot marks which had riddled the boat, Munro-Ferguson was told the story of the famous journey. The lower deck had been barricaded with the cargo of flour and cordwood. "The engineer and the captain were the chief objects of aim and had a lively time. The captain lay flat on the floor of the wheelhouse and steered so – looking through a crack! Several spokes were shot off his wheel and the cabin was honeycombed. The rebels lowered a steel cable and caught the *Northcote* after funnels at a narrow point of the river, but she pulled through."

If the story of the *Northcote* aroused Munro-Ferguson's spirit of adventure, the two Hudson's Bay Company men at Cumberland House who told it to him touched another heart string. The retiring factor, MacFarlane, and his replacement, MacDougall, were both fellow Scots. As they sat late into the night talking of the old country the inherent sentimentality of exiled Scots was awakened. He wrote in his diary "it quite broke one up leaving there. Two men who had spent such lonesome lives and hard in the furthest northern wilderness who yet had such a warm corner left in their hearts for a countryman." The feeling was mutual. At Cumberland House there were two old guns, relics of its days as a fort. The guns had reached such venerable age that they had been given names – Thunder and Lightning. As the explorers left the post on the next lap of their journey the guns were ordered loaded and a two-gun salute was fired – Thunder first and then Lightning.

CHAPTER 7

Days of disillusion

Disenchantment came on the heels of glory. The five years that followed the conclusion of his work in the Barren Lands were anticlimactic for Tyrrell. He had reached the pinnacle of his chosen profession and there was no place left to go but down. In the light of his single-minded dedication to his work that was undesirable. In the light of his ambition and vanity it was intolerable. The disenchantment did not set in immediately, rather it grew slowly. Had it overwhelmed him at once, he would probably have recovered from it and stayed with the Survey for the rest of his working life. But, growing slowly on him, it took over his thinking bit by bit, each layer being firmly set as a foundation for the next, until finally he decided that if he were to live the kind of life he yearned for, he would have to leave the Geological Survey and strike out on his own.

When he arrived back from his second Barren Lands expedition he had no inclination of what the future would hold. Once more his emergence from the wilderness was greeted by the public with enthusiastic interest. The press, ever ready to cater to the demand of its readership for adventure, served up liberal helpings of the stories of his exploits suitably adorned for the occasion. "Last evening," began the *Winnipeg Free Press* of January 9, 1895 "a conveyance drew up at Government House from which two fur-clad gentlemen alighted, and at once proceeded to employ themselves in unloading their baggage, consisting of snow-shoes, blankets and similar articles, which, to the onlookers, conjured up thoughts of remote northern regions." The editors of the *Toronto World* knew a good story when they saw one, so they picked it up and reran it the following week.

The pattern of January 1894 was repeated in January 1895. Their return had again been preceded by speculation that they had perished. Doll was inundated with letters assuring her that she ought not to worry. Later she recalled "I had the feeling that they would not have written to me if they themselves had not lost heart." Then early in December an incident convinced her that she had indeed become a widow after less than a year of marriage and less than four months of living with her husband. Joe had left the insurance policy which he had taken out before his departure with a friend at the Geological Survey with instructions to send it to Doll "if anything happened." When the policy and the letter of explanation arrived in the mail, Doll conjectured that if J. B.'s seasoned fellow explorers on the Survey had given him up for lost, he must have perished indeed. Even Sir John Schultz was genuinely worried: so much so that he arranged with the men carrying a mail packet going up to Oxford House that if by the end of their journey their path had not crossed Tyrrell's they would carry on to Fort Churchill in search of him.

The speculation into his death assured a lively public interest on his return and a renewal of the celebrity status he had revelled in the year before. That in itself would have been enough to have kept disenchantment at bay for the time being. Reinforcing that aspect there was the news that reached him on the way back to Ottawa. The leadership of the Geological Survey had changed. Like most of the staff on the Survey, Tyrrell had been in conflict with the director, Dr. Selwyn. Selwyn was caught between the demands of his men for more of everything and the parliamentary and mining industry demands for less of everything (especially money) except identification of workable ore deposits. In retrospect the accomplishments of the Survey under his leadership were remarkable – especially when seen in the context of the limited resources at his disposal. In 1894, however, he made a serious error of judgment. After twenty-five years with the Survey, he let go the reins of office to make an extended visit to his native England. The long knives that had been only just sheathed for years were suddenly bared. By the time Selwyn arrived back in Canada he had been summarily retired and replaced by George Dawson.

Tyrrell greeted this news with enthusiasm when he learned of it at Sudbury on the train back to Ottawa. He had not been active in the campaign against Selwyn that had raged within the Survey during all the years he had been on its staff. His father had advised him, even before he led his first expedition to the west, to stay well clear of the dispute and he had assiduously followed that rule. Tyrrell was, however, a simple man in many ways and he had identified all his personal difficulties of salary and career with Selwyn personally. Thus when he heard of Selwyn's demise he thought his problems were solved. The new director, George Dawson, was sure to be much better. Tyrrell wrote to Doll that he was "delighted" at the news. Dawson, he said, "will be strict, but he will be rational, and if I cannot get along with him it will be largely my own fault."

His optimism was not well founded. Dawson not only succeeded Selwyn as director, he inherited all the same problems and was as unable to find solutions as his predecessor had been. If the job had not changed, neither had J. B. Tyrrell. Still without the promotion and pay increase that would have been tangible recognition of his accomplishments, Tyrrell's dissatisfaction grew and he continued to place the blame on the director. Before the year 1895 was out Tyrrell had changed his mind about Dawson. The new director did nothing to improve his position or his pay. Nor had he provided any secretarial help in writing up his reports of the work of recent years. This failure of Dawson's, Tyrrell saw in terms of the director's jealousy at the degree of public prominence Tyrrell had achieved. Undoubtedly Dawson, as had Selwyn before him, saw Tyrrell's penchant for publicity as unnecessarily complicating his job in dealing with other members of the staff. But Tyrrell's real problems were money and the nature of the work assigned to him in the years after 1894.

Almost from the day he married Doll the added financial responsibilities began to complicate his life. His first letters to Doll as he set out for the second Barren Lands trip are full of comments on the house they are planning to rent in Ottawa and the cost of rent and the need to install a new furnace. Earning around $1,700.00 a year at the time, the house they had chosen on Alexander Street near Government House and the present Prime Minister's residence was well beyond their means, but in keeping with their social status and ambitions. When their first child, Mary, was born at the end of January 1896, the pressures were even greater. During the weeks surrounding the birth and the long confinement so typical of medical opinion of the time, extra domestic help was essential. From his small salary a maid and a nurse had to be hired – the nurse only complicating life further when, the day after Mary was born, she accidentally set the curtains in Doll's room on fire with a candle. No harm came to the mother or child, but another bill was added to an already strained budget. Over the course of the following winter Tyrrell estimated he went $250.00 in the hole.

His celebrity status also brought expenses that he could ill afford. To be part of the coterie that frequented Government House required a certain standard of life, that strained the budget even further. In February 1896 alone, while Doll was still confined to her bedroom, Joe was at Government House four times: for a dinner, for an at home, and for two formal balls. In between, another ball at the house of George Foster and numerous other engagements that all added to the expense of living as well as to its enjoyment. His duties as a militia captain in the Governor-General's Foot Guards drained his funds even further. The prestige of commanding his own company, the challenge of inter-company competitions and the opportunity of acting as captain of the guard on State occasions such as the opening and closing of Parliament, all sat well with Tyrrell. The cost of mess bills, of uniforms, of out of town excursions and of providing prizes for his men did not. At West Selkirk on the way out on his 1896 expedition he commented, "I have now $1.88 in the bank."

At home every effort was made to cut domestic costs to a minimum. Chickens were kept to supply eggs and meat and, when Doll left to spend the summer with her parents, J. B. lived frugally before setting out on his field work. He had read an article setting out a diet that a man could live on for only nine cents a day. With Doll off to stay with her mother and the two maids laid off for the summer, Tyrrell tried his nine-cents-a-day subsistence diet. Never much of a gourmet (though he did on occasion import smoked caribou tongues from the west) and experienced in living at below subsistence level, Tyrrell found he could make do on such fare "quite pleasantly and comfortably." But, even for him, two weeks of it was enough. During a typical Ottawa heat wave in 1897 he went out to buy a new straw hat. The first store he went to was asking $1.25 for them. He left there and went to a cheaper store where he got one for twenty-five cents. About the only luxury he allowed himself during those days was a visit to Buffalo Bill's Wild West Show when it came to town.

If his personal finances were a cause of concern, the resulting pressures were not eased by the fiscal restraint forced on the director of the Survey and in turn passed by him to his subordinates. At the first level Tyrrell felt the consequences in his inability to get a much needed salary increase. But both under Selwyn and Dawson the consequences went further and intruded into the funding of expeditions. The $1,300.00 which Selwyn had approved for the 1894 Barren Lands expedition was simply inadequate. Even with contributions from Munro-Ferguson, Lord Aberdeen and Sir John Schultz, it was impossible to carry out the work assigned on $1,300.00. To pay off the men and settle his bills with the Hudson's Bay Company, Tyrrell had to dig deeply into his own pocket using up almost all of the salary that had been deposited into his bank account during his absence. Naturally anxious to be reunited with his bride with whom he had only managed to spend four of the eleven months they had been married, he found himself unable to renew their relationship immediately. Doll was in New Brunswick with her parents and Joe had to write to her the day after he arrived back in Winnipeg, "I cannot tell you when to meet me, dearest, for I have used up every cent of money I have in helping to pay the expenses of this trip and I cannot send you any to bring you up until I return to Ottawa. You know that I had only a limited sum from the Survey and I have been obliged to draw all my summer's salary to pay the wages of the men. Probably I shall get it back, after a while."

Nor did things improve once Dawson had succeeded Selwyn. Just before he set out from Selkirk on July 1, 1896, for his summer's work, Tyrrell received a letter from Dawson informing him that the 1896-97 appropriation had not yet been passed by Parliament. The old appropriation had expired the day before Tyrrell and his men set out for the north. Until he returned to Ottawa in the middle of October he was not informed that the Survey would meet his expenses. While he could reasonably expect that Parliament would approve the funds, he was also aware that if it did not he would be personally liable. Dawson's letter had removed the onus from himself.

As the financial pressures mounted Tyrrell was forced into a distasteful program of retrenchment. Keeping chickens and eating on nine cents a day was not enough. Debts were mounting and more basic cuts had to be made in the family budget. The house on Alexander Street was beyond his means and eventually he gave it up for cheaper accommodation on Metcalfe Street. The price of staying on as a captain in the Foot Guards was too much and he resigned his commission. Even so, his salary remained inadequate. By the time he finally left the Survey it was still only $1,850.00 *per annum* – on average about $1,000.00 a year less than former colleagues who had left the Survey for greener fields in the United States and the universities were earning. Doll, by now aware of their straitened circumstances, began to pressure him, and that only increased his tensions. The accounts he left of his life in this period are sprinkled with references to his health. A series of bad colds were interspersed with an attack of lumbago on one day, the grippe on another. The illnesses were probably a heightening of the mild case of hypochondria he carried with him all his life. They were no less real for being psychosomatic. Then, on top of the aches and pains, there was the humiliating necessity of taking a doctor's certificate to the director to justify any absence from work.

Money, or the lack of it, was not, however, his only concern. His deteriorating relationship with Doll also plagued his mind. Long before the predictable life crisis of the seventh year of marriage they had hit stormy times. Their problems had financial roots but went much deeper. Faced with the reality of living together the romantic notions that they had built the relationship on were proving inadequate. The problems were compounded by his long sojourns in the wilderness which interrupted their efforts to build a life together.

"Shall we never be able to spend the summers together until I am old and not fit for this work any longer?" Joe asked. He hoped desperately that if only they could be together everything would work out. "We are going to have a lovely time at home this winter," he told her in a letter. He knew, however, that the separations were not the only problem. By 1897 her annual visits with her mother were starting before they had to and lasting longer. While he was still in Ottawa he wrote to her in Port Rowan saying how much he wished they were together. He went on to acknowledge "but you should very soon tire of being here alone with a stupid old fool like me." The "stupid old fool" reference was typical of his self-denigration in his letters to Doll of this period. For perhaps the only time in his life he was lacking in self-confidence. He was not sure that Doll would attend the meetings of the British Association for the Advancement of Science to support him when he delivered his *magnum opus*. He urged her that by coming she would meet "nice ladies" and find out what kind of life a successful scientist leads. He went on, however, "whether you would enjoy that life or not seems to be a little uncertain."

As so often happens in marital upheavals petty jealousies crept in. Joe had to reassure his wife that a certain Miss Clark had left to spend the summer in England. "You need not be in fear of my spending any time with her."

His troubles were compounded by the nature and pressure of his job while in Ottawa. His prolonged travels in 1893 and

1894 had kept him from finishing the reports of work done during the preceding years. Then his collection of rocks and specimens from the two Barren Lands expeditions did not reach Ottawa until late in 1895. Thus it was impossible to write his report of his greatest endeavours until long after the work itself had been completed. He was frustrated at not getting his reports published early. The frustration was compounded by the fact that writing the reports kept him bound to a desk well into the evening hours and left him with a feeling of claustrophobia. Sitting at a desk was never his idea of a satisfying lifestyle – he longed to be free and to be moving in the outdoors. The help of an able secretary would have eased the load. But Dawson, like Selwyn before him, was continually turning down requests for such assistance from all his staff. There was simply not enough money for such luxuries.

Even when summer came and he was able to return to the field, he was only marginally happier. The territories assigned to him were all areas with which he was already familiar. For Tyrrell, always restless in the search of new challenges, to return to Manitoba and Lake Winnipeg was somewhat less than satisfying. In 1895 he was sent to explore Playgreen Lake (the northern extension of Lake Winnipeg) and its rivers. "The work" wrote Tyrrell, "was rather monotonous."

Eighteen ninety-six proved a little better. In that year he was sent into the territory north of the Saskatchewan River and west of the Nelson. Part of his assignment was to be on the look-out for signs of Huronian rock and to try to determine its extensiveness and mineral potential. His explorations that summer took him along the Nelson, Grass and Burntwood Rivers, among others, and to Snow Lake, Cross Lake and, once more, Split Lake, with crossings at Thicket Portage and Cranberry Portage. "The rocks proved to be rather interesting," he said. They should have – he was examining the geology of one of the richest mineral areas in Canada, identifying the extensive Huronian deposits that today support the mining industries of the Thompson and Flin Flon areas of Manitoba. In other places he was again surveying sections of what would later be the route of the Hudson Bay Railway line. If the *Mining Review* and the industry's lobby had been able to criticize the lack of tangible returns from his work in the Barren Lands they had no cause for complaint in 1897. He had repaid them a thousandfold. So much so that a Minister of Mines in Manitoba later referred to him as the "Father of Mining" in that province. Even his work in that rich mineral field, however, did not satisfy his longings. "At times," he told Doll, "I think of the preparations necessary for some distant expedition which is not likely to be undertaken." He was depressed. One phrase sums it up. In a letter to Doll describing the "picturesque and beautiful" scenery of the Nelson River area he calls it "this dreary country." The dreariness was in the soul of J. B. Tyrrell.

The summer of 1897 brought welcome change of pace for Tyrrell. Instead of the usual spring departure for the field, he did not go west until late in August. The British Association for the Advancement of Science annual meeting was being held in Toronto and, once the various reports of work done in previous summers were out of the way, J. B. turned his attention to the preparation of two papers which he would deliver to one of the world's most august scientific bodies. The first paper, and the more important, was entitled *Glaciation of North Central Canada*. Here Tyrrell presented a new theory of the process of glaciation that had occurred during the ice age.

With the publication of Darwin's *Origin of the Species* earlier in the nineteenth century doors had been opened for new avenues of thought in all branches of science. Until Darwin science had been constrained to produce hypotheses that were not incompatible with the biblical record. Darwin, however, had ventured into an explanation of creation that did not jibe with the "six days" account in Genesis. Those involved in other branches of science were quick to follow suit. For geologists this meant that they were no longer bound to measure the earth's age in terms of the 6,000 years or so covered by the biblical record. It also meant that in explaining the evidence of the ice age they were no longer forced to place it in the context of Noah's Flood. The Swiss scientist, Louis Agassiz (whose memory is perpetuated in the name of the prehistoric body of water that once had its bed on the Canadian prairies, Lake Agassiz) introduced the theory of glaciation to account for the ice age. Of all natural phenomenon, Agassiz maintained, only the glacier could offer an explanation of the ice age that took into account all the evidence left behind from prehistory. Thousands of years before, according to Agassiz, giant glaciers had formed in the north and moved south scraping the land to bedrock.

The revolutionary new theory which Agassiz propounded touched off a long debate amongst geological scientists, especially in the older, more established scientific communities of Europe and the United States. In Canada, however, the debate was relatively less heated. Canadian geologists were still too few in number and too busy discovering the composition of the land to have much time or energy to devote to a theoretical debate of what had happened thousands of years before in the pleistocene age. It was enough for them, by and large, that an ice age had once existed. With that knowledge the age of rocks could be determined and its effects noted. Reinforcing this pragmatic approach was the fact that the dean of Canadian geologists, Sir John William Dawson, refused to embrace the Agassiz hypothesis. Instead he was a firm adherent of the uniformitarian school of geology which maintained that the causes and effects of physical phenomena were the same in the past as they are in the present. That being the case the only observable phenomena that would explain the ice age were icebergs. These, Dawson and others maintained, had drifted in the prehistoric inland seas until they were left behind on the shores as the continent rose and the waters drained away. With the knowledge available today the first part of the uniformitarian position is still not far off the mark. It is now known for example that the mean temperature of the areas covered by ice was only some $10°$ below what we have known in the twentieth century. But Dawson and the other Uniformitarians knew nothing of this cooling of the earth's surface. Thus instead of recognizing a cooling process as the constant then and now, they turned to the more readily visible contemporary phenomenon of icebergs for their consistent explanation.

The elder Dawson's whole-hearted adoption of uniformitarianism effectively stifled public debate on glaciation in the Canadian geological community – at least until Tyrrell appeared on the scene. The younger Dawson, typical of his generation of geologists, at first adopted unquestioningly his father's position on the iceberg theory. Gradually and slowly, as a result of his explorations, he was converted to the glacial theory of Agassiz, though he never publicly challenged the authorized version held by his father. In the course of the work that led to G. M. Dawson's conversion, the young Tyrrell was his eager student. Unlike his teacher, though, he was not intimidated at the thought of a public debate with the older Dawson nor averse to the notoriety within the scientific community that would surround such a controversy. Tyrrell was not, however, merely a propagandist for the younger Dawson's theories. Instead Tyrrell developed his own ideas which differed substantially from any that had gone before.

Previously geologists who had rejected the iceberg theory had believed that the ice age had seen giant ice sheets move southward over the land on a solid front. From his observations Tyrrell had developed a new theory and, in the Barren Lands in 1893 and 1894, he had found evidence to confirm his explanation. One of the basic pieces of evidence that an area was long ago covered by glacial ice is found in the *striae* or scratches in granites and other hard rocks. As an ice field ground its way across the land it seized huge boulders and rocks in its grip. The hardest of them it held firm and carried with it as it advanced and retreated across the continent. The softer rocks, under the tremendous weight of hundreds of feet of ice were ground to dust and sand which, as the ice melted and water again flowed, were washed away as silt. But, as Tyrrell put it, "the foundations of the earth stood firm." As the irrestible force of the glacial ice slowly moved its way forward and back across the immovable hard rock "foundations" of the earth, the equally hard boulders and rocks which the glacier had in its grip, gouged and scraped at the surface. As a result the earth, where the ice passed, was left scratched.

The development of Tyrrell's concept of glaciation was a gradual thing. As late as 1887 he was still hedging on whether occasional rocks of "eastern origin" had found their way into northern Alberta as a result of glaciers or icebergs. But once his field of exploration was switched to Manitoba the evidence of the ice age more and more pointed away from the iceberg theory and towards glaciation as a feasible explanation.

In his trips of the late 1880s and early '90s to Riding Mountain and Lakes Winnipeg and Manitoba he had observed the *striae* always running north and south. He knew too that in Northern Ontario the direction of the *striae* is from northeast to southwest. Tyrrell staked out his position on the glacial debate at the 1889 meeting of the Geological Society of America. The official critic of the paper told the audience that it brought the question of North American pleistocene geology into "beautiful consonance." In 1891 Tyrrell carried his position a step further with another paper, this time on the pleistocene age in the Winnipeg area. The big leap forward, however, came in 1897 with his paper to the British Association for the Advancement of Science. On that occasion he established once and for all his reputation as a scientist of note. In the meantime he had made his two trips to the Barren Lands. There, where the "foundations of the earth" were clearly exposed to view, he noticed that the pattern of the *striae* all running in one direction did not hold. Instead they pointed in all directions. From this, and from other evidence such as the contours of valleys, the slope of the land and the erosion of the rocks, he concluded that previous glacial theory was not adequate. Instead he proposed an alternative. Rather than a single massive ice field that had once advanced and retired on a long front, there had been centres of glaciation where not once, but on several occasions, the ice had formed and radiated out to cover vast stretches of the continent. One of these gathering places had been in the Barren Lands of the Keewatin District west of Hudson Bay. From here, he argued, it had stretched north to the Arctic, east to the Hudson Bay, west almost to the foothills and south across the lakes to the valleys of the Ohio and the Mississippi Rivers.

This was to be Tyrrell's biggest single contribution to the advancement of scientific knowledge. Typically, he had at first moved cautiously in presenting the hypothesis. In papers written between 1894 and 1896 he had tentatively broached the subject. Then, having thought the theory through still more and having considered the comments of others, he just as typically abandoned caution and at the 1897 meeting of the British Association staked his scientific reputation on the theory. Naming the centre of glaciation west of Hudson Bay the Keewatin Centre he went on to suggest that there had been others, in particular the Labradorean in Labrador and the Cordilleran in British Columbia. Fifteen years later, travelling in the area south of Hudson Bay for the Ontario government he once again observed the phenomena of multi-directional *striae* and concluded that here too, south of the Bay, there had been a centre of glaciation. This one he named the Patrician Glacier.

The presentation of Tyrrell's glacial theory marked a major step forward in the understanding of the prehistoric development of the continent. That he presented his theory at the 1897 meetings was ample testimony that his courage did not only extend to the way he faced physical danger, but also carried over into the realm of the intellect. Not only were the greatest scientists of the day gathered in Toronto but amongst the Canadian contingent were the doctors Dawson – father and son. Tyrrell's theory contradicted the views of both Dawsons, the younger of whom was his boss, and the older of whom was the most respected figure in Canadian geology. Their attendance at the 1897 meeting did nothing to deter Tyrrell. Having once concluded that his theory was valid, he met his opponents head on.

For years after the scientific community debated the pros and cons of Tyrrell's explanation before it eventually found universal acceptance. By that time Tyrrell's claim to a place of honour in the annals of Canadian science was secure, though his day of glory, August 23, 1897, had long since faded except in Tyrrell's memory. In the morning he had attended the meetings of the Geological Section of the Association, listening to papers and then reading his own on glaciation. Then in the afternoon he attended the Geographical Section where he presented his other paper which dealt with the natural resources of the Barren Lands. In this paper, perhaps in answer to the criticism of the *Mining Review*, he showed that large areas of the Barrens were underlain by precambrian rock which was likely to prove a storehouse of mineral wealth. Then a garden party with Dollie at a "beautiful home" and in the evening a "conversazione" at the university.

Always an able self-publicist and a bit of a social snob Tyrrell was delighted at the opportunities afforded by the meetings of the Association to make new contacts. In an account of the meeting, written years later, Tyrrell spent a half page on his theory of glaciation and five pages on the people he met – professors of mineralogy and geography, explorers and scientists, and the inevitable big game hunter. Knights and baronets and, even one lord – but what a lord that was – Kelvin the great Scottish physicist.

His contact with Lord Kelvin actually came about after the conference was over. To wind things up the Association had arranged for two excursions to take the members across the country to the west coast. Tyrrell was invited to accompany one of the excursions as a guide but Dr. Dawson refused to give him more time off work, thereby adding yet another irritant to their relationship. Instead Tyrrell was instructed to proceed to Winnipeg and continue his explorations of Lake Manitoba and the surrounding area. Tyrrell grudgingly complied with the order. In doing so, however, he made certain that he was booked on the same train as the group from the Association on the trip west. Perhaps to his surprise, and certainly to his delight, Lord Kelvin was travelling on the same car. At breakfast the next morning when Tyrrell was sitting alone in the dining car Kelvin came in and sat beside him. As could be expected, a question came up about the country they were passing through and Kelvin found out he had touched a vast reservoir of knowledge in J. B. Tyrrell. As Tyrrell poured forth his great body of information on the Canadian Shield and lands to the north; their mineral and animal and forest wealth; their great water highways and huge range of flora and fauna the Scottish scientist sat dumbfounded. Throughout breakfast he listened intently, an ardent student of an able teacher. By the time breakfast was over Kelvin's insatiable thirst for knowledge had been aroused and he knew he had found just the man to assuage that thirst. For the rest of the trip to Winnipeg, Tyrrell was happy to accept Kelvin's invitation to sit with him and his wife. From that meeting began a friendship between the two men that continued until Kelvin's death some ten years later.

After the stimulation of being amongst the high society of science, his explorations of 1897 were again anticlimactic. He did, however, manage to outline more of the shoreline of the great post glacial inland sea of Lake Agassiz. He also discovered a new body of thick limestone that promised to provide a source of good quality building stone. In addition he identified the source of water for the artesian wells of the Winnipeg area. Between Lakes Dennis and St. Martin he came across a "great area of porous rocks which takes in rainfall like a sponge." The water thus absorbed, flows down to large underground rocks where it stays under pressure to surge out of the ground when a hole is drilled in the surface clay. It was all grist for the mill, but he would much rather have continued west on the CPR with Lord Kelvin and the other scientists. That he was unable to do so only deepened his dissatisfaction with the Survey.

By 1897, Tyrrell was totally convinced that his colleagues in the Survey were all jealous of his fame and his reputation. Dawson in particular, he saw as resenting his erstwhile protégé's accomplishments. As he had done with Selwyn, so with Dawson he personalized his dissatisfaction with his job. But with Dawson there was a viciousness that had not been there before. It never left him. Looking back on these years, he wrote, "Dawson was an able scientist but a very poor executive. Probably his great infirmity, for he was a hunchback dwarf, had begun to tell on him in these years, though he was only forty-five years old, but he died six years later." What Dawson's size, deformity and early death had to do with his capacity as an executive is hard to imagine. But a "hunchback dwarf" is an easy figure to despise – especially for one raised in the tradition of Victorian manliness. There is no indication that Tyrrell ever thought back to his earlier letter to Doll when he had written "if I cannot get along with him it will be largely my own fault."

The charge that Dawson was a poor executive, however, was not without substance. It is revealed in the way he handled Tyrrell. Admittedly Tyrrell was not an easy man to get along with. He was vain and snobbish; self-righteous and ambitious; hungry for publicity and more than a little pompous. Nonetheless he was a dedicated and untiring worker, as tough-minded as he was tough.

In short an able professional who had done as much to advance the work of the Survey as he had ever done to advance his own cause. His achievements were already widely recognized, not only in the popular press, but in the most prestigious bodies of their common profession. It was not for nothing that the Royal Geographic Society had given him one of its brightest honours, the Back Award, for his work in the Barren Lands. It was a fitting tribute. Sir George Back was the English naval officer who in the 1820s and 1830s had explored the Arctic coast. For a time during his first Barren Lands trip, Tyrrell feared that he might in fact be on the Back River which had been named after the earlier explorer. The Royal Geographical Society's decision to give the Back Award to Tyrrell was an appropriate recognition of the work of both explorers. In the years that followed similar honours were freely bestowed. Yet Dawson, who should have known the nature and personality of his former student better than any other colleague, showed a distinct lack of judgment in dealing with his temperamental subordinate. Nowhere does the new director's lack of tact come through more clearly than in his handling of the publication of Tyrrell's report on the Barren Lands.

The lateness of Tyrrell's return from the field trips of 1893 and 1894, the long wait for the rock samples collected along the way to arrive from Churchill, and the full schedule of work carried out in 1895 and 1896, had delayed the completion of the official report of the Barren Lands expeditions. It was not until early 1897 that Tyrrell had the time to finish it and present it to Dawson for publication. Even so, time had only been found for writing by regularly working late into the night, transcribing the logs and notes he had kept along the way into reasonably polished though technical language.

In addition, to accompany the report, Tyrrell laboriously prepared highly detailed maps of the area on a scale of two miles to the inch. After the 1893 trip James had prepared large scale base maps of the route they had followed. Starting with these J. B. now added in colour all the geological information he had gathered in the course of the long trek. Then, since he himself had done the surveying of the 1894 route, he prepared his own base map of the ground covered. Again he adopted James's painfully detailed scale of two miles to the inch indicating all the geographic information he had gleaned of the rivers, lakes and portages he had travelled and the surrounding countryside and hills. On this black and white base map he again coloured in the wealth of geological information he had acquired.

On both these expeditions Tyrrell as always had spared himself nothing in checking and double-checking the accuracy of his observations. The result of his labours was a series of painstakingly informative and extremely accurate maps containing a wealth of information on a previously unknown part of Canada.

On May 10, 1897 he presented the finished report and maps to Dr. Dawson for inclusion in the Survey's official *Report*. Later in the year, when the proofs of his work were sent to him for correction, Tyrrell was dismayed to discover that his maps had been arbitrarily reduced from the careful two miles to the inch that he had prepared to the much less detailed scale of twenty-five miles to the inch. Tyrrell considered the new scale much too small to allow a proper presentation of the information he had gathered. He remonstrated with Dawson, arguing that even his maps of Manitoba had been published on a scale more than three times the size of the proposed one. But his cry was in vain. Dawson refused to reconsider and stood firm by his earlier decision.

That in itself would have been enough to have left Tyrrell in an unhappy frame of mind. He plied his craft with great thoroughness and he wanted the results of his work to be made available in the greatest possible detail. Dawson's decision hurt his professional pride. Another decision by Dawson concerning the maps hurt more than his professional pride. It also hurt his personal pride. In the past survey maps containing geological information carried the name of the man who had supplied the information. But in the proofs of the Barren Lands maps the only credit was a line in "small type" which read "To accompany Report by J. Burr Tyrrell."

Again Tyrrell protested in vain to Dr. Dawson. In future, the director told him, all maps published by the Geological Survey of Canada would be anonymous. Anonymity was not for J. B. Tyrrell – especially in connection with his great northern exploration. He relished the reputation his Barren Lands trips had brought him, and Dawson should have known his man well enough to recognize that to deny him due credit was to wound him deeply.

By the time the incident with the maps had occurred Tyrrell would gladly have quit the Geological Survey if he could have found a decent job. One obvious alternative source of employment was the universities, but inquiries and applications to Toronto, McGill, Cornell, Manitoba and possibly others, had been to no avail.

Tyrrell was restless. His fortieth birthday (that age when so many men look back over their lives with disgruntlement) was fast approaching. Underpaid and under-appreciated, uneasy with his colleagues and in conflict with his superior and pushed on by Doll's nagging, he was in need of a new challenge. Then the word filtered through and, in Joe's words "gold was dazzling everyone's eyes" – his own included.

CHAPTER 8

Goldrush

"Gold! There's gold in the Klondike." That cry, first heard on the streams of the Yukon in 1896 took a year to reach the outside world. Once it reached San Francisco on July 16, 1897 and Seattle the next day, it had grown to a roar. The roar echoed around the world: it was even heard in Ottawa's somnolent Rideau Club. The whole *pot-pourri* of humanity – the proverbial soldier, sailor, tinker, tailor, richman, poorman, beggarman, thief – heard the cry and more than 100,000 of them gathered up all they wanted of their belongings and headed north. The gold rush was on. They came from every province of Canada, every state of the Union and every continent of the world; all of them dazzled by the gold that flowed from the pokes on Seattle's harbourfront. Nuggets as big as a man's fist lying around like pebbles on a beach, gold dust in mountains like gravel pits waiting to be shovelled into bags. By the tens of thousands they packed their belongings and headed north through Alaska to the Yukon in what was to become the last great romantic surge of the nineteenth century.

From the first it appeared that J. B. Tyrrell was destined to take part. As imbued with the romantic spirit as any of his generation, the response of "Ho, for the Klondike" was as natural to his lips as to those of any man. The spirit of adventure that had motivated him in his explorations could not but be aroused by what the Klondike held in store. The relative poverty of living on $1,800.00 a year laid the basis for dreams of the wealth that the new gold-field promised.

Tyrrell, however, was an experienced geologist. He knew that the gold was not just lying there in sufficient quantities for a hundred thousand pairs of hands to pick it up in abundance. He was also a civil servant. His salary may have been inadequate to his needs but still it was there. Month after month for fifteen years, his pay had been assured and during his long sojourns in the field each summer it had accumulated in Ottawa, so that when he returned he was able to enjoy a better standard of living than his $35.00 a week would suggest. Caught up in the excitement of the times, his eyes as dazzled by the giant lottery of Klondike gold as any other man's, he was still not a candidate for the Chilkoot Pass in 1897.

Nonetheless, the Klondike beckoned. It was not just the attention of the little man blinded by the yellow glare of gold that was riveted on the wealthy northern frontier. The Canadian government also focused its gaze on the northwestern corner of the kingdom. Matters of high policy were at stake. Canadian sovereignty over the area was neither firmly established nor universally recognized. The Alaskan boundary dispute had been simmering in the background of Canadian-American relations ever since Confederation. The United States' purchase of Alaska from the Russians coincided with the Confederation of British North America. The treaty that sold Alaska for $7,200,000.00 was signed on March 30, 1867 and the actual transfer of territory took place on October 18, 1867. Almost exactly in the middle of those two dates, on July 1, the British North America Act came into effect and the new nation of Canada came into existence. For the next thirty years, the question of where Canada left off and the United States began was more or less quiescent coming to the fore briefly in the mid-1870s when the prospect of extensive gold deposits in the Cassiar district drew attention to the north only to fade once again. In 1897 when news got out that gold had been discovered in the Klondike, the question of sovereignty immediately became important.

The concept of sovereignty is an abstract thing resting on such elements as prior discovery and exploration, occupation and effective administration. Almost as soon as the reports of gold came out of the Klondike the Canadian government turned its attention to the boundary between Alaska and the Yukon Territory. For the next six years that question would plague Canadian-American relations on the diplomatic front. In the meantime the government moved quickly to establish *de facto* sovereignty. Nowhere is the old chestnut of possession being nine points of the law truer than in the area of sovereignty. From the first Canadians were flocking to the Klondike; but they were vastly outnumbered by Americans and the rumblings of annexationists were soon being

144

heard. The first interest of the government was to establish effective occupation of the territory to administer Canadian regulations and enforce Canadian law.

Before the end of September 1897, the task was well in hand. Clifford Sifton, Laurier's Minister of the Interior was off on the CPR for Vancouver and from there north on the steamer *Quadra* for Dyea, one of the major take off points for crossing the Coastal Mountains into the interior. Preliminary arrangements had already been made for the administration of the territory. Accompanying Sifton on the *Quadra* were a dozen members of the NWMP under Inspector Wood. Their job would be to enforce the law. With them was Judge Maguire who would try offenders and Fred C. Wade an Ottawa lawyer who had been appointed as registrar of Maguire's court and who would later loom large in Tyrrell's life. Also on board the *Quadra* were Major Walsh, the new administrator of the Yukon Territory, and William Ogilvie, soon to be appointed Gold Commissioner and who, as much as any man, was responsible for preventing the boom town of Dawson from degenerating into a Deadwood or a Tombstone. Prior to the discovery of gold on the Klondike, Ogilvie and William King, the Dominion Astronomer, had been in the area delineating the Canadian boundary claim. They were able to give a first-hand briefing on the problems involved so that within the Cabinet one man would be well versed on what was at stake.

The visit of Clifford Sifton, Laurier's super-minister, to Dyea in his blue flannel shirt, prospector's coat and parka symbolized the determination of the Canadian government to maintain their claim to sovereignty over the Yukon Territory. New regulations on staking claims and paying royalties on gold mined had already been proclaimed. Asked when the government intended enforcing these regulations Sifton replied simply, "They are in force now." Quick, firm action was the key to success and Sifton's trip dramatized that approach.

Back in Ottawa, in the meantime, the second stage of action was being planned. It was in these follow-up plans that Tyrrell's destiny began to be linked with the Klondike. The best routes into the gold-fields were via Skagway over the White Pass or via Dyea and over the Chilkoot Pass. Terrible as these routes were with their huge toll of human and animal suffering they were the most direct and thousands flocked into the two instant towns and over the treacherous trails. From the point of view of the stampeders the routes had a thousand disadvantages and one advantage – they were the gateway to wealth. From the point of view of the

Canadian government they had one major disadvantage: they siphoned off wealth. Both towns were in Alaska and U.S. customs exacted their toll on everything going in and out. Under pressure from west coast merchants and in keeping with its general policy the government set out to find an all Canadian route to the Klondike. A dozen possibilities were identified and stampeders tried each of them, but one in particular, the most ambitious of them all, won the backing of the government. Sifton examined the first part of the route in October 1897 and gave it his approval. The plan was to go up the Stikine River by steamboat and wagon trail to Telegraph Creek. From there a railway would be built to cover the 150 miles to Teslin Lake which would be the terminus for a shuttle service of steamers that would carry the travellers down the Teslin River (with numerous portages) to the Yukon River and on to Dawson City. The key to the plan was the proposed 150 mile stretch of rail line from Telegraph Creek to Teslin Lake.

"In those times whenever the word 'railway' was mentioned, Mackenzie and Mann bobbed up." Tyrrell knew what he was talking about. Early in January 1898 while lunching at the Rideau Club, Sir William Mackenzie "bobbed" into Tyrrell's life for the first time. Always willing to make new contacts with the powerful, Tyrrell was no doubt delighted to court the attention of Canada's intrepid railway builder. Identifying new railway routes could be a lucrative business and Tyrrell always liked to keep his options open. Even he, however, was probably surprised at the job offer that came out of that casual meeting.

Identifying themselves with the government's desire for an all Canadian route to the Klondike, Canada's terrible twosome of the twin track had quickly latched on to the 150 mile Telegraph Creek to Teslin Lake idea. They would build the railroad and put up a quarter of a million dollars to guarantee their performance. In return all they asked was a land grant of almost four million acres – 25,000 acres for every mile of track – and a five year monopoly in the area. It was here that Mackenzie offered to bring Tyrrell into the arrangement. The land grant was to be taken in blocks six miles wide by twenty-four miles deep separated by similar blocks that would remain as Crown land. But Mackenzie was not willing to risk picking the wrong blocks of land. Others would survey the railway track and its route; he wanted an expert to survey the land grant and evaluate its potential. J. B. Tyrrell was just the expert he needed. Tyrrell always maintained that he had protested to Mackenzie that as a civil servant he could not consider such an offer to which Sir William had replied, "Oh that's all right, I'm friendly with the government and the minister will release you if I ask him." No doubt Sifton would have done so but it is hardly likely that such a request would have been necessary except perhaps to permit Tyrrell to hedge his bet. He was by that time thoroughly disenchanted with the Geological Survey and the outlook for his future in government service. To strike out as Mackenzie and Mann's mining engineer, choosing the more than 20,000 square miles and controlling its development would have been good enough reason to resign from the Survey.

The contract between the government and Mackenzie and Mann was signed on January 26, 1898. To all intents and purposes the deal was concluded. Construction was started on the railroad: surveying the route, building the road-bed and taking delivery of track and ties. All that was needed now was parliamentary approval – a mere formality. But one that was just important enough to keep Mackenzie sitting in Ottawa until it was attained.

Across the street from Parliament Hill, Mackenzie made his headquarters in the Rideau Club. There Tyrrell met with him almost daily to discuss the task that he would take on. No formal offer of employment was ever made or accepted – not until the detail of parliamentary approval had been taken care of. As Tyrrell noted, however, that did not seem to bother Mackenzie, who talked as though the explorer was already in his employ. When asked how much he wanted, Tyrrell had blurted out "$10,000 a year" and Mackenzie had not even blinked. "It would be so nice to have a good comfortable income" he told Doll.

Both arrangements – Tyrrell's with Mackenzie and Mackenzie's with the government – were doomed. Sifton had no difficulty getting the contract approved by the House of Commons. A year and a half before, for only the second time since Confederation, the Liberal party had managed to form a government. With a clear majority of 117 in the 213 seat House the Laurier government had little problem in having the contract approved there. The majority, however, did not carry over into the Senate. Just as today a Conservative government inherits a Senate stocked by long years of Liberal rule, so the Liberals in 1898 were faced with a Senate appointed by the Conservative administrations that had governed for twenty-four of the first thirty years of the nation's history. There in the chamber of "sober second thought" the Conservative majority gave the Liberal scheme the six month heist thus effectively killing the plan. Hastily devised, the Stikine to Teslin railway scheme had several drawbacks, but for the

Senate the stumbling block was the land grant provisions – the very aspect that Tyrrell was to have administered.

Looking back on the proposed railroad – by that time having lived in the Klondike for six years – Tyrrell was still convinced that the plan had been a good one which would have benefited the area and its people. He also, however, felt a certain relief that he had not become a party to it. Had he selected and controlled the land and then turned it over to the company his position, he felt, would have been "very unpleasant and perhaps impossible." Land grants to railways have not always been very popular in Canada. The stone wall of the Conservative Senate saved him from ever having to worry about that. It also destroyed his first opportunity to take part in the gold rush.

For a while Tyrrell's second opportunity to go to the Klondike seemed doomed to be as ill-fated as the first. A small part of the government's response to the demands of the gold rush was to send a member of the Geological Survey to report on the area and to verify the extensiveness of the gold strike. R. G. McConnell, Tyrrell's closest friend among his colleagues, was assigned to the task by G. M. Dawson. Tyrrell and McConnell had much in common and though they had never gone on a field trip together, they had shared the same fate in Ottawa. Both were of roughly the same age and had joined the Survey around the same time, had advanced through the ranks as clerks and had been unable to persuade their superiors that they should be promoted to the rank of Technical Officer and thereby have the way opened to an increased salary. Together they had fought and cajoled to improve their lot and together they had become disenchanted first with Selwyn and then with Dawson for the failure to promote them to Technical Officer even though, as Tyrrell said, they had been "engaged in highly technical work for many years." They felt undervalued and underpaid but at least they could commiserate with each other and share that strange *camaraderie* of misfortune. At more or less the same time the two explorers had reached the conclusion that the only way to advance their careers was to leave the Survey. Until the spring of 1898 neither had much success in his search for another job. Then McConnell, after Dawson had assigned him to the Klondike, was offered the position as British Columbia's Provincial Mineralogist and accepted.

Dawson's response to McConnell's decision to resign was twofold. First, and most immediate, a replacement had to be found to conduct the summer's work in the Klondike. Here again destiny seemed to call for a rendezvous between Tyrrell and the gold-fields. J. B. was assigned to the area. Dawson's next move was to avoid losing the services of McConnell. Finally, when all else failed, the director capitulated to McConnell's demands. He would be promoted to Technical Officer with the new salary level of $2,250.00. McConnell accepted and Tyrrell wrote, "Now I was left behind." McConnell's promotion filled Tyrrell with rancour. Of his friend he wrote, when he "considered the fleshpots of Ottawa" the prospect of living in Victoria seemed a "bleak prospect" and he changed his mind.

At the time it appeared that McConnell's decision had not only left Tyrrell behind in the ranks of the Survey but had also robbed him of his second opportunity to take part in the excitement of the gold rush. Once McConnell had agreed to stay on, Dawson reassigned him to the Klondike for the summer. Once more it seemed the gold of the Klondike would only dazzle Tyrrell from a distance. However, in the end Dawson, perhaps because he did not know what else to do with him in 1898, decided to send Tyrrell to the Yukon anyway. McConnell was instructed to go to Dawson City and afterwards to explore the region of the Big Salmon River while Tyrrell was sent to the southwest corner of the Territory with instructions to go in over the Dalton Trail and make a survey of the area between the Yukon River and the Alaska boundary south of Fort Selkirk and only incidentally to go to the Klondike if an opportunity presented itself. Dawson's decision sealed Tyrrell's fate.

The events of the spring of 1898 had finally brought Tyrrell's mounting dissatisfaction to a head. He was earning $1,850.00 a year and if he remained as a clerk in the government service this was the maximum he could expect. The only prospect for advancement, like McConnell, was to have his classification changed from Clerk to Technical Officer. For years he and McConnell had been stuck in position without promotion or significant financial advance. Ever since the success of his expeditions to the Barren Lands, Tyrrell had felt that both the nature of his work and the recognition it had received at home and abroad had given him every right to expect promotion. Now that McConnell had received it, J. B. felt he had no choice but to leave the Survey if he was not given the same treatment.

Having watched McConnell's experience of that spring there may have been an element of bluff in Tyrrell's manoeuvre. Whether there was or not, however, before he left for the Yukon he called on Dawson with an ultimatum. Unless the year 1898 brought the promotion to him he would quit the Geological Survey. Dawson assured him "there would be no need of that." He would recommend J. B.'s promotion to the Minister. With the understanding that his "status would be improved when the summer's work was over" Tyrrell left for the Yukon. He was mistaken.

"A mad jumble of shanties, separated by wide layers of mud which did service for roads." Such was the town of Skagway that Tyrrell found on May 27, 1898. Two weeks before, he had left Ottawa by train for Vancouver and from there made a short side trip to Victoria in the hope that he could pick up the job of Provincial Mineralogist that McConnell had turned down. The position, however, had already been filled by an American. When Tyrrell found out that the man had been hired on George Dawson's recommendation, he was disgusted. "He had thus found another friend at the expense of the Survey," he told Doll. He felt gloomy and depressed. Suddenly all of life seemed "so selfish."

Back in Vancouver he met McConnell again. Together they set off on the *S.S. City of Seattle*, crowded with would-be prospectors, he for Skagway and the Dalton Trail, McConnell for Dyea and the infamous Chilkoot Pass.

The steamer with the two explorers pulled up alongside the wharf at Skagway at 2 o'clock in the morning. On its first few runs into Skagway the *City of Seattle* had let its passengers stay on board until morning. The hotel owners in town, however, had protested that by doing so the ship owners were stealing their business by allowing passengers to stay on board. In response the owners obligingly agreed to disgorge their passengers as soon as the ship arrived at the dock. So at 2 AM Tyrrell bade farewell to McConnell (who was carrying on to Dyea) and, with his "considerable outfit" of supplies and equipment dumped on the shore, he stepped on to the wharf of the wildest town in North America – with $2,000.00 of government money in his pocket.

Somewhere amid that "mad jumble of shanties" was one that housed a sergeant and two constables of the NWMP. The three Mounties were living as civilians in the American town, with the assignment of helping Canadians en route to the Klondike pass safely through the lawless wilderness of Skagway. Tyrrell's first task was to find the undercover Mounties and deposit his $2,000.00

with them for safekeeping. To reach them, however, he would first have to pass through "Soapy" Smith's sophisticated laundry, designed for the express purpose of cleaning travellers of their last dollar.

Skagway, Alaska, was the typical gold rush boom town. A year before there had been nothing there but the tidal mud flats of the upper Lynn Canal and unbroken pine forests. Overnight the town had sprung into existence to accommodate the thousands of stampeders who poured off the boats to climb the White Pass to the interior. Into that instant town, in the late summer of 1897, came Jeff "Soapy" Smith, "a soft-spoken, black-bearded bandit" and five henchmen. He must have thought he had landed in heaven. In a way he had: Skagway was a con man's paradise; a bunko artist's Eden. Six months earlier the town had not existed. Stumps of trees still dotted the muddy streets. Before law and order could be established or a meaningful municipal government formed, Smith had taken over. By the time Tyrrell arrived at Skagway in the spring of 1898, Smith had turned that remote corner of the great republic into a lawless feudal kingdom which he ruled with impunity.

According to one account, Smith originally acquired his nickname as a street salesman selling packages of soap flakes. Into this seemingly legitimate business he injected a variation of the shell game. Instead of a pea under a shell to capture the unwary, Smith used his sleight of hand in putting a five dollar bill into one package of soap flakes. He would then persuade the gullible to try and pick the right package. Before 1897 Smith had practised his con games up and down the continent. But those days were far away for "Soapy" Smith. He no longer went to the suckers; they came to him and the army of henchmen who aided him in lightening them of their load. His closest associates were the five cohorts he had brought with him to the north. Each had names as colourful and meaningful as his own: "Doc" Baggs, the "Reverend" Bowers, "Old Man" Tripp, the "Bishop" and "Slim Jim" Foster.

Saloons were the con man's natural habitat but Smith and his cronies were not to be confined to their natural habitat in Skagway. The church, struggling for a foothold to minister to the souls of an ever-shifting community, was an acceptable place of business for Smith, as was a phony information bureau, a news-paper office, a telegraph office and the trails to the interior. Skagway was the perfect site for Smith's operations. Most of its transient population of would-be prospectors were as inexperienced in the ways of the world as they were in the art of mining. They poured through the town by the thousands and to a man they had but one goal. To get rich quick. It was this common element, even more than the lack of adequate law enforcement, that made them ripe for Smith's plucking. He offered to help them reach their goal of instant wealth before they ever made it to the gold-fields. Those who were naive enough and gullible enough to fall for his schemes were quickly relieved of their poke and spared the tortuous path across the Coastal Mountains and down the Yukon River.

As an agent of the Canadian government, Tyrrell had undoubtedly been forewarned of the dangers that lay in store for the unwary in Skagway. Rather than risk heading through the town alone in search of the Mounties, he therefore decided to enlist the help of "a pleasant-looking young man."

It just happened that the neatly dressed young man was going right past the Mounties' office and would be happy to show Tyrrell the way. As they passed a saloon on the main street his youthful guide asked Tyrrell if he would mind waiting for a couple of minutes while he went in to hunt up a friend. By sheer coincidence, just inside the open door of the crowded saloon, four men were betting $20.00 gold pieces in a crap game and one of them was losing badly. As Tyrrell looked on from outside the door, the loser caught his eye.

"Here stranger, throw the dice for me, you may change my luck."

Tyrrell stepped closer, took the dice in his hand and threw them. The heavy loser let out a roar of joy.

"Here" he said, "half of this is yours" holding out a handful of gold coins to Tyrrell as the crowd inside surged forward to see what the noise was about.

It had just happened that his young guide had been going right past the Mounties' office. It also just happened that Tyrrell realized in time that a phony fight was about to break out in which he would be relieved of $2,000.00 in Canadian government funds. Fortunately he was still standing at the door and could make a quick exit, his "pleasant-looking young man" following behind urging him to come back for his reward. J. B. declined. If he could make his way through the backwaters of Lake Athabasca without Moberly, he could find the Mounties in Skagway without a guide. By the time he hunted down the sergeant in charge of the unofficial NWMP detail, Tyrrell was well aware of what he had almost been caught in. The sergeant filled in the details. The

152

"pleasant-looking young man" was none other than "Slim Jim" Foster whose specialty was picking up new-comers on the dock and leading them into one of "Soapy's" establishments for fleecing. The saloon he had stopped at was known locally as the "Slaughter House" so named because often those lured inside never emerged onto the street again. The back of the saloon was built over the tidal river into which a body could be conveniently dropped to be carried to sea with the ebbing tide. Joseph Burr Tyrrell had had a narrow escape from being looted and possibly killed.

After his brush with "Soapy" Smith's gang and the relief of making contact with the Mounties, Tyrrell was ready for a night's sleep. The Pacific Hotel had rooms with two bunks at fifty cents a bunk. Tyrrell decided that since he was on a government expense account he would live in greater style. For $1.50 he got the best room in the house – a room with a view. The room was crude but clean. Its furnishings were meagre consisting of a folding bed, two chairs and a small table that doubled as a wash-stand. The walls were of unpainted boards ventilated with knot holes and bullet holes. The floor was covered with Chinese rush matting. It was sufficient. Tyrrell fell exhausted on the bed for a long much-needed sleep.

From the window the next morning he absorbed the magnificent sight of the Lynn Canal sweeping out to the ocean. Even the piles of garbage in the foreground awaiting the twice daily pick-up by the tide did not spoil the view. For the first time in months he felt the depression that had gripped his soul begin to lessen its hold. It was not instantaneous. He still could not help but comment that the clouds hanging low over the mountains made "everything appear gloomy and desolate," though he had to admit that the snow-capped mountains rising from the edge of the water on every side "were exceedingly good and picturesque." His initial response to Skagway was to describe it as a "villainous hole." He wrote to Doll, "if being a mining engineer would mean living in such surroundings as these and in such company as is to be met with here then it would be better to settle down quietly on a farm or be a clerk in a small office in a decent city." Pretty soon, though, he was admitting to himself that with a decent job he could become oblivious to his surroundings. A similar change occurred in his attitude to the people around him. At first he saw them as a group whose "rush for wealth has dried up most of the humanity in their natures." After a few days he was calculating that among such people his geological knowledge "ought to be of some value." He could feel the change within. The excitement of the times, the stimulation of the crowd, the hope for a new life were all combining to end his long night of despair.

Tyrrell's instructions from Dawson were to go into the Yukon Territory from Skagway via the 300 mile Dalton Trail. Once in he was to explore the southwestern part of the district with a particular eye to whether the geological conditions were such that there might be gold, coal or other ore deposits worth searching for. Almost as an afterthought his instructions permitted him, if it were convenient, to "pay a brief visit" to the Klondike, in order that he might be able to compare the two areas.

To conduct the operation Tyrrell had arranged for a party of three men and fourteen horses to meet him near Haines Mission about fifteen miles from Skagway on the opposite side of the inlet. The plan to use horses, however, meant that he could not set out immediately. Snow still covered much of the ground along the Dalton Trail and the spring growth of grass was not sufficiently advanced to provide adequate grazing for the animals. But if the trail was not yet open, one night of Skagway and the Pacific Hotel was enough for Tyrrell. The next day he took the little steamer *Pilgrim* to Haines Mission, the starting point of the Dalton Trail, to check that his men were in place and that the horses, equipment and supplies were all taken care of. Never one to waste time, once he had satisfied himself that everything was in readiness for his expedition, he set about exploring the other trails until conditions on the Dalton Trail permitted him to set out on his journey.

McConnell had already headed over the Chilkoot Pass but a mutual friend who had travelled to Vancouver with them and had stayed over an extra day was due to arrive in Skagway. Arthur Treadgold was exactly Tyrrell's choice in men – a well-connected Englishman of good family who had left the comfortable life of an Oxford don to venture into the Klondike. Treadgold's plan was to go over the Chilkoot Pass to join McConnell at Dawson and Tyrrell decided to return to Skagway to search him out and accompany him on the first stage of his journey. Successful in finding him among the thronging hubbub of Skagway's muddy streets, they set out together for Dyea at the head of the inlet, and the jumping off point for Chilkoot trail. Dyea, like Skagway, had sprung up overnight to accommodate the throngs of stampeders but prided itself in having remained free of "Soapy" Smith's orbit – though not outside his sphere of influence. From Dyea in that year more than 20,000 succeeded in travelling over the Chilkoot Pass to the interior. Higher than the White Pass route that led from Skagway, the Chilkoot had remained open throughout the winter of 1897-98. All year long the flow of men continued to file over the Pass. Eric Hegg's photographs of them snaking up the snowy hillside has become the hallmark of the Klondike stampede. From Dyea, Tyrrell and Treadgold drove up the gorge as far as Canyon City where the trail steepened and the real challenge of the Chilkoot began. Tyrrell, as always a keen observer, measured the grade and found that it sloped upwards at an angle of 22 degrees which, he conceded, was fairly steep but hardly sufficient to deserve the description given by one traveller who said that although, from reports, he had prepared to find it went straight up and down, he had not been prepared to find that in fact it leaned over backwards. But, as Tyrrell noted, it was not the steepness of the grade that had given the Chilkoot Pass its reputation; rather it was "the misery suffered by many of those who had struggled over it carrying their heavy packs up the narrow slippery path, or who had been discouraged by those unexpected difficulties, and had abandoned their trip to the new Eldorado far beyond."

Amidst the tents and stacks of baggage of Canyon City, after arranging to meet again later in Dawson, Tyrrell and Treadgold parted. The latter continuing up the steepest part of the trail where weeks before an avalanche had torn a path through the thin serpentine line of humanity sweeping sixty-three to a suffocating death. Meanwhile Tyrrell headed back to Haines Mission via the corruption of Skagway by now aware that "Soapy" Smith's operations were not confined by the city limits. All along the trail in the lengthening summer days members of his gang had set up tables where they tried to entice the would-be gold seekers to make their fortune the easy way with a throw of the dice or a guess at which walnut shell the pea was under.

The Dalton Trail, which would be Tyrrell's path to the interior, was in many ways the easiest route to the Yukon, and also the most expensive. Of all who tried, only Jack Dalton proved strong enough to seize one of the gateways to the gold-fields and not only impose, but collect a toll from all who would use it. The trail, which today is a spur of the Alaska Highway, ran north from Pyramid Harbour up the valleys of the Chilkat and Klehini

Rivers and over the Coastal Mountains to the Yukon Plateau. For centuries the Chilkat Indians had used the trail as a trading route in their commerce with the inland Stick Indians. Six years before the gold rush to the Klondike began, Jack Dalton, a local trader, had gone over the trail that later bore his name. Not only that but he had done it with four pack-horses much to the amusement and later amazement of the other traders and prospectors. Nor were the Chilkat Indians any more encouraging. Sensing that Dalton's success would strip them of their trading monopoly they at first tried to dissuade him by ridiculing his proposal and telling him of the raging torrents that lay in his path and of slopes so steep that even the Indian hunters had to climb them on their hands and knees. When that failed and the Chilkats held a war council, Dalton simply buckled on his six-shooter and with his companions rode into the interior.

The trail was no paved highway and the Indian warnings, although exaggerated, were not altogether groundless. Nonetheless Dalton made it through and back in the summer of 1891. From then on he had journeyed back and forth each summer clearing the trail to the Lewes River, the upper part of the Yukon, where he had established a trading post. When the gold rush began Dalton offered his trail as an alternative route to the Yukon River for a price – the toll was $250. E. J. Glove who had pioneered the trail with him in 1891 described Dalton as being "cool and deliberate." Those who tried to avoid his toll found out just how cool and deliberate he could be.

As soon as the trail was passable and the new growth of grass sufficient to sustain the horses, Tyrrell with the three men he had hired in Vancouver and equipped with fourteen pack-horses to carry them and their provisions set out. For many the Dalton Trail, like all the other trails leading into the Klondike, was the path to hell, but unlike the biblical path to hell its gates were not wide nor its way easy. Tyrrell, always a master of under-statement, described the Dalton Trail in one word – "obscure." Adequate pasture was sparse along the stony flats of the rivers, and snow still covered much of the ground in mid-June. The Chilkat and Klehini Rivers were at times raging torrents and they and their tributaries had to be crossed and recrossed along the way. No matter how one travelled to the interior from the Alaskan Panhandle, the Coastal Mountains stood as a mighty sentinel seeking to forbid entry.

The Dalton Trail in that summer of '98 was a busy place and as Tyrrell travelled up towards the pass he kept getting reports

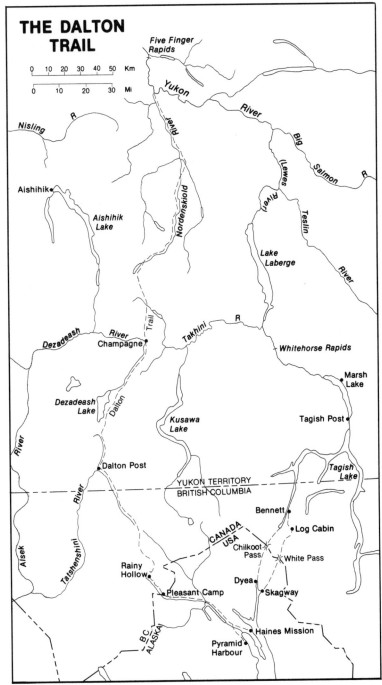

THE DALTON TRAIL

Five Finger Rapids

0 10 20 30 40 50 Km
0   10   20   30 Mi

Yukon

Nisling R.

Yukon River

Big (Lewes) Salmon R.

Aishihik

Nordenskiold River

Aishihik Lake

Teslin River

Lake Laberge

Dezadeash River

Trail

Takhini R.

Champagne

Whitehorse Rapids

Marsh Lake

Dezadeash Lake

Dalton

Kusawa Lake

Tagish Post

River

Dalton Post

YUKON TERRITORY
BRITISH COLUMBIA

Tagish Lake

River

Bennett

CANADA
USA

Log Cabin

Alsek

Tatshenshini

Chilkoot Pass

White Pass

Rainy Hollow

Dyea

Pleasant Camp

Skagway

B.C.
ALASKA

Haines Mission

Pyramid Harbour

Map of the Dalton Trail.

from those travelling the other way that because of snow the summit was still impassable for horses and the grazing on the other side, away from the lush Pacific growth, was sparse. Since there was good grazing where he was camped Tyrrell decided to leave the pack-horses and supplies there while he rode on to the recently established Mounted Police post at Pleasant Camp to check the lay of the land.

Recounting his ride to Pleasant Camp later Tyrrell noted that late in the day he "crossed the invisible boundary line between Alaska and Canada." Not only was the border line invisible, it was also non-existent. The Alaskan boundary was still in dispute between Canada and the United States and, although the gold rush gave both sides the necessary impetus to reach a compromise settlement, would remain in dispute for another five years. In the meantime, Tyrrell's "invisible boundary line" lay far to the south and west of the one claimed by the United States. But possession being even more important in international law than in civil law, the NWMP establishment at Pleasant Camp, like its counterparts at the other mountain passes, helped determine where that border would be.

Tyrrell described the NWMP station at Pleasant Camp as being "in a very picturesque situation in the middle of a forest of magnificent pines and firs." Behind the post the mountains soared 6,000 feet into the air and, on the other side of the river, a valley with a large glacier which Tyrrell later named the Jarvis Glacier after the NWMP inspector in charge of the post. Jarvis impressed Tyrrell not only as a policeman but as a master builder. The officers' quarters was a "beautiful building of . . . long straight logs." All it lacked was a fireplace and Tyrrell made that possible.

"Why don't you build a fireplace?" he asked.

"But" Jarvis complained "where would I get lime for the fire bricks?"

"Burn some limestone," said Tyrrell.

"Where would we get limestone?" asked the inspector.

"There" replied Tyrrell, pointing to a big red boulder which, it had been assumed was granite but which he recognized as red, crystalline limestone.

The good inspector was doubtful of the advice but still, in the course of the summer ordered his men, to their amazement, to try it. By the time Tyrrell returned in the fall the barrack room at Pleasant Camp had been made more pleasant by the addition of a log burning fireplace and supplies of lime were being sent to the other NWMP posts in the area.

From Pleasant Camp Tyrrell continued northward over the summit of the pass to Rainy Hollow on the Klehini River to check whether it would be possible to collect the rest of his party and move on. Although the gullies were still full of snow and the streams flowing beneath made them dangerous to cross, the hills were clear and the spring growth of grass was showing green. So Tyrrell returned through Pleasant Camp to gather up his party and a few days later, their horses reshod by a grateful NWMP inspector, they were off on the Dalton Trail for the Indian village of Westkatahin and Dalton's trading post. Along the way Tyrrell carried out the first part of his duties. As the men and horses travelled down the deep valley of the Klehini, Tyrrell scrambled over the rock face rising 3,000 feet above the river, searching out the history of their formation, chipping at them to see what they contained and estimating the likelihood of valuable ore deposits. Granites, quartzite, fossil-bearing sandstone, all were grist for the geologist's mill.

In this way he slowly worked his way to the Yukon River. Others paying much less attention to the rocks and moving much more quickly, passed them along the way. The Dalton Trail was a busy place in that summer of 1898 – and it was a two-way street. Even then, in June, as men and women continued their unthinking migration to the new Jerusalem, City of Gold, others, who had already been there were heading back, exhausted and disillusioned and to all who would listen they had one message "Turn back, there is nothing there." The closer they got to the Yukon the more disillusioned and disheartened evacuees of Dawson they met.

> All abused the country [and] said that there was little or no gold there, that even if there was gold all the mining claims of any value had already been taken up, that there was not work for half the men in the country, and if you did get a mining claim of any value the officials were so grasping that they would manage in some way to take it away from you.

While others were still struggling over the Chilkoot Pass and White Pass those who had gone before were returning, their spirits broken that the great effort which had summoned up every last vestige of energy had been for nought. "These men" wrote Tyrrell, "were walking along the trail without tents or blankets, with no covering but what they had on, and often with very little food. In the daytime they would lie down on the dry ground in the sunshine, and sleep, and travel at night when it was cool, though there was no darkness there at that time of year."

These stories of doom and gloom and the helpless condition of those who told them had their effect on some. The men whom Tyrrell had hired in Vancouver had been excited at the prospect that they too would reach the Klondike – all expenses paid. By the time they reached the Yukon River none of them cared to descend it to Dawson City. One man they met along the way had brought a number of pack-horses loaded down with goods to sell in Dawson. He had come all the way from Vancouver, waited until the Dalton Trail was open and then travelled its hundreds of miles only to decide after reaching the Yukon River that there was no point in going further. Tyrrell watched as he sold off everything for what he could get, which for the most part was less than he had paid, then turned his face to the south, defeated without ever having reached Dawson City.

Joe Tyrrell was made of sterner stuff. He continued his survey, descending the Nordenskield River, pacing out his distance and examining the rocks and formations as he went. Where the Nordenskield meets the Yukon he had a problem. Under Dawson's instructions he should probably have turned into the upper Yukon valley to retrace the river's path and examine its valley. That accomplished, he would have come back down stream, to where the Nordenskield empties into it. Then and only then, if time permitted was he free to go on to Dawson. However, despite the fact that his instructions made it plain that a visit to Dawson was to be considered a side trip, secondary in importance to all his other work of that summer of '98, Tyrrell was determined that nothing would stop him from seeing the new El Dorado for himself. The Mackenzie and Mann railway may have fallen through, and McConnell's change of heart may have robbed him of the opportunity of spending a whole summer on the gold-fields. But nothing would stop him now from being part of Dawson City in 1898, that town which had gripped the imagination of a whole generation and sent 100,000 of its most daring in search of the Grail. Nothing would deter him from going to Dawson. Reaching the Yukon River he turned inland and followed it downstream to Five Fingers Rapids.

Joe Tyrrell was not to be daunted, and if he were the sight of the Yukon River would have overcome discouragement. As he stood on the bank he watched the "great procession" of 7,124 boats going downstream. Aboard were the 28,000 men and women who had crossed the mountains by the White and Chilkoot Passes the previous fall and winter and on reaching Lakes Bennett and Tagish had stopped to cut timber, whipsaw it into lumber and hammer it together into something that resembled a boat if in no other way, at least in the fact that like a boat it floated. Then they had waited all through the long winter for the ice to melt and the water to flow and when it did they were off to Dawson. "The great stampede to the Klondike was at its height," and the sight was enough for Tyrrell. If doubts about what would be gained from going to Dawson had entered his mind they quickly vanished. Joe Tyrrell was a man who at the end of a sixteen hour hike through virgin territory would climb a high hill to see the sun set on a picturesque lake. Having feasted his eyes on the sight of that magnificent flotilla he finally picked out a boat that seemed seaworthy and called out to it asking if he could come along as a passenger. The boat he chose was a large, flat-bottomed pointer piled high with baggage and carrying six men and a sheet iron stove. But there was still room aboard for one more.

In reply to Tyrrell's request for a ride came back a question in a heavily accented voice.

"Can you steer?"

The boat was powered by oars and, instead of a rudder, a heavier oar was used at the square stern for steering. For the most part the work was straightforward. The river carried them downstream and by the strength of their arms they could increase their speed. Steering, however, required skill and the six stampeders who had built the boat and now manned it had already discovered that none of them were very adept at the task. Like so many others on the river that summer, what they lacked in experience they made up in determination. Without a capable helmsman they had managed to make their way from Bennett Lake, where they had built the boat, to Five Fingers Rapids. If their journey had not been without mishap, it had at least been without disaster. Now their troubles were over.

"Yes, I can steer," Tyrrell assured them and for $10.00 plus his labour they offered him passage.

The voyage from Five Fingers Rapids to Dawson took the argonauts three days and two nights. During that time the six adventurers soon discovered they were no longer masters of their own ship. The stranger they had taken aboard quickly took command. They in turn became the "passengers," obeying his orders, moving at the pace he set, and, as a result, arriving safely in Dawson.

If there was any doubt in their minds who was captain it was firmly removed at the end of the second day when the owners wanted to continue through the night to reach Dawson the next

Tyrrell's party fording the upper Chilcat River on the Dawson Trail. (TFRBL)

morning. To do so, however, would have meant that they would have taken turns steering while Tyrrell slept. That he would not allow. During the previous day, whenever he had "permitted" one of them to steer they invariably ended up stuck on one of the Yukon River's innumerable bars. So Captain Tyrrell commanded that the boat be tied up for the night and the crew-owners obeyed. Only when they reached Dawson did the roles return to the previous order and Tyrrell the passenger paid the boat-owners $10.00 for his fare before bidding them farewell.

CHAPTER 9

Appointment with destiny

The time was 7 PM on Saturday, July 16, 1898. The place was the crowded waterfront of Dawson. The occasion was Joe Tyrrell's appointment with destiny. From that moment the whole course of his life changed. The sights and sounds and experiences of the next three days etched themselves so deeply on his mind that he would never forget them. Years later he could still hear the rattle of gravel being washed down sluice boxes. He could still see the glistening yellow gold lying at the bottom of a pan that minutes before had contained dirty gravel. He could still feel the smoothness of the huge oblong nugget newly dug out of the ground where it had lain for untold thousands of years.

He was at the cross-roads of his life. The long grey depression had lifted. Everything that had gone before, it seemed, had been in preparation for this moment in time. His experience in northern survival, his wide knowledge of geology, his reputation, his dissatisfaction with his job and salary – all of them came together now like the sounds from the separate instruments that blend to make a symphony or the single brush strokes that combine to make a painting. They belonged together.

"You've wasted your time."

"There's nothing here."

"Keep going while the weather holds."

The unasked-for advice was hurled at them from the throngs along the shore as they pulled in amongst the hundreds of boats that had beaten them in the race to Dawson. Tens of thousands reached the Klondike in that summer of 1898. Disillusionment arrived with them. A very few found the gold they had come looking for. Some of them found it in the ground; more found it in the pokes of the miners who poured it out to meet the highly inflated price of everything or to sustain the wild spree that characterized the boom days of the Klondike. Most of those who struck it rich, by either method had arrived in 1896 or 1897. Only a handful of the stampeders who arrived in 1898 came away with more than when they started. For the rest it was either hard work to earn enough to survive, or turning around and going home empty-handed. Some, like the man Tyrrell saw on the trail, did not even bother to finish the journey before turning back. Others struggled valiantly on to the gold-fields before going home. To the latter, reaching Dawson had become the goal in itself. Once there they realized the futility of their endeavour. As they dragged themselves homeward, they advised all they met, "Go back."

The advice was wasted. Few having come that far, were going to admit defeat without having at least set foot in Dawson.

The motley crew who owned the boat that Tyrrell had commandeered were no exception. They had come too far to turn back now. Nor was their passenger-captain about to be dissuaded. He was there on official business and already in his mind there were the seeds of personal business that were soon to sprout, take root, and change the pattern of his life. For thousands, indeed for most, there really was nothing in Dawson. But for Joe Tyrrell there was the beginning of a new life.

His first task in Dawson was to rendezvous with Treadgold, whom he had last seen heading up the steep Chilkoot Pass, and McConnell from whom he had parted at the wharfside in Skagway. With every bed and cabin in Dawson, "this dirty city of tents," taken up by the gold rushers who were still arriving in droves, he sought out his companions and successfully traced them to their campsite on the banks of the river.

Determined to see and learn as much as he could in the short time available to him, Tyrrell set out with Treadgold the next evening for the very heart of the gold rush – Discovery on Bonanza Creek. It was there that it had all started and it was close by there that the richest plot of gold-bearing gravel was to be found. Discovery was the claim that George Carmack had staked less than two years before and thereby touched off the great stampede. It was a full day's journey from Dawson City on foot. Up the Klondike River a couple of miles from where it flows into the Yukon and then due south along the valley of Bonanza Creek until just below its junction with Eldorado Creek, at the foot of Cheechako Hill. Then, about a quarter of a mile upstream from Carmack's Discovery, they pitched camp on a tiny piece of land known as Dick Low's fraction – "the richest single piece of ground ever discovered." By the time Tyrrell and Treadgold pitched their tent on it, Low knew that he indeed had a gold-mine, but just how rich it was had yet to be established. Dick Low's fraction was less than ninety feet wide and lay wedged between claims, Two Above and Three Above on Bonanza Creek.

When gold was found and a claim staked, the first claim was labelled "Discovery." That first claim was taken as the central point and subsequent claims running up and down stream from it were labelled One, Two, Three and so on, "Above" Discovery or "Below" Discovery as the case might be. According to the mining law of the day prospectors were allowed to stake one claim in each mining district and that claim could be for a maximum of 500 feet measured in a straight line. Dick Low had been in the Yukon when gold was discovered on Bonanza. Even so, arriving in the Klondike well ahead of the stampede he was already too late to stake a claim on Bonanza Creek. There was still time, he hoped to search out another gold-bearing plot. But before he could find what he was looking for he got involved with Commissioner Ogilvie who had agreed to straighten out the tangled web of over-lapping claims and counter-claims that had been erratically staked in the rush of the first prospectors to get a piece of the action. Ogilvie hired Low as his chainman in making the survey.

As it happened even the first claims staked – those between Discovery and the fork of Bonanza and Eldorado – had been over-staked by George Carmack and his two Indian companions. Ogilvie's survey established that a fraction eighty-nine feet wide existed between Two and Three Above. There was an excellent prospect that the fraction would have gold on it. There was paydirt all around it. The problem was that it amounted to only 18 per cent of a normal claim. However, each miner was not allowed 500 feet; he was allowed one claim to a maximum of 500 feet. So whoever staked the eighty-nine foot fraction would give up his right to stake any other ground in the district.

Commissioner Ogilvie had no problem about it. As a government official with a scrupulous sense of duty and an absolute determination not to become involved in any conflict of interest, the fraction of land offered no temptation to him. Dick Low had no such restrictions on him. His primary purpose was to strike it rich as he had done once before in the Black Hills of Dakota. He was in a quandary. Bonanza Creek was pretty well sewn up but there were other streams in the area that looked promising and that were still open. But they had not yet been proven to have gold-bearing gravels. There was also the danger that before he could find a proven ground the great flood-gate would break and the thousands of stampeders who were poised awaiting the arrival of spring would pour in and every piece of gravel would be forever lost to him.

Low decided to take his chances on the tiny fraction between two proven claims. According to Tyrrell, Ogilvie tried to dissuade him from using up his one chance on such a tiny area, and according to other sources, Low himself must have had second thoughts about the wisdom of his action and tried to get out of it. He first tried to sell it for $900 but there were no takers. Then he tried to lease it but again to no avail. A few months later he would have had no trouble in doing either. Fortunately for him, he had by that time started working the fraction for himself.

In the late winter and spring he sank two shafts. It was hard work. The permafrost in the Klondike can run to depths of over 200 feet. In the winter, the top soil is frozen too. To sink a shaft, the miners had to build fires to melt the ground underneath, dig through the inches of thawed ground and then light another fire to thaw the next layer. It was slow, monotonous and back-breaking, and when it yielded poor results the process had to be started over again in another spot. The earth hauled from Dick Low's first shaft was bereft of anything more than mere traces of gold. He started over again, this time with different results. The second shaft hit pay dirt. It was obviously rich ground; but how rich nobody yet knew. Spring would have to arrive before they could find out. Until then the winter's diggings would be piled up in heaps waiting for the water in the creeks and streams to start flowing. Once it did flumes would carry it to the sluice boxes – long narrow boxes across the bottom of which spars or riffles had been placed. Into these the gravel would be shovelled and the water turned on. By the same process that nature had used in depositing the gold in the first place, it would now be separated from the gravel. As the water poured through the boxes, the gravel was washed away and the heavier gold sank to the bottom to be caught in the riffles, just as nature had once caught it behind boulders on the beds of the flowing streams.

Dick Low's cleanup had begun when Tyrrell arrived on the scene. Water was running through the flume and the accumulated gravel was being shovelled in to be washed through the sluice boxes. While the work was going on Tyrrell asked Low if he could try his hand at panning some of the gravel. He shovelled about 15 pounds of gravel into a prospector's pan and started to wash it in the water of Bonanza Creek. The soil he chose may have been from Low's first pit, for it yielded little. Low then suggested another panful from a different spot and Tyrrell obliged.

It was his first experience in panning and he was clumsy and slow. The sight of what was being left behind in the pan as the gravel was washed away added to his clumsiness. Tyrrell displayed so little of his usual dexterity that Low's foreman, Joe Irvine, took the pan from him to finish the job. From that one panful of dirt weighing about 15 pounds there remained at the bottom no less than 40½ ounces of gold. At the 1898 values that was $648.00 worth of gold: at the 1975 high for gold of $198.50 per ounce, it would have fetched over $8,000.00.

All day long they watched the operation as shovel after shovel of gravel was dumped in at the top and muddy water poured out at the bottom. Then about 10.00 o'clock, the sun still in the sky, Tyrrell and Treadgold retired to their tent and, rolled in their blankets, went off to sleep. They had hiked up the valley all the previous night and had not slept for almost forty hours. In the normal course of things they should have slept soundly for the next six to eight hours. Even the racket outside their tent as gravel was shovelled into the sluice to be bounced noisily against the sides on the way down would not have disturbed them. Nonetheless, after about one hour, Tyrrell awakened. The noise outside the tent had changed. There were sounds that he had not heard before. The only explanation he could think of was that Low had stopped loading gravel into the sluice boxes and was about to remove the riffles and clean out the gold. Never having seen the operation he awakened Treadgold.

"You're mistaken," Treadgold told him, "go back to sleep."

Low himself had promised them that he would not be cleaning out the sluices until the next morning. Tyrrell refused to accept Treadgold's advice.

"I pulled on my boots, and went out to see for myself what was going on just as I would have done when travelling on the plains of Alberta if there had been a disturbance among the horses." His thoroughness paid off. The water had been diverted from the flumes. The riffle bars which had lined the bottom of the sluice boxes to trap the gold were being removed. For the next two and a half hours Tyrrell stood transfixed watching the biggest cleanup ever to have taken place in the Klondike to that time – over $40,000.00 worth (about half a million dollars in 1975 terms).

In the months ahead as Tyrrell faced the decision of quitting the Survey and returning to the Klondike to search out his own fortune the memory of that day on Dick Low's fraction remained riveted in his mind. The cleanup of 150 pounds of gold was spectacular. The single pan with its 40 ounces was perhaps even more so. The $648.00 value of that panful of gravel was equal to more than a third of his annual salary and Tyrrell could never forget the experience.

In the years that followed, Dick Low took over half a million dollars from his eighty-nine foot fraction. He squandered every cent of it and left the Klondike as poor as he entered it. A few years after that first cleanup on Dick Low's fraction which had inspired him to try his hand at mining, Low wandered on to a claim Tyrrell was working on Hunker Creek. Tyrrell was delighted to see him and together they watched the work in progress. Low by this time had spent every ounce of his wealth. Booze and gambling had taken up a lot of it but, by Tyrrell's account, $100,000.00 of it had gone as "a down" on the dance hall girl he married who afterwards left him taking as much more as she could get. Low was not dismayed. He had already struck it rich twice.

"What do you propose doing now?" Tyrrell asked.

"Oh, I'm going to find another claim like the last one" he replied.

He never did. Instead he died in poverty in San Francisco in 1907.

After their experience on Dick Low's fraction Tyrrell and Treadgold set off on a week-long exploration of the Klondike gold-fields. Tyrrell was short of time. He was determined to use what little he had to cover as much ground as possible and to pick up as much information as he could. The gold-bearing area of the Klondike was a small rectangle of land about twenty-eight miles at its widest and thirty-six miles at its longest. In all it covered an area of about 800 square miles bounded by the Yukon River to the west, the Klondike River to the north and a ridge of hills to the south and east. Dominating this ridge, about twenty miles southeast of Dawson was King Solomon's Dome, a 3,000 foot hill whose summit had once, long eons before, been the level of all the surrounding territory. On this ancient plain, which miraculously escaped the glaciation of the ice age, the prehistoric animals had found sanctuary. Extinct species like the hairy mammoth; ancient

Dick Low's foreman Joe Irvine with the pan containing 40½ ounces of gold that Tyrrell had loaded. (TFRBL)

Low and Irvine outside the cabin on Dick Low's fraction. (TFRBL)

ancestors of animals no longer indigenous to North America, like the elephant and the lion; the predecessors of lines which have continued uninterrupted on the continent like the bison and horse, the bear and man; all of these once took refuge here.

If the plain's escape from the weight of the ice age had provided a last retreat for animals it had also left its minerals in place free from the scraping action of the glaciers that would have carried its wealth to other places. Ice may have left the plain untouched, but other forces were constantly at work before, during and after the recurring periods of glaciation. From time immemorial the Yukon River had drained the area. As it cut its way into the face of the earth so, over the millennia, the streams that drained into it had gouged deep V-shaped valleys into the flat land changing it beyond recognition. In time the land had changed again. As the softest elements were washed away the streams slowly broadened and deepened the valley bottoms. At the same time the weather was eroding the tops and sides of the valleys until the contour of most were changed into the U-shaped configurations which Tyrrell now toured. All that remained of the ancient plain was the Dome. From it streams and valleys radiated out in every direction. Tyrrell estimated that as these streams had cut through the plain they had carried away no less than 136 cubic miles of rock and earth. Thinly scattered through that mass had been a minuscule portion of gold – less than 300 tons in a total of 1,500 billion. But the streams had been nature's sluice boxes and as the earth and gravel had been washed away the gold had stayed behind trapped behind obstructions and then buried over. Not only was there gold on the river beds where George Carmack had first found it, but up on the hillsides where once the creek beds had lain, the gold lay buried too. Its discovery had touched off a new wave of staking only two months earlier. Now the hills resounded with the sounds of digging.

Little of this was known to the stampeders of 1898. All that mattered to them was that there was gold in the Klondike and they wanted to find it. Tyrrell, however, wanted more. From the first as he and Treadgold trekked up Bonanza Creek to its source on the Dome he was in search not only of experience of how the miners operated, but for knowledge of how the gold had got there. His search added greatly to the understanding of the processes that had been at work.

From the top of the Dome he looked over the entire territory. Creeks and streams radiated in every direction. Stretching out from the Dome to the Yukon River he could see the ridge of hills that separated the Klondike and its tributaries from the Indian River and its tributaries. A clearly defined watershed, and by a fluke of nature, a clearly defined goldshed. Only the Klondike was rich in the yellow metal. The Indian River and its creeks, although scoured by prospectors, yielded nothing comparable.

From the summit of the Dome Tyrrell and Treadgold walked down Dominion Creek, a tributary of the Indian River, and reascended it. Then they returned back down Bonanza to the junction with Eldorado Creek and went up the valley of Eldorado, still retaining its ancient V-shape, examining its gold-bearing gravels.

During that summer of 1898 as the gold seekers poured into Dawson, many stayed there, many did an about face and returned home, but some set out into the mining areas. There were enough of this last group to make the trails crowded. Some were like Tyrrell and Treadgold who for the time being were only on the trails to see as much as they could. Others, the miners and their hired help, were digging up the soil or washing it through sluice boxes. All around were still more who had not yet given up hope of finding new claims to stake. Wherever there was unclaimed property they were to be found kneeling by the rivers and creeks panning the gravel or toiling with pick and shovel on the hillsides. And these were only the half of it. The demand for food, lumber, supplies and equipment was intense. Hundreds were employed freighting goods into the established mines. Supplies and equipment were loaded on donkeys, horses and dogs, and on the backs of the freighters themselves as they wound their way up the trails.

Everywhere there was the excitement of gold being found. On Sam Stanley's million dollar claim, Tyrrell simply bent over and picked up a nugget weighing over 4½ ounces. As he held it in his hand he realized that its value was equivalent to his pay for two weeks' work. Shortly afterwards, as they reached Thirty-six Above on Eldorado they were attracted by noise from the open pit where the gravel was being excavated. Tyrrell and Treadgold climbed down into the pit to discover that a huge nugget weighing almost 24 ounces had just been dug out of the pit wall, the hole from which it had been removed still being visible for the geologist to inspect. The nugget itself Tyrrell described as looking "very much like potato, thick and oblong, with well rounded surface." It was the second largest nugget to have been found in the Klondike until that time.

Tyrrell's first experience of the Klondike was short. All too soon he was on the other side of the Yukon River, miles upstream, reunited with his men and horses. He was in a hurry now. As quickly as he could he finished off the summer's work and headed back to Skagway. He found a much different place from the town he had last seen. "Soapy" Smith had at last met his match in the vigilante Frank Reid. The famous shoot out between the two men that would have done justice to any of the frontier towns of the mid-west, had occurred just a week before Tyrrell arrived in Dawson. Both Smith and Reid had died in the fight and while Tyrrell tramped the creeks of the Klondike, the citizens of Skagway imposed a rough municipal order on their town before another Smith could rise and take over.

The removal of Skagway's crooked tyrant mattered less to Tyrrell, however, than the fact that he might soon be passing through the town yet again on his way back to the Klondike. While in Dawson, Tyrrell had met Major Walsh, the Commissioner of the Yukon Territory. Walsh was undoubtedly impressed by Tyrrell's knowledge and the amount of information he had gleaned during his short visit to the area. Before the explorer left for home Walsh raised with him the possibility of his staying in the area for a full year to study in detail the conditions in which gold was being found. The idea appealed tremendously to Tyrrell and he arranged with Walsh that the proposal should be put to the Minister. Walsh accordingly wrote to Sifton suggesting the arrangement. But when Sifton consulted the director of the Survey, Dawson flatly rejected the idea. Dawson could not agree to Tyrrell's returning to the Klondike for the winter. But whether Dawson could agree or not Tyrrell would return, albeit as a private citizen.

Dawson's rejection of Walsh's proposal was the second last in Tyrrell's long list of complaints. The final one was the outcome of his ultimatum for a promotion and a salary increase. It was the middle of October before Tyrrell arrived back in Ottawa and Hallowe'en before he had a chance to talk with the director about his future in the Survey. Dawson told him that he had made the recommendation to the Minister but the Minister had decided against it. By Tyrrell's account, he immediately called on Sifton to ask him why he had refused the promotion and was told by the Minister that he would have been happy to promote him but that Dawson had never suggested it. Whatever the truth of the matter, Tyrrell concluded rightly that his bluff had been called. He had in the past used the threat of resignation to get his own

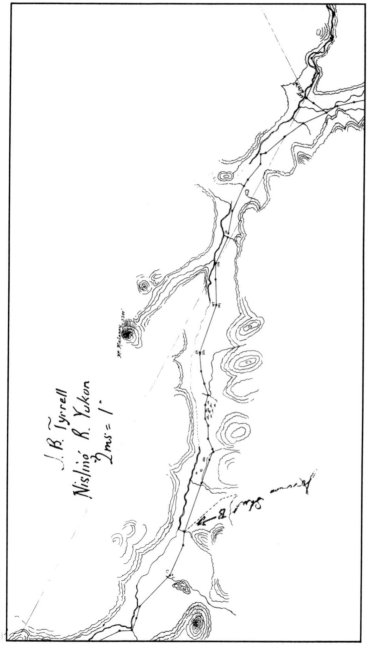

Tyrrell's two mile to the inch map of the Nisling River area of the Yukon.

way with the Survey. But that Hallowe'en was the first time he had ever been called upon to carry out his threat. To have accepted the decision and stayed would have left his position on the Survey even weaker than it had been in the past. It was trick or treat time. If there was to be no treat in the form of promotion then the only trick open to him was his resignation. Thus ended almost eighteen years of dedication and a career of great distinction in the Canadian public service. He would write as much of his report of his summer's work as he could by the end of December and then he would be gone. There was no doubt in his mind what he would do next. For the next seven years the Klondike which he had seen that summer would be his home and for the rest of his long life the search for gold would loom large.

The day after Dawson rejected his salary demands and touched off the crisis in his career, Joe Tyrrell celebrated his fortieth birthday. Many people as they approach the age of forty feel despondent and discontented with their lot and their accomplishments. Suddenly life is passing them by. The activities that have engrossed them and into which they have unstintingly poured their energies seem meaningless and they wonder how, as strength diminishes, they will be able to continue. Tyrrell was no exception. His accomplishments had been great, but he seemed to have passed the pinnacle of his chosen career while the rewards had remained minimal and showed no sign of ever increasing. As this feeling had spread over him and consumed him, little irritants had become major problems. When it became obvious that if he remained in the Survey nothing would be done to improve his lot, Tyrrell was typical of most men in doubting the value of what he was doing as middle age approached. He was characteristically atypical in that he did something about it. On his fortieth birthday he decided to take the drastic step of resigning from his job.

Perhaps his superiors had thought he was bluffing – perhaps he had been. But once his bluff was called and he had taken the final step he considered it irrevocable. Clifford Sifton, realizing the loss that the Survey was about to experience, urged him to reconsider.

"It's too late," Tyrrell told him bluntly.

If they had wanted him to stay they should have acted sooner. Before November was out he was running newspaper ads announcing that he was setting up shop in the Klondike as a mining consultant. The ads were almost unnecessary for his decision was news in itself and the story was carried in newspapers across the country and abroad. The future may have been full of unknowns but always in Tyrrell's mind was the memory of that moment on Dick Low's fraction when a single panful of gravel had yielded more than four months' salary. He knew he was worth more than $1,850.00 a year, and now he was going to prove it for he had little doubt that he could make money in that northern country where "gold is so thickly sprinkled."

Tyrrell's resignation from the Geological Survey took effect on January 1, 1899. He left Ottawa for the Yukon on January 19. In the less than three weeks that intervened he carried his new business as far forward as possible. The first task was to raise some money. He was broke but he was not without friends. Amongst these was Fred Wade the Ottawa lawyer who had gone up to the Klondike with Sifton's party the year before as registrar of the court in Dawson. Wade had enough confidence in Tyrrell and in the Klondike to risk his money on the enterprise. With apparently no strings attached he loaned Tyrrell $2,000.00. This would be Tyrrell's working capital for his new venture. Then, with his grubstake secured, he signed a contract with two Ottawa businessmen, E. H. Bronson and C. C. Ray, which made the three men equal partners in a mining venture that was to be the central feature of Tyrrell's seven years in the Klondike – and the biggest single failure of those years. He also arranged with the general manager of the Bank of Commerce that the Dawson office would be instructed to use him to investigate mining properties on behalf of the bank. Finally, for good measure, he made sure the government knew that although he had resigned from the Survey there were no hard feelings and his services would still be available to them, but only in the Klondike, and only for a fee.

This was the business side of his last weeks in Ottawa. There was also the social side. His retirement from the Survey brought on a round of farewell dinners and parties. The highlight of these, as usual, was at Government House. The Governor-General and his wife invited the Tyrrells to dine. At Rideau Hall where J. B. had once danced his twenty-two miles with the pick of Ottawa society and where he had held the household entranced with his accounts of the Barren Lands, he was once more the guest of honour. As a farewell gift Lady Aberdeen presented him with a copy of her little book *Where Dwells Our Lady of the Sunshine?* It was an appropriate gift: a short allegorical tale of an old Queen (representing the nineteenth century and the British Empire) "whose reign had been so matchless in the annals of the world's history." It told of "bright faced youths and maidens" in search of a new sovereign, and of their finding this new Queen in the

175

old Queen's daughter, Our Lady of the Sunshine (representing Canada and the twentieth century).

Says the old Queen:

> You may shrink from her in her fierce consuming midsummer mood, you may love her as she prevails over you in her sweet spring garb, you may rejoice over her rich handiwork in the autumn, but you will see her in her glory as you perceive that 'Our Lady of the Sunshine' is also 'Our Lady of the Snows'. . . . Her realms are wide, her resources are vast, and sown within her borders are the seeds of a mighty nation. . . . I would fain live to see the golden future of the people reigned over by my daughter of the Sunshine. But beware ye of marrying her work – she will fill the land with plenty, she will endue her subjects with strength of body and strength of mind through her gracious influences, but she needs loyal followers for the perfecting of her work. Will ye serve her?

Joseph Burr Tyrrell at forty years of age answered "Yes." He had already shown himself a loyal servant of Our Lady of the Sunshine and the Snows. Until now his service to her had been in her guise of Canada. The land with its vast unexplored forests and plains and their watery highways had been his mistress. Now her role in his life would change, but she would remain his mistress as he gave over his energy to the harvesting of her mineral wealth.

Of the tens of thousands of brave souls who had left for the Klondike over the preceding eighteen months, few had been fool-hardy enough to set out on the long trek in the middle of winter. That much they knew. They set out in summer and when winter came untold thousands were caught on the Chilkoot Pass and the White Pass and the long trails of the all Canadian routes. That preceding winter of 1897-98 had waged a physical toll on the romantic men who would moil for gold. It took an even heavier toll in dreams that were shattered and souls that were scarred. But for Joe Tyrrell, boarding the CPR train in Ottawa on Thursday, January 19, 1899, the journey to the treasure laden Klondike was a different matter. For one thing, although there was still a heavy traffic to and from the Klondike, the stampede was over. The gold boom itself went on. In 1898 the value of gold taken out of the Yukon Territory was four times what it had been the

The scenes of the Dawson waterfront as Tyrrell found it in 1898. (GSC)

year before and more than thirty times what it had been in 1896. It was still two years away from its peak, in 1900, when it amounted to over $22 million. For six years it remained higher than it had been in that first great clean-up that Tyrrell had witnessed in 1898. But the gold rush itself, with its crowded trails and human misery, was over.

Tyrrell also had the advantage of having been there before. Better still he had braved a winter and a terrain far more severe in his journeys through the Barren Lands. Years later, as he looked back on his trek to the Klondike, he wrote "I had had considerable experience travelling with sleighs drawn by dogs in northern Canada." That experience was to prove invaluable. Not only would it get him to Dawson in condition to start his new career, it would also get him there in one piece. Some of those who accompanied him part of the way were not so lucky. The trail to the Klondike in 1899 may have been quieter than the trail in 1898, it was no less fraught with danger. Tyrrell's advantage was twofold. He knew from experience what to expect, and he knew how to handle the unexpected. Even so, the path was not an easy one. The journey north took him close to two months to complete. And when it was over there was still the challenge of a new life to be hewn from the permanently frozen ground, less than three degrees from the Arctic Circle. No longer would he be secure in the knowledge that, however inadequately, the government of Canada would be paying its servant each month. No longer would he know that however long his travels might be or where they might lead, his wife and child were provided for. Doll, still very much a Victorian in her view of life was staying behind with Mary until later in the summer when they too would journey north for the first time. By that time the White Pass and Yukon Railway would be completed and the trip, though still a major undertaking would be less hazardous. She was, however, very much behind her husband in his new endeavour. To show her support in a tangible way she packed two huge boxes of food for him to eat on the train and stuffed his pockets with apples. In her first letters to him after he left she took great pains to assure him he was doing the right thing. McConnell and all his other colleagues at the Survey, she informed him, were jealous of what he was doing.

Before leaving Ottawa Tyrrell wrote to West Selkirk, Manitoba, and hired Roderick Thomas to go with him. Thomas had worked for Tyrrell during the exploration of the interlake district. He knew him to be "a good, reliable halfbreed who . . . could drive dogs, paddle a canoe, pitch camp, cook a good meal etc.

etc." Thomas was told to secure a sleigh and a team of four good dogs and wait for Tyrrell in Winnipeg. Tyrrell knew his man. When he arrived in Winnipeg, Roderick was awaiting him with "as fine a team of dogs" as he had ever seen. They should have been for they cost him over $200.00 before he got them out of Winnipeg; but that included $15.00 to pay for a bunch of pigs they killed when they escaped from their kennel. They were worth the price, however, for all four of them made it all the way to Dawson via the White Pass and its infamous Dead Horse Trail where thousands of wretched beasts had perished the year before. Fine animals they undoubtedly were: Roderick Thomas could tell a good dog when he saw one. But the dogs also had the advantage of having Joe Tyrrell as their master. He summed up his attitude towards handling the animals; "it is the pace, and not the distance travelled that kills dogs as well as horses." Knowing that, Tyrrell set the appropriate pace each day on the 600 miles (or in Tyrrell's terms "one million, two hundred thousand paces") from Skagway to Dawson. The load was heavy, the road was long, and in addition to the usual provisions, this new miner's sleigh was piled with books and instruments. But Tyrrell was careful of his animals. He made sure they were not strained and watched their feet to detect sores before they could develop into crippling problems. At the first opportunity he acquired the use of additional dogs to share the burden.

All of that, however, was on the trail between Skagway and Dawson. Skagway was still half a continent away. The half continent was filled with memories. In Winnipeg the dogs and sleigh were loaded on the CPR train with the rest of the supplies and the iron snake carried the party across the prairies, past the new land which Tyrrell had helped map and which was now filling up with settlers. Only slightly to the north of the railway line was where he had discovered the dinosaur remains, and the huge coal deposits. All around was the territory he had paced for Dr. Dawson, Calgary was no longer just a few shacks on the banks of the Bow River. By the time the train chugged into the Rogers Pass, named after the inexhaustible surveyor who had once entertained them in camp, Tyrrell could not have helped but marvel at how the world had changed. Only the Rockies it seemed remained unchanged and unchanging. Crossing them in mid-winter he was confined to the coach. The previous summer, however, he had spent much of his time in the "observation car" – not the glassed-in dome of the sleek, modern transcontinental but a flat car with benches running lengthwise and no roof. Even from within the coach, however, nothing could diminish the awesome majesty of those snow-crowned peaks.

At Vancouver they delayed their journey for a week as Tyrrell demonstrated the versatility which was to stand him in good stead in his new life. He was going to the Klondike to search for gold, to become an expert in mining technology, and to sell the geological expertise he already possessed. Along the way, however, he had agreed to act as a courier or mail man for the federal government. On the train journey west of Winnipeg a telegram from the Minister of the Interior, Clifford Sifton, caught up with him. It was a request that he wait in Vancouver until some "important" government despatches could arrive and then to carry them with him into the Klondike for Commissioner Ogilvie.

Never one to miss an opportunity, Tyrrell immediately agreed. It was a small task but it demonstrated that his assurances that he was leaving without ill-will had been accepted. It also provided him with an opportunity to do a favour for an important Cabinet Minister. Tyrrell was well aware of the long-term advantages of doing favours for Ministers of the Crown. He also knew the short-term advantages. As an unofficial courier of official despatches he could expect preferential treatment from the Mounties along the way and, in particular he could expect to have any obstacles removed from his path when crossing into the Yukon from Alaska at the head of the White Pass. When the despatches arrived in Vancouver he was disappointed that they did not carry with them a letter instructing all and sundry to assist him on the way. In the meantime, however, he had been in touch with Major Perry of the NWMP in Vancouver who had assured him that the police would put him through as quickly and easily as possible even though he had no official status as courier.

That Saturday, after the papers arrived from Ottawa, Tyrrell with Roderick Thomas and the dogs boarded the steamer *Rosalie* for the five day journey up the coast to Skagway which was still the closest one could get to Dawson by public transportation in winter. By the summer of 1899 the precarious White Pass Railway would be in operation and Doll would ride over its narrow gauge track, but for J. B. in early February there was no such luxury. The sleigh was loaded, the dogs were hitched and the long trek to Dawson begun. In all it would take them exactly four weeks and although Tyrrell would complain that "progress at times seemed somewhat slow," he could still boast later that, with one team of dogs, they had reached Dawson faster than the mail which had also arrived at Skagway aboard the *Rosalie* and from there was carried into Dawson by teams of policemen who had the advantage of changing dogs at each police post along the way.

True to the principle that it was the pace and not the distance travelled that killed dogs, and well aware of the need to cover as much ground as possible while the weather permitted they began from that first day the pattern they would follow. It was strikingly similar to the routine of his earlier explorations. They rose early each day and covered as many miles as possible in the morning. Around noon they would stop to cook a meal and let the dogs rest before setting out again, continuing until within an hour of sunset when they would pitch camp on the bank of the river near a source of dry wood for fire. For the most part the weather held fine, fuel was abundant, and there was even companionship along the trail. It would have still been a month of deprivation and hardship for most travellers. But for Tyrrell, as he himself described it in a letter to his wife, this Yukon country was "a paradise" compared with the Barren Lands west of Hudson Bay that he had traversed twice in that decade.

From Skagway they ascended to White Pass City, five miles from the summit of the White Pass and the relative luxury of a hotel "where we had good meals and were made very comfortable." The "hotel" was a tent, and the "city" was a stopping place where the winter before the thousands of ill-prepared men in search of instant wealth had rested before setting out on the tortuous path to the summit. Ahead lay the infamous Dead Horse Gulch where it has been estimated 3,000 animals met their death in the few short months that the gold rush was at its height. Early the next morning, with another team of dogs hired to haul half his load up the deadly trail to the summit, Tyrrell set off. For him the trail that had broken so many men the year before and had seen the death of thousands of animals and not a few humans, held no horror or particular challenge. It was merely a part of the route through this northern "paradise." Recalling the trip in his later years he recounts the day he crossed the summit simply. "Next morning we were able to have half our load hauled to the summit by another team, and then from there we drove on to Log Cabin, a total distance of twenty miles."

The previous winter, at the height of the stampede Colonel Steele of the Mounties had set up a post at the summit of White Pass. Now with traffic reduced to a trickle the police post and customs house were located further inland at Log Cabin. Steele's initiative had established the border at the crest of the Coastal Mountains. It had also secured peace and order in the Yukon. It was more than nationalism that led Tyrrell to comment, "We felt more at home again for we were now back into Canadian Territory." "Soapy" Smith had been dead seven months and his gang broken up. But the memory lingered in Skagway and along the White Pass trail. Here at Log Cabin was the symbol of the only authority that had effectively kept Smith and his kind in check. Here too was another comfortable night for the latest of the gold hunters, his companion and his dogs.

At Log Cabin and at Tagish Post Colonel Steele's order that no one would enter the Klondike without either $1,000.00 or a year's supply of provisions was still being enforced. The order had prevented starvation from decimating those who reached Dawson in those first hectic days. By the time Tyrrell went across the border on his own account, Steele's order had the backing of legislation. When he had first issued it, Steele himself admitted to Tyrrell, he had no legal authority to do so. Steele also told Tyrrell, however, that he had acted secure in the knowledge that he had sufficient strength to enforce it and that before anyone could have his order overturned by higher authority or challenged in the courts the spring would have returned with its flow of goods and the emergency would have passed. Steele like "Soapy" Smith knew the nature of naked power in those hectic days. But Steele used his knowledge to a much better end. Without the control the deprivation suffered in the Klondike during that winter of shortage would have been much greater.

From Log Cabin to Bennett where two more dogs were acquired for $55.00 and then on to Tagish Post – a matter of three days. There Tyrrell readily undertook to increase his activities as a government courier. In addition to the despatches he was carrying for Clifford Sifton he willingly agreed to deliver four dogs and a sled from Major Wood at Tagish to the police post at Dawson. Leaving Tagish on Saturday, February 11, 1899, they were a week out of Skagway and still three weeks from their destination. The two dog teams and sleds made for lighter work for the dogs, though it did little to increase their rate of travel which was governed not only by the strain on the animals but also by the speed at which Tyrrell and Thomas could walk or run behind the sleds as they drove them. From Tagish to Marsh Lake, past the Whitehorse Rapids where soon the town of Whitehorse would arise, stormbound for a day on the legendary Lake Laberge which Robert Service had not yet laid eyes on, and on down the Yukon River to where it is joined by the Salmon River. Here they met up with two Mounties who were also heading downstream. Since congenial companionship in facing the hazards of the trail was always a welcome commodity, the four men agreed to travel together.

The weather to that point had been mild. In fact it had been so warm that one day in mid-February Tyrrell had stripped down to his shirt sleeves. "I brought my Hudson Bay clothes with me," he complained, "and so far I haven't been able to use them." His complaint was a little premature for at Salmon River the weather changed. A series of storms broke on them and then the bottom fell out of the thermometer. The mild weather that had gone before had made the journey heavy going through wet snow. Now that difficulty disappeared and was replaced by others – extreme cold and deep drifts that blocked their path. Undaunted, the enlarged party set out for Five Fingers Rapids and what to Tyrrell was familiar territory.

This sixty mile section of the journey took them three days in temperatures that dipped to 60° below zero Fahrenheit. For Tyrrell and Thomas this leg of the journey contained a mishap that cost them several hours of travelling time. For the two Mounties the cost of the same mishap was much higher. Using the frozen river as a highway the party's progress was halted when they suddenly ran into a layer of thin ice. The river itself was solidly frozen but on top of the ice the recent mild weather had left about a foot of water. Now, with the return of cold weather that too had frozen over, but at one spot not sufficiently so to take the combined weight of four men, ten dogs and two sleds loaded with over 1,000 pounds of supplies. The whole group crashed through the ice and found themselves calf-deep in icy water. Tyrrell knew that to continue with wet feet at these bitter temperatures was to court disaster. As quickly as they could he and Thomas headed for the bank of the river to gather wood for a fire at which they could dry themselves. Despite his urgings, however, the two Mounties decided they did not want to lose the time. The next police post was, they said, only a matter of three or four miles further on and they struck out for it while Tyrrell and Thomas made a fire and dried their feet, socks and moccasins. After an hour or two's delay they resumed their journey only to discover that the two policemen had arrived at the next post suffering severe frostbite. Tyrrell later reported that as a result of the accident both had parts of their feet amputated.

From Selkirk at the mouth of the Pelly River to Split Up City at the mouth of the Stewart and on until finally, early on the afternoon of March 4, 1899, four weeks after leaving Skagway and more than seven weeks after leaving Ottawa, J. B. Tyrrell, Mining Consultant, had arrived at his destination. Ahead of him was a very different life from that which he had known in the Survey. Eventually his new career would make him a wealthy man – but that was a quarter of a century down the road. In the meantime, in the Klondike over the next seven years, Tyrrell was to earn large amounts of money. His expenses were also high, however, and although he left the promised land much wealthier than he arrived he was still far from being a rich man. He would not leave the Klondike with money only, however. He would also take from it a wide experience of mining techniques and procedures which he would later use to great advantage on the outside.

In March, 1899, Dawson's new mining consultant was an accomplished explorer and geographer and a learned geologist who knew almost nothing about mining operations. His entire practical experience had been gained in the week he had spent on the gold-fields the previous summer. He had, however, several major advantages over most. First, as his trip from Skagway demonstrated, he knew well how to convert the skills he had developed in his explorations into the techniques of survival in the Yukon. Second, he knew more about the phenomena of geological formations than any other man residing in the Klondike. Third, he had a considerable reputation which made him credible to those who sought professional advice. Finally, he had known nothing of geology when he went to work for the Survey, and had taught himself. He had known nothing of geography when he went on his first expedition with Dr. Dawson and he had taught himself. Now, in Dawson City, he knew nothing of mining and immediately set about finding out all there was to learn. He knew how to teach himself.

Armed with these four qualities, Joseph Burr Tyrrell took up his new life in "the world's most extravagant mining town." To aid him in the transition he had brought with him one assistant from Manitoba, two sleighs, six dogs, a load of provisions, books, papers and instruments and some borrowed money. His greatest asset, however, was that he had also brought with him the twentieth century. Later he would claim that he was the originator of Laurier's phrase that "the twentieth century belongs to Canada." He, like a number of others who got caught up in the rhetoric of the turn of the century, sent a copy of his rather purplish prose to the Prime Minister, and when Laurier predictably uttered a similar sentiment, Tyrrell, like the others, was happy to assume the pride of authorship. His pride was misplaced. He was undoubtedly not the originator of the phrase and with more than three quarters of the century behind us the prediction has yet to be fulfilled. But whether or not the twentieth century ends up belonging to Canada, in Dawson in 1899 the twentieth century did belong to J. B. Tyrrell.

When George Carmack, Tagish Charley and Skookum Jim pulled that fateful nugget from Bonanza Creek and touched off the gold rush they had been plying the age-old technique of panning for gold. The first wave of claim stakers were the other prospectors already on the Yukon and its tributaries. They too brought their pans with them. The next wave, also by and large northerners, came from all around the Yukon Territory and Alaska and were similarly equipped. So were the first lucky few from outside and the unlucky host that followed. They scooped up the gravels of the Klondike and its tributaries and panned it in search of the elusive yellow promise. When they found it they staked out their claim to 500 feet of river frontage and set up their primitive mining operations. First cleaning out the river-bed and then thawing the frozen ground with fire and hacking away at it until they reached gold-bearing gravel just above bedrock. With the arrival of the spring thaw and enough water to operate the primitive sluice boxes, the stockpiled diggings were shovelled in by hand. The gold was caught in the riffles while the sludge still containing unreclaimed wealth that had escaped the rudimentary recovery process, was discarded back into the stream or into ever-increasing piles.

The Klondike gold rush was the last great romantic adventure of the nineteenth century. In its first two years it was man, without technology, seeking to wrest a fortune from nature. By the end of the century the place of the solitary man was passing from the Klondike. The industrial techniques of the twentieth century were taking over and J. B. Tyrrell was in the vanguard of the change. Tyrrell's plan was to introduce large scale hydraulic mining to the area. No longer would the unit of operation be 500 feet of river frontage. Rather it would be a single acreage, encompassing what previously would have been numerous claims, granted as a concession within which no other mining could take place. In place of the laborious excavation of hand-heated earth, steam shovels would break through the still frozen ground and scoop it up. In place of the total reliance on the spring runoff of the adjoining river or stream, other waterways would be diverted to the concession by a system of ditches, aqueducts and pipes so that a greater and more regular, if not a constant source of water could extend the cleanup period from a few weeks to several months. And with better designed sluice boxes and a higher level of water availability even the sludge of the first processing could be run through again and a second skimming of gold retrieved. Before such a concession was granted the law required that the applicant demonstrate that the concentration of gold was not sufficient to support retrieval by hand methods. After the concession was granted, the holder was required to spend at least $5,000.00 a year in developing the operation.

If the twentieth century methods of retrieval that Tyrrell sought to introduce to the Klondike are not as romantically attractive as the panhandling methods of the first prospectors, that is as it should be. When he set foot in Dawson on that sunny winter's morning in March, 1899, it was a much different experience from his arrival the previous summer as part of that rough hewn armada that had been assembled on the shores of Lake Bennett. The gold rush of 1898 was the last flowering of nineteenth century romantic adventure. Men motivated by dreams of wealth forsook their families and careers to dash off in search of their fortune. For the most part they were untutored in the harshness of the northern climate and unprepared either by experience or study for the rigours of mining. Their maps failed to show the way and their equipment could not tackle the terrain. They went out by the tens of thousands to find the golden fleece. Too often all they found was that they themselves were the golden fleece – to con men and profiteers.

Tyrrell was the opposite. He too was in search of wealth. But he knew that it was not lying around under rocks with little signs saying "pick me up." He was no stranger to the harsh northern winter and short summer. For a decade and a half he had raced against time between spring and fall to accomplish all he had to do. For part of that time he had survived the onset of winters that howled out of the Arctic across Hudson Bay and a wild rock strewn tundra bereft of game. He was, it is true, as devoid of mining experience as they. But he had studied well and was as capable a geologist as Canada had produced to that time. In short he came not with a romantic notion that wealth was waiting for him but with the conviction that he was well-equipped to extract it from the ground. "If I can't make it here," he admitted, "I can't make it anywhere."

To be sure there was in Tyrrell a romantic streak. He would have liked, as would so many others, to unearth the mythical mother lode of the Klondike gold from which all the other gold was thought to have come. Unlike the others his geological studies prevented him from wasting much time on so futile a search. He quickly concluded that there was no mother lode in the Klondike. The concentration of gold in the creeks and hillsides had been the result of the erosion of billions of tons of earth and rock. In this, as in everything else in Tyrrell's life, the romantic gave way in the face of the practical. Only in one respect was this not true for him in 1899. Nothing could remove the romance of starting a new life.

CHAPTER 10

Life in the Klondike

She was "strong, straight and hardboiled." She had to be. Belinda Mulroney was a coal miner's daughter from Pennsylvania. Of all the jobs that fed the nineteenth century industrial revolution the most crushing were in the coal mines. The work itself was backbreaking and the working conditions inhumane. The desperate and perpetual gloom of the pits carried over into the life of the mining communities. The towns that housed them were caked in coal dust. Much worse was the cloud of poverty that hung over them. King Coal was in the forefront of the heavy industry that had changed the face of western civilization. He was also in the forefront of the recurring recessions and depressions that characterized the process. In the boom and bust economy of the era, every slowdown was felt first and hardest by the miners.

Growing up in that environment was no guarantee that a man or woman would end up "straight." The righteous fervour of the sons and daughters of coal miners who led the demand for social justice in the first half of the twentieth century is testimony, however, that the quality was not uncommon. Belinda Mulroney's straightness did not take the form of a crusader. It did, however, influence every dealing in her long entrepreneurial career. As for being strong and hardboiled, only the strong survived a childhood in the mining towns. The weak died young or grew up enfeebled. And if you were strong and survived then hardboiled you would most certainly be. Growing up in a tough environment has its advantages. The genteel world outside is unprepared for the onslaught of those who emerge to force down its barriers. Belinda Mulroney typified the breed. Her appearance in Dawson City at the onset of the gold rush with a load of hot water bottles for sale demonstrated her entrepreneurialism. A quick 600 per cent profit from the hot water bottles set her on the road to becoming "the richest woman in the Klondike." She never worked a claim herself, although once her future was made, she dabbled in the ownership of mines. Her real gold mine was in her hostelries. First her roadhouse on the trails, where a "spring bed" could be had for $1.00 a night, and then the most famous and luxurious of Dawson's hotels, the Fairview, with its canvas-walled interior rooms.

Arriving in the bright winter sunshine of March 4, 1899, Tyrrell sought out Miss Mulroney's Fairview Hotel on Main Street. Joe Tyrrell had probably met Belinda Mulroney the previous year when he was in Dawson, and, unbeknown to either of them, their paths had also crossed some years before when Tyrrell went to the Chicago Exposition for the Survey. Indeed Tyrrell may have eaten at her board at that time, for in 1893 she had opened a successful restaurant at the World's Fair and he, en route to the Barren Lands, had stopped off to lend a hand at the Canadian geological display. Despite any previous encounters, however, it was not until Tyrrell took up residence in Dawson that they came to know each other. Although they were never close friends, each could recognize elements of their own personality in the other and, not unnaturally, they held each other in fair esteem. In his eyes to say someone was "strong, straight and hardboiled" was a compliment indeed. "She was" he wrote "a young woman of enterprise and character."

Belinda showed her friendship in a more tangible and, typically, more flamboyant manner. While Joe was in Ottawa in February 1902 with his family, Belinda breezed into town, no longer plain Miss Mulroney but now Countess of Carbonneau – the count being a champagne salesman who had come to Dawson some time before and catching the eye of the Klondike's richest woman decided to stay. On their way back from one of their numerous trips to Paris where they rented a carriage and pair ornamented with gold and complete with a footman as part of an attempt to raise French capital for investment in the Klondike, the "aristocrats" stopped off in Ottawa to visit Belinda's younger sister who was a student at Ottawa's rather staid Sacred Heart Convent. When Belinda found out that Joe and Doll would be celebrating their wedding anniversary on St. Valentine's Day she decided that nothing would do but that an appropriate dinner should be held at the Russell Hotel with Joe and Doll as guests of honour.

Doll described the occasion as the "most marvellous party I

ever attended." Roses had been brought in by the bushel basket and simply dumped on the tables covering everything. The menu, Doll recalled, had "about sixteen courses" with "dainties . . . from all over the continent." One course was canvas-back duck from New York which, the Count decided, must have walked to Ottawa. Another had been intended to be turtle soup. To this end a live turtle had been brought in from Florida. But since the method of killing turtles was beyond the ken of the Russell's chef, canned soup was substituted and the turtle stayed on as a pet of the Russell's kitchen staff for years after.

If the hosts, the flamboyant Carbonneaus, and the guests of honour, the Tyrrells, *habitués* of Rideau Hall, were oddly assorted, the other guests were no less so. They ranged from the collection of Klondike sourdoughs who happened to be in Ottawa, to Belinda's sister and a group of her teenage friends from the convent "all prettily dressed in white muslin frocks." The girls dined on simpler fare and were generally more decorous – at least until the good count emptied a bottle of champagne into the jug of lemonade en route to their table. Doll summed it all up – "a riotous party."

Belinda's dinner party demonstrates the change that the Klondike wrought on Joe Tyrrell. Going into the Klondike for the first time, he was shocked at the "frightful amount of liquor" being taken over the passes. "The Dominion Alliance should send a man up to investigate the liquor question in the Canadian Yukon at once." His strait-laced attitude was also reflected a year later when he had moved to Dawson. He told Doll "I have not been inside a saloon since coming here and it is doubtful if it will be necessary for me to go into one." He soon found out that if he boycotted the saloons he was boycotting the boardrooms of Dawson. A few months later he was to be found in the saloons conducting business with everyone else. His snobbery took a beating too. From the train on the first lap of his journey to a new life he wrote, "There does not seem to be anyone on board whom I would care to know." Less than six months later he was writing to Doll that Big Alex Macdonald had just married a nineteen year old dance hall girl. "If you were here you could probably make a friend of her, and in that way we might get some work from him." He told an old friend and earlier biographer that he had gone into the Klondike "a modest, unassuming, amiable fellow" and came out of it "devoid of grace and filled with unbelief." The description is only partly true. Modest and unassuming Tyrrell never was. Neither was he "devoid of grace" afterwards. Nonetheless the Klondike left its mark on him as it did on everyone who went there in those frantic years. By the time Belinda threw the party for him in Ottawa, the transition was complete. He certainly no longer cared what the neighbours thought.

Belinda's party was still almost three years off, however. In the meantime Joe was finding her rates of $9.00 a night each at the Fairview Hotel pretty steep for himself and Roderick Thomas. He had about $500.00 of his original grubstake left. Until his business was established he would have to watch his expenses carefully. The first task was to find other accommodation. It came in the form of a small log cabin at $50.00 a month for which he had to buy a sheet iron cooking stove and cord of wood to burn. The next purchase was enough pine boards and nails to put together some furniture – two bunks, a kitchen table with some boxes for chairs, a writing table, drawing board and book shelves. Then he hung a shingle outside the door. The log cabin, measuring fourteen feet by twenty on the inside and boasting two windows was not only his home, it was his office.

Four months later, in July, knowing that business was picking up and also knowing that soon Doll and their two year old daughter Mary would be joining him, he found somewhat larger accommodation at a good price. A Miner's Institute which had been forming had obtained permission to build a two-storey structure as a meeting hall on the northeast corner of the Police Reserve and a promise that the portion of land would be severed. The Institute had gone bankrupt before that was done, however, and Tyrrell bought the house at the sheriff's sale with an oral promise that he would be able to continue leasing the land on which it stood.

Tyrrell's stay in the Klondike was marked by numerous conflicts and battles. In so dynamic a community as that which had sprung up from nothing on the banks of the Yukon there would inevitably be plenty of dissension as the town tried to set aside its stampede origins and settle into a more regular pattern of existence. Relationships between individuals and ill-defined ownership of property were bound to cause disputes among the ambitious citizens whose only common element was the desire to cash in on the boom. Men and women who can brave an unsettled frontier are likely to be highly individualistic. Dawson, in fact, was a whole community of individualists and conflicts among them were inevitable. Tyrrell was no exception and battles of one sort or another became an accepted part of his life in the Klondike. He was, nonetheless, filled with dismay when one of the elements

191

in a dispute became his lease on the Police Reserve lot and he was forced to find another location and move his house to it.

It was perhaps appropriate at the beginning of his new life in the Klondike that the day after he arrived Tyrrell attended the local Presbyterian Church. Never a religious man he was all his life a churchman, his morality founded deep in the Mosaic Law and the Golden Rule. Although raised in the Methodist tradition, when he married Doll – the daughter of a Baptist preacher – they made sure there would be no future disputes over their different religious backgrounds by settling on a neutral third option, the Presbyterian Church. In Dawson, Tyrrell's associations with the church were varied. It was there he was elected to the eldership taking his seat on the basic governing council of the presbyterian system. It was also in the church that he found a convenient way to dispose of all his mining properties on leaving the Klondike. He did not leave them as an endowment to the church or its charities; philanthropy would come later in his life. Rather he sold them at a fair profit to the minister, the Reverend A. S. Grant.

The appropriateness of his attendance at the Presbyterian Church on March 5, 1899 went further than his own relationship with the church, however. A part of the service that Sunday provided him with a vivid lesson on the nature of the Klondike with its sharp mixture of harshness and tenderness. An element of the worship of the presbyterians of Dawson that Sunday was the celebration of the sacrament of baptism – the baby girl being given the unlikely name "Edna Eldorado." The exact details of her birth are not clear for they quickly became shrouded in a cloak of folklore. Tyrrell's version of the events is as good as any. A young couple both sickly and the wife expecting, had gone out on the trails east of Dawson just before Christmas 1898. When the pregnant wife went into labour, perhaps brought on pre- maturely through the exertion of hiking up and down the valleys of the gold-fields, the husband deposited her in an empty unheated shack on Eldorado Creek while he went to search out the NWMP doctor. Before he could return the mother gave birth, but the exertions of labour and the sub-zero temperatures that penetrated the logs of the cabin were too much for her frail body. As she lay close to death her feeble moans were heard by three of the Eldorado miners making their way back up the trail after picking up supplies in Dawson. Johnny Lind, "Skiff" Mitchell and Bill Wilkinson, burst into the tiny cabin. While Lind tried to revive the mother with brandy, Bill Wilkinson peeled off his woollen undershirt and handed it to "Skiff" to wrap the baby in. Nothing could be done for the mother and by the time her boy-husband arrived back with the doctor she was already dead. The gentle treatment from the rough hands of the three miners, however, had saved the baby's life.

The father, already suffering from pneumonia and now stricken by grief was unable to take care of the child. So, while he was taken back to Dawson by the doctor, the three miners set off with the baby on their dogsled for one of their own cabins. The doctor had written out instructions on how to handle the baby through the night and gave them strict orders to find one of the local women to take over from them in the morning. News of the birth set the trails of the Klondike agog. By next day there were no fewer than sixteen applicants for the job of foster mother. As Johnny, "Skiff" and Bill tried to resurrect the wisdom of Solomon in deciding who the mother should be, Mrs. Brock from the next claim over, shouldered her way through the crowd and picked the baby up.

"I'll take care of her. You boys take up a collection to pay for the milk."

While the miners poured out $400.00 worth of gold dust, Mrs. Brock carried the infant to her own cabin. As Tyrrell watched the sacrament being performed a few months later, the harshness of the northern trail stood starkly before him. So too did the bond of humanity that tied together the people of the trail. The honesty and plain dealing of the Yukon prospector is fabled, but here was the morality of the trail in its positive aspect, in its care for the helpless.

Once in Dawson there was no time to be wasted. One night at the Fairview at $9.00 a night, the first part of Sunday for the observance of the Sabbath and then it was down to the business of finding accommodation. By Monday evening the rough furniture was hammered together and a shingle hanging outside – J. B. Tyrrell Mining Consultant. Soon it was replaced by another – Tyrrell and Green, Mining Engineers and Surveyors. There were three prongs to Tyrrell's business endeavours in his new life. The first was his business as a mining consultant. Here he would sell his know-how and experience for a cash return that he hoped would provide the basis for his livelihood. It was slow at first – very slow.

Tyrrell, however, was not idle. First there was the task of developing business contacts and to this he applied himself as assiduously as he had ever done in developing his social contacts in Ottawa or his professional ones at the meetings of the British Association. He followed through with his introductory letter to the Bank of Commerce, and hunted down many of the people he had met the year before. He also made contact with Commissioner Ogilvie and the other government officials but, almost to a man, he found the reception from them cool. It was, he concluded, a case of them leaning over backwards to avoid giving anyone the impression that they were favouring a former government colleague. For new contacts Tyrrell soon realized that he had to go where everyone else met – the saloons. Never a heavy drinker he learned to haunt the bars of Dawson in those early days meeting as many of the miners as possible. It was there, in the saloons, that he received his first commission as a mining consultant.

There was also, in those early days, the task of learning as much as he could about the gold-fields. "It is necessary for me to become thoroughly conversant with the details of the workings on the creeks as soon as possible, for people expect you to know what you are talking about." Out on the trails he was as meticulous in making notes and collecting specimens as he ever was on an expedition. Within a month he could boast that he had "a collection of rocks that would make almost any geologist's mouth water." Others benefited from his approach to his new work. He continued to send specimens of plant and animal life to various museums and institutions. Interesting bones and fossils of prehistoric animals were similarly shipped east and into the United States. He benefited too, as did his future customers, from his thoroughness. He worked his way up and down the creeks, examining operations, collecting and examining rocks, making an accurate map of the area and finding out everything he could of the gold found in preceding years. He wanted to know how much had come off every claim, where it had been found and in what density, what form, what colour. Each piece of information he carefully noted for future reference.

By the time he picked up his first commission on May 13 he was ready for it. The job was to examine and report on a claim on Hunker Creek for four miners. He set his fee at $100.00 a day plus expenses and after four days on the creeks submitted his bill for $580.50. A few days later one of the miners came in with a check for $145.00. Joe was euphoric. He rushed a money order for $50.00 to Doll and assured her there would be lots more to come. He was right. By early September he was able to earn $2,500.00 in two weeks. The gamble had paid off.

From then on the demand for his services grew steadily. He quickly became known for his fairness and honesty as well as for his knowledge of the gold-fields. Others had been there longer and had more experience in searching for gold or mining. But Joe Tyrrell was unique in having made it his business to find out everything he could about the area in general and about as many claims as possible. With each succeeding commission he became more knowledgeable. In the Klondike that made him a wise man to consult before buying in on a mining operation.

During the height of the gold rush a consultant would have starved. Claims were bought and sold, partnerships formed and dissolved, operations begun and halted with such tumultuous rapidity that there was no room for a mining consultant. Before any investigation of a claim could have been made it would probably have been sold and resold two or three times. With the end of the stampede Dawson, although still a boom town, settled into the more stable patterns of a bustling, thriving, northern mining community. Claims still changed hands frequently. Partnerships came and went at a pace that would have left the business communities of Toronto and Montreal flabbergasted. There was time now, however, to consider what one was buying or selling.

If J. B. Tyrrell was not the only man in Dawson trying to sell his advice he was certainly one of the most qualified. He also wisely recognized the limitations of his own qualifications due to his inexperience in mining operations. Hence his first partnership. Tom Green was everything Tyrrell was not. A full-blooded Mohawk Indian from Brantford, Ontario, Green was a civil engineer, who had graduated from McGill and was in the Klondike for much the same purposes as Tyrrell. The alliance of the two men strengthened each of them during that first year in the Klondike for each had a different range of knowledge and ability to bring to the business.

Throughout his six years in the Klondike the consultancy business formed the base for his operations. When he left in 1905 it was because he had come to the conclusion that the Klondike had passed its peak. Mining production in the Yukon reached a high point of over a million ounces of gold in 1900. From there it fell steadily until by 1904 it was down to just over 400,000 ounces and still falling. There were now greener, or at least yellower, pastures elsewhere.

Tyrrell had not only gone to the Klondike to earn a livelihood. He had also gone with the dream of striking it rich. When he left Ottawa he was still dreaming of finding the "mother lode" of Klondike gold. He quickly realized that he would not get rich that way. But he also knew that he would not do so by peddling advice to other people either. If there were to be any hopes of earning his fortune he would also have to strike out for himself into the gold-fields and moil with the other miners on individual claims. Even before he reached Dawson he had taken some steps in that direction. In Skagway he had met up with one of R. G. McConnell's brothers who owned four claims in the Klondike. Tyrrell agreed to look after the claims in return for a one-third interest in them. He also had his partnership with Bronson and Ray by which he would operate the Dawson end of a mining concession. In addition, he had a 10 per cent share in another concession. But these were all straws in the wind. What was needed was a good working claim of his own. The opportunity he was looking for came soon after his first job as a consultant.

While on Hunker Creek he had had an opportunity to see the workings of Thirty-Nine Below. It looked impressive and when a few weeks later it was put up for sale Tyrrell did not hesitate. The asking price was $30,000.00, well beyond Tyrrell's assets, but nothing fearing, Tyrrell went to the Bank of Commerce to borrow the money. By this time he was a known quantity and he had come to the area highly recommended by the bank's president. As a result he got the money at the most favourable interest rate going, 24 per cent per annum. He must have spent some sleepless nights over that arrangement. The $600.00 a month interest payment was as much as he would have earned in four months only a year before. But the Klondike was another world, where values were measured in ounces not in dollars. In fact Tyrrell had judged his first investment well.

In the years that followed, alternating between mining it himself and turning it over to laymen who were allowed to mine it in return for a percentage of what they took out of it, Thirty-Nine Below on Hunker was the basis of Tyrrell's success. In the spring cleanup of 1901, for example, when he had worked himself, it yielded a gross in excess of $25,000.00 before expenses, including wages. Even as late as the spring of 1903, when he had left it to laymen to work his clear share was almost $5,000.00. Though in the two years that followed it never again paid so richly, none-theless by then it was his own property. Indeed he had repaid the bank completely within the first two years just as he had also

Top: Working the claim at Thirty-nine Below on Hunker. (TFRBL) Bottom: The constant lineup outside the Gold Commissioner's office at Dawson where the claims were registered and transferred. (PAC)

repaid Fred Wade his initial grub stake of $2,000.00. From this base of operations as a miner he got involved in numerous other claims sometimes with a single partner and sometimes with a group of co-owners. His expenses were high, but so was his income and he ended each year better off than the one before. If he lived off the income from his consultancy it was the operation of his mines that enabled him to leave the Klondike at the end of six years with some $50 – $60,000.00 to his name. Thirty-Nine Below on Hunker was a valuable paying property, but it was not Dick Low's fraction where the gold return was over $5,000.00 per foot frontage and a single pan could yield well in excess of $600.00.

The price was in the lifestyle. Conditions in the Klondike were tough. During the winter of 1901, for example, there were whole weeks at a time when the temperature never got above 60 degrees below zero. Living conditions were not the best. Tyrrell described the little cabin on Hunker Creek where he spent the winter of 1900-01 while mining his claim.

> My cabin, built of peeled poplar logs, had a little window in the east wall, in front of which I had a rough table on which were the gold scales etc. The glass used to get so thickly covered with frost that it would let in very little light, so I hung a bag inside of it which I let down at night and while it was down the frost would thaw and clear from the window. Then in the day time I would pull up this outside blind and the cleared glass would admit a nice amount of light.

To complicate life further an outbreak of rabies had induced Commissioner Ogilvie to order all the population vaccinated with anti-rabies serum brought in for the occasion. A painful precaution that saw men unable to work for a month afterwards. Klondike gold was never cheap.

The third element of his business was the one that held the greatest hope for the future. "We have a fortune in our Concession when it goes through," he optimistically forecast. In fact it yielded nothing but expense, trouble and the consumption of a great deal of time during those six years. The gold rush and the initial boom of the Klondike were rooted in the age-old methods of placer mining – named after the "placers" or deposits of gravel in which the gold was found. Placer mining techniques work well, provided they are used on rich highly concentrated deposits. As the concentration of gold diminishes, however, the techniques become economically unfeasible. Either the thinner concentration of gold is left untouched or new mechanized methods of retrieval have to be instituted which are capable of handling large amounts of ore bearing gravel and extracting from it the tiny proportion of gold it may contain. The newly developed technique of hydraulic mining was just such an operation, digging up the soil with steam shovels and washing it through enlarged sluices with large amounts of water. To institute the new technique, however, required a fundamental change from the traditional unit of operation. The 500 foot creekside claim permitted under existing mining laws was an inadequate base of operations. To justify the expenditure on equipment a larger operation was essential. To this end the government had introduced its concession policy.

Where it could be established that an area contained only a thin concentration of gold that was not economically viable for hand exploitation, and where such hand exploitation was not in fact under way, an applicant could be granted a concession to mine a larger area within which the staking of individual claims under the other mining laws would be forbidden. During the years in the Klondike Tyrrell was involved in various capacities with several concessions, but the particular operation which predominated was the one which he had set up before he ever left Ottawa. It occupied much of his time while he was in the Klondike and the final settlement of the problems that arose did not reach the courts until after he had returned to the outside.

Drumming up business in Ottawa before he left for his new life, Tyrrell had entered into a three-way equal partnership with C. C. Ray and E. H. Bronson to set up a concession for hydraulic mining in the Klondike. In essence the agreement was that Bronson and Ray would put up the money and look after getting approval for the operation in Ottawa while Tyrrell would manage the working end of the partnership in Dawson. All went well at the beginning. Through the intercession of Napolean Belcourt, Clifford Sifton agreed in principle to the granting of the concession. In many ways Belcourt was the key figure in granting the concession. A Liberal Member of Parliament, future Speaker of the House of Commons and Senator, he was without doubt one of the great agents of patronage of his day. His Ottawa law firm unabashedly billed itself "parliamentary and departmental agents."

Almost from the day Tyrrell arrived in Dawson, he was caught up in the affairs of the concession. Before the actual permit could be issued two certificates had to be acquired from the officials in the Klondike. One from William Ogilvie, by now Commissioner of the Yukon Territory, and the other from E. C. Senkler, the Gold Commissioner, certifying that the ground in question could not otherwise be economically worked. Ogilvie had little difficulty in issuing the certificate though he waited until after Senkler had issued his before he acted. Senkler, however, at first refused and Tyrrell had to persuade him by taking him on a tour of the area in question before he would agree. But agree he did and on May 5, 1899, Tyrrell was able to stake the concession. At the time, the difficulty with Senkler loomed large as an obstacle to Tyrrell's dreams. By the time his dealings with Bronson and Ray were over, he wished he had accepted Senkler's first ruling.

The concession policy was unpopular with the miners since it closed land to their use. And although there were several concessions in the area the one granted to the Bonanza Creek Hydraulic Company was amongst the most visible and therefore bore the brunt of much of the criticism. Throughout his stay in the Klondike, Tyrrell's position in the community was coloured by his association with the B.C.H.C. operation. The land they had applied for ran for five miles from the mouth of Bonanza Creek just opposite the town of Dawson. Since there were two applications for the same territory, however, the government compromised by giving each applicant half their request. The B.C.H.C. lease therefore covered the second two and a half miles of the creek up the both sides of the valley to the summit. Later, the company appears to have managed to acquire the whole five miles. In any event it was still more or less within sight of Dawson and a constant reminder to the population as production levels fell that valuable land was being kept out of production. Whether the ground in fact could have been worked by hand on small claims is a moot point. There is no doubt, however, that the ground was being kept out of production. One condition of the lease was that $5,000.00 a year would be spent on developing the concession. But Bronson and Ray had no interest in pouring their money into the operation. Their interest was speculative. Having secured a lease on a potentially valuable mining property they were from the first in search of a purchaser. Tyrrell on the other hand was in the business of reaping a mineral harvest. He tried to bring the B.C.H.C. concession to production. To this end he went after and secured the rights to divert additional water from farther up the valley and spent a good deal of his own money in channelling it to the concession. But it still was not a sufficient water supply for the type of mining operation he wanted to establish. In any event, it soon became obvious to him that his partners were only interested in a free ride. Without their capital, he knew he could not finance the required outlay.

200

As the return from his own properties on Hunker Creek dwindled, Tyrrell's determination to develop the B.C.H.C. concession grew. At one point he negotiated with Ray to buy out the two Ottawa partners. The negotiations took place in Dawson and the two men finally agreed on a price of $50,000.00. Tyrrell asked for twenty minutes to raise the money, left Ray in the hotel and went across the road to the bank. In fifteen minutes, the loan arranged, he returned to close the deal. But fifteen minutes had been too long. Ray had raised the price to $100,000.00 and the deal fell through.

Negotiations were renewed at various points and a half-hearted attempt was made to institute work. By that time, however, the whole concession policy was under fire and a royal commission had been appointed to investigate the situation. While awaiting the report of the commission Ray reconsidered the haste with which he had rejected Tyrrell's $50,000.00 and offered it to him again. Like the haberdasher he was, he reduced the price. Tyrrell could have it for $49,600.00. By now the minimal work done on the property and Tyrrell's own claims against it left the company with a debt of $18,000.00. In addition it was already clear that the B.C.H.C. concession would be coming under heavy fire from the royal commission and might even have its lease revoked. Tyrrell wrote back turning down the proposition. "If you can persuade anyone to pay any such figure for a concession without title, without water, without dumping ground, and with a deficit of about $18,000 on it I should advise you to sell without a moment's hesitation."

That was the end of the road for the partnership that had begun with such great promise. Soon after, Tyrrell resigned as manager and filed a claim against the company for what was owed to him. The lawsuit that followed dragged on after Tyrrell had left the Klondike and by the time the courts found in his favour he had sold all his interests in the area and the money awarded went to the new owners. Tyrrell had, however, the satisfaction of having been vindicated in the battle and to him that was not unimportant.

The fight with Bronson and Ray aroused a good deal of acrimony on both sides. Much of this fell on Doll's shoulders rather than on J. B.'s. Throughout his stay in Dawson the Tyrrells maintained a home in Ottawa. From there Doll, who handled much of their relationship with the two businessmen, wrote telling her husband how much she hated the sight of their adversaries. At one point it got so bad, she said, that she could scarcely sit near them in church. Her reaction is testimony not only to the intensity of her feelings towards the two men but also to how strongly committed she was in supporting her husband's venture into private enterprise. Throughout his years in the Klondike she stood firmly with him. She alone knew of his fears that his resignation had lowered him in the eyes of his former colleagues, she wrote to him shortly after he first left Ottawa assuring him that everyone admired what he was doing. Twice, although she continued to make her home in Ottawa, she ventured up to the Klondike to join him. Like everyone else who went there, her life was never the same again. Late in life she wrote a book about her experience and entitled it simply *I Was There*.

Edith Mary Carey was younger than Joe. The daughter of a Baptist minister and a well-to-do mother, she was given a genteel upbringing in a variety of small Ontario and Maritime towns with a few years of English life and education thrown in for good measure. It was not until after the family had returned from England that she met and married Tyrrell.

From the first their life together was punctuated by long separations from one another. Their courtship had endured the first Barren Lands trip. Their first year of married life was marked by the eight months of the second Barren Lands trip. The separations of the next four years had varied only in their length. The initial hope of the Klondike was that they would be able to make their life together. In fact, it did not work out that way and, if anything, they had even less time under the same roof from 1899 to 1905, than they had enjoyed previously. But the intention was there and as soon as Joe had made enough money he sent for Doll to join him. With Mary in tow, and a draft on a bank in Dawson for enough money to guarantee return passage sown into her petticoat, she set out.

When she left Ottawa in August 1899 she was the typical late Victorian young matron. Prim and proper as a lady ought to be, hers had been a sheltered life. A daughter of the parsonage she considered herself a "fragile" person. She was also, by her own admission "a prig." The Yukon would change much of that. Before the venture began the ride by Pullman to Vancouver "seemed a terrible undertaking." By the time she reached Dawson City the Pullman car would be remembered as the very height of luxury. With her two year old daughter, she travelled across the country to Vancouver and then by boat to Skagway. From there it was over the Coastal Mountains by the precipitous, narrow gauge White Pass Railroad and then by steamer to where a "primitive open tram" carried them, seated on stacks of champagne cases, for a three mile portage to Whitehorse and on by boat to Dawson.

The crowded steamer to Skagway was her first real taste of what the Klondike was all about. There were but half a dozen women on board, and Mary was the only child. Doll later claimed that Mary was the first white child in Dawson. An exaggerated claim, but not by much. Children were so few and far between in that northern nirvana that Mary was often presented with gifts by the miners – usually in the form of gold nuggets. Of more immediate benefit to Doll than any number of nuggets was the fact that Mary was an insurance policy for their safe passage. Years later Doll told how on the first night of her voyage she had just put Mary to bed in their cabin when someone began banging at the door. Terrified, Doll managed to find the courage to tell the intruder that it was she and the baby inside. She concluded the story, "At once the man apologized saying 'I wouldn't disturb a frightened little girl for anything.' "

If the steamer to Skagway was out of Doll's ambit of previous experience, Skagway itself was even more so – "The most unusual place I had ever seen." Its fire-trap shacks, its tents occupied by whole families and its bustling raised wooden sidewalks with churned up mud streets were enough to inspire a mixture of fear and awe. She described the scene, "Filth lay around everywhere. Men with packs on their backs, pack-trains of horses and mules and many dog-teams were going about. Indians and squaws were scattered among the crowd and all languages were being spoken." Fortunately Skagway was a one night stop. The next day they would be aboard the train that would take them across the White Pass to Lake Tagish. But if Doll thought she was off on another Pullman ride, the conductor soon put her straight. As they pulled out of Skagway he walked through the coach warning the passengers to stay in their seats and not to move from one side of the car to the other. If they did there was a danger that the narrow gauge train would go over the side of the mountain into the gorge.

It was at the end of that ride on the White Pass Railroad that she displayed the last element of her narrow upbringing. She described a man she met on the train. He was "of gentlemanly manners who had taken a great fancy to Mary and made himself very agreeable to us." In the course of the conversation he told her of his own five year old daughter whom he had left behind. That struck a responsive chord in Doll's heart. By the time they reached Tagish they had struck up a reasonable friendship. As he helped her transfer her baggage to the overnight steamer for Whitehorse, however, Doll made the mistake of asking him if he would be bringing his wife and daughter to the Klondike. He told her no, he would not, since he and his wife were getting a divorce. That did it. "I turned from him in disgust."

Years later reflecting on these events she acknowledged the effects of the Yukon on her puritan training, "I wouldn't be so shocked today as I was then." The undoing of her priggishness was not far around the corner. Indeed her first lesson in the roughness of the new life came on her very first night in Dawson. But that was still three days away. First the stern-wheel steamer had to get them to Whitehorse with passengers debarking from time to time along the lake to help the crew load fuel cut in the surrounding forests. Doll's rectitude was still safe, for she was in good society. A happy band of twelve civil servants were on board heading from Ottawa to Dawson to help add "good government" to the peace and order that had gone before.

There was also on board the boat a company of police troops under the command of Colonel Evans. That night when the boat reached Whitehorse the Colonel allowed his men to strike up a band to provide music for a dance. Doll tells the story,

Men crowded in from the store, the warehouses and tents until it seemed as if there were hundreds of them. There were only four women besides myself. The men were great, strong-looking fellows, most of them unshaven, and they wore broad hats which they never removed even while they were dancing. Their long riding-boots had spikes in them, and a considerable number had revolvers in their hip pockets. I had gone to bed with Mary, but Colonel Evans came to my door and asked me to get up, saying that I would never see another dance like this one. I certainly never have. The Colonel and I danced together once or twice, then he said, 'Just stand by me and no one will bother you.' A man would come up to one of the women with his arms outstretched, saying, as he spat out tobacco juice, 'Dance, pardner?' One or two came up to me, but the Colonel sternly refused to allow me to dance with them though I am sure, from my subsequent knowledge of these men, that I would have been treated with the utmost respect. The oil lanterns shining dimly, the music of the band, the wail of the Arctic wind, and the splash of the water against the boat, made a weird scene which I have never forgotten.

Nor did she ever forget her arrival three days later at Dawson. It was 11.00 o'clock at night and no doubt her romantic heart was aflutter. "I stood at the rail looking eagerly for my husband among the crowds of men waiting on the wharf. The other women on the boat with us were literally carried off by triumphant and happy husbands, but I was left standing alone. There was no one to meet me."

Meanwhile back in Vancouver a letter addressed to her had arrived at a friend's house. Its message was simple: "Don't come any farther, I'm coming out." Fortunately, Doll knew nothing of this message as she and Mary made their way along the wooden catwalks of Dawson past the false-fronted buildings in search of Belinda Mulroney's Fairview Hotel.

That Dawson was separated from Ottawa by miles of rocks, streams, mountains, forests, prairies, more rocks, streams and forests was already clear to Doll. It had taken her many days to cross that mass of land. In one night she would cross an even greater barrier. For Ottawa's society was a million miles from the Klondike's. That night at Belinda Mulroney's hostelry, she was baptized by immersion. Afraid to undress she put Mary to bed, and sat listening to the noise of midnight merriment through the canvas walls of the room.

> Then a party of men and women came in from the mines and took the adjoining room, which opened into mine by a door having no lock on it. They ordered up champagne and other drinks and soon the place was bedlam let loose. Furniture was being flung around and the language was such as I had never heard before. I buried my face under the pillow and prayed that I might not hear what they were saying and that Mary might not awaken. Soon the party became so uproarious that every moment I expected them to burst into my room.

Fortunately someone got the idea that she might need help and contacted Faith Fenton of the Toronto *Globe*. The intrepid Miss Fenton, who was known slightly to Doll, appeared at the hotel room door and succeeded in getting the almost hysterical Mrs. Tyrrell calmed down. She also got word out on the trail to Joe that his family had arrived and soon the Tyrrells were reunited.

The first visit to the Klondike was mercifully brief. Shortly before Doll arrived J. B. had received and accepted the best offer to date for his services. The owner of four rich claims on Hunker Creek was going to London for the winter and wanted Tyrrell to go with him in case he needed the services of an expert on the Klondike during any of his business dealings. An all expense paid trip to England and a fee of $1,500.00 in return for being on hand was too good an opportunity to miss. So nine days after she arrived in the Klondike, Doll was heading back east, this time accompanied by her husband. She too would spend the winter in Britain. But even London, the heart of empire and civilization, could not erase the memory of the new world that she had ventured into – however briefly.

Four years later, in 1903, when Doll ventured back into the Yukon she stayed for the whole summer. By then the community had further settled down and Doll was more experienced in some of the not-so-fine points in life. She fitted easily into Dawson's society and regretted leaving it as winter set in. She never went back after that, but the Klondike stayed with her all her life. Never again would she turn away in disgust from someone of whose life she did not approve.

"Dawson" wrote Tyrrell "reeks with lawyers." He was talking from experience. Tyrrell was well aware of that aspect of his adopted home. His lawsuit over the Bronson and Ray concession after he had left the Klondike was the final episode in seven years during which it appeared at times as if he spent more hours in the courtrooms than in the gold-fields. The Klondikers were litigation happy. In any frontier community that springs suddenly into existence disputes over property and reputation are bound to be frequent. In the fabled frontier of the American west when such disputes arose a man reached for his revolver. In the Klondike, no doubt reflecting the influence of the NWMP, a man reached for his lawyer. Tyrrell was involved in his share of these courtroom battles, mostly dealing with conflicting claims. On one notable occasion however, he became involved in a major lawsuit that had nothing to do with property, though it was related to the unpopular concession policy.

Concessions were under heavy fire in the local newspapers. But Tyrrell had first-hand experience that revealed clearly that the papers were not always motivated by the highest principle of

206

what was best for the community. W. A. Beddoe, the editor of the *Dawson Daily News*, had approached Tyrrell with a proposal for a deal. If Tyrrell agreed to a piece of the Bronson and Ray concession going to a third party, Beddoe would see to it that the *News* ceased its attack on the concession. Tyrrell refused and, by his account, went to Richard Roediger, the owner and publisher of the *News*, to see if he had approved the approach. Roediger denied all knowledge of the deal and told Tyrrell if there was any truth to his story he should make a public statement of it and he, Roediger, would order Beddoe to either clear his name or be fired.

On May 5, 1903, Tyrrell swore out his affidavit and the next day Beddoe issued a statement denying Tyrrell's accusation. By Beddoe's account he had only spoken to Tyrrell on behalf of Senkler, the Gold Commissioner, in an effort to clear up conflicting claims to a piece of property. Beddoe vehemently denied that he had offered to end the newspaper's criticism of the concession and announced that the courts would settle the matter. He then launched a libel suit claiming $10,000.00 in damages.

The opposition papers had a field day. "No offense in the eyes of reputable newspaper men is more henious [*sic*] than the one of which the editor of the News is accused." thundered the *Nugget* and went on to say that if Tyrrell's charges were upheld the *News* was "unworthy of public confidence" and "guilty of a foul betrayal of trust." The court case was a bitter one. The fact that Roediger had an interest in two newspapers with opposing editorial policies was dragged up. So were Tyrrell's various government reports on the Klondike. One account has Beddoe's lawyer making a "fiery speech" and with "forcible gestures and a face like marble" pointing his finger at Tyrrell and saying, "That man lied." But the jury found otherwise. It took Tyrrell's word, dismissed the suit, and awarded him costs which amounted to $873.60 – none of which Tyrrell ever managed to collect.

Beddoe's libel suit itself was over, but it was the precursor of a longer fight with the recently appointed Commissioner, Frederick Congdon, which led Tyrrell into a brief sojourn in the world of newspaper ownership and of politics. Congdon and Tyrrell had been at the University of Toronto at the same time and had known each other slightly. When Congdon came to the Yukon in 1901 as Legal Adviser to the Commissioner and the Territorial Council, Tyrrell worked hard at renewing the acquaintance. He even gave Congdon the use of his house in Dawson until he could find suitable accommodation of his own. It appeared to

Tyrrell that at last he had a friend in high office – an asset which he would not hesitate to use to good advantage. To his dismay, however, he found that Congdon's presence did nothing to lessen the local authorities' continued opposition to the concession policy. By the time Congdon was appointed Commissioner in 1903 it was obvious to Tyrrell that he would be receiving no benefit from his old school mate. Indeed, the very opposite was true. The attacks on the concessions increased. As they did relations between the two men deteriorated until they were locked in a desperate power struggle.

Where precisely the enmity between the two men began is not clear but various elements in its deepening stand out starkly. Had he had his way Tyrrell would have used his influence to his own advantage just as he had done years before in having his father intercede in getting his appointment with the Survey and, similarly, in mobilizing Lord Aberdeen's assistance to acquire authorization for the second Barren Lands trip. More recently there had been Belcourt's intercession on behalf of the B.C.H.C. concession. Tyrrell, as a consultant, had also used Belcourt as an advocate in winning leases for other concessionaires. Tyrrell saw nothing wrong with this type of influence, provided always it stayed within the letter of the law. At the same time he would never countenance going beyond the letter of the law. It is impossible to imagine Tyrrell taking a bribe or falsifying a document. Such actions were beyond the pale of gentlemanly conduct even in the Klondike. If Congdon had belonged to a new wave of public officials who eschewed the use of patronage and favour, Tyrrell would have accepted the situation. Congdon, however, was no such reformer. As far as Tyrrell was concerned, he was nothing but a political hack – and acted like it. His administration was rife with corruption. To make matters worse it was inefficient. Tyrrell's struggle with Congdon, however, stems more from the personal enmity that grew between them than from Tyrrell's objection to the "unrestricted graft and dishonesty among many of the officials in the Yukon Territories."

The declaration of war between the two men came in the wake of Beddoe's libel suit. Tyrrell's fight with Beddoe had been bloody and he had not relished the experience of being called a liar in court. Yet the case was hardly over, and Beddoe's dismissal as editor of the *News* hardly accomplished, when Congdon gave the erstwhile editor a job in the Territorial administration. When Congdon followed this up a little later by appointing Beddoe the editor of *The World*, "the organ of the local government, and

The steamer *Tyrrell* coming in to the wharf at Dawson in 1903. (TFRBL)

Seventh Avenue, Dawson in October, 1905. Tyrrell's house is on the extreme left. (TFRBL)

mouthpiece of the Commissioner," the insult was as much as Tyrrell could stand. It was difficult for Tyrrell to imagine a more outrageous affront than the refuge granted to Beddoe. He soon discovered the limitations of his own imagination. Congdon had more in store for him and with his next ploy the Commissioner won Tyrrell's undying enmity.

When Tyrrell bought his house on the corner of the Police Reserve in 1899, he was assured by Commissioner Ogilvie that, provided the police did not need the land for their own use, there would be no difficulty in renewing the lease indefinitely. Although the police still had no use for the land, when the lease expired in 1904, Congdon, who now held Ogilvie's old job, refused to renew it. Tyrrell was furious. He remonstrated with the Commissioner that he would probably not be much longer in the Klondike – to no avail. He cast up the fact that he had loaned the house to Congdon when the latter first arrived in Dawson – to no avail. He even reminded the Commissioner that he had on occasion loaned him money when he needed it – to no avail. Congdon was adamant in his refusal to renew the lease and Tyrrell had to find another site for his house. It cost Tyrrell over $1,000.00 to move the house to its new location. "It was an entirely unnecessary expenditure, and it left me with a very bitter antagonism towards an old acquaintance," wrote Tyrrell. Congdon would have been wise to have chosen his enemies more carefully. Once aroused Tyrrell could be a bitter, unforgiving opponent as the Commissioner was to learn.

The first opportunity to join battle came with the impending closure of *The Sun*, one of Dawson's two daily newspapers. Unable in the flagging economy of the district to keep up its payments on the linotype machine the newspaper had been told that the typesetting equipment would be repossessed if payment was not forthcoming. Generally Roediger's *Daily News* supported Congdon's administration and, as Tyrrell put it, if the *Sun* folded, "the opponents of the government" would have no daily newspaper to espouse their cause. That was reason enough for Tyrrell to get together with his old friend the Reverend A. S. Grant to put up $4,500.00 between them to keep the paper going. In fact, however, Tyrrell's motive was not to ensure an opposition press. It was to get at Congdon by the best means available. As soon as a better method presented itself, he had no compunction about selling the linotype machine, and thereby the "opposition" press, to Captain Roediger.

The better opportunity was the calling of an election in 1904.

210

The first Member of Parliament for the Yukon, J. H. Ross had been Commissioner of the Yukon Territory after Ogilvie and it was on his resignation to run for Parliament that Congdon had been appointed to the job. Now Congdon decided that he should follow even further in his predecessor's footsteps. Accordingly he resigned the Commissionership and announced that he would be running for Parliament as the Liberal candidate. Tyrrell immediately joined in an active campaign to run Dr. Alfred Thompson not as a Conservative opponent, but as an independent whom both Conservatives and disgruntled Liberals (of whom there were quite a few) could vote.

The election campaign was a dirty one with stolen voters' lists, a complaint by Thompson that his supporters had been denied co-operation by the returning officer and more than one threat that a general uprising and bloodshed were imminent. One common aspect of dirty politics was absent from the Yukon in 1904, however. Tyrrell and Dr. Grant saw to that. Between them they organized a system of scrutineers to sit at the polling stations and make sure the ballot boxes were not stuffed. By Tyrrell's account in the previous election at one poll far back in the forest, the government candidate had taken a majority of 500 by this method. Tyrrell was undoubtedly exaggerating. Ross had only won that election by a majority of 829 in the whole constituency. Nonetheless the practice was common and Tyrrell and Grant between them made sure that it did not result in Congdon's election in 1904. Tyrrell himself went out to one of the polls on the trails. The deputy returning officer was a good friend and a genial companion so, with the help of a box of cigars, the two men spent "a quiet and pleasant day." No ballots were stuffed and Thompson won with a clear majority.

Tyrrell's revenge on Congdon was not over yet, however. Soon after the election Congdon was heard around Dawson boasting that he had nothing to worry about; the government would soon reappoint him as Commissioner of the Territory. Even before the official returns were in, Tyrrell wrote to Clifford Sifton to head off Congdon's reappointment by drawing the Minister's attention "to a few facts in connection with the late regime." According to Tyrrell, Ross had been a popular Commissioner and Congdon had inherited that popularity. He had, however, quickly lost all the goodwill by a series of bad policy decisions while at the same time maintaining a poor administrative structure. A bloated government payroll was balanced against neglected work on the roads and trails. Then Beddoe, a man who was "heartily despised and hated throughout the length and breadth of the territory" was added to the payroll. "Since that time the belief has been general throughout the Klondike that the country has been ruled by Beddoe and a number of other unprincipled and irresponsible men who have had the direction of all Mr. Congdon's acts."

From this personal attack on Beddoe, Tyrrell went on to describe how Congdon had arbitrarily removed the town charter that Ross had bestowed on Dawson. Tyrrell's complaint was not against the act itself but the way it had been done. In the depressed condition of the area there had been a general feeling that revocation of the charter was necessary. But Congdon had jumped the gun and as a result had earned "the very decided illwill of the ratepayers, when he might just as well have had their goodwill and thanks."

Without going into detail Tyrrell went on to catalogue Congdon's other misdemeanours including his handling of the Dawson Fire Commission, the License Commission, the Police Wood Contract, the Police Hay Contract and, just in case he had missed anything, the "other villainous transactions of the past regime, where the rudimentary principles of justice and fair-play were openly and offensively brushed aside." The recent election had not been a contest between Congdon and Thompson. It had been a contest between Congdon and anyone else. If this man were reappointed, wrote Tyrrell, it would be "utterly disastrous to the peace, welfare and progress of this community which he has been pushing down to ruin."

Congdon had not known the measure of Tyrrell when he made an enemy of him. But Sifton did know the measure of his former employee. He was vain, ambitious and self-righteous. But he was also tough-minded and practical and, above all not given to overstatement and hyperbole. From a thousand others such a ranting letter of denunciation might be written off as hysteria. From Tyrrell a carefully worded appeal to reason might have been analyzed to see what he was really after. But this letter, from this man, could not be ignored. Congdon never did get his old job back.

Tyrrell had asked in his letter that the appointment be given to "some honest and independent man." That's what they got in W. W. B. McInnes. By July the *Dawson Daily News* was carrying a massive front page headline of the "sweeping reforms" he had announced. The opening paragraph read:

Yukon's emancipation proclamation was announced last night. It came from Governor William Wallace Bruce McInnes. Like William the Conqueror and Wallace and Bruce of old – whose significant name he bears – the new commissioner enunciates the principles of glorious conquest for a struggling land.

Not a bad reception for a speech announcing clean politics.

Tyrrell's venture into the political arena was not quite over with his letter to Sifton. There remained one last task. Thompson had been elected as an independent and although the government candidate had been defeated Tyrrell was anxious to ensure that the Conservatives did not claim the victory. Thompson, in fact, was a Conservative and Tyrrell himself, although he never joined any party, was a life-long Conservative supporter. He even managed to join Toronto's Albany Club, without taking out a party membership. Early in 1905, before Thompson himself had headed east, Tyrrell went to Ottawa to arrange for the new members reception.

The Conservatives were already claiming the victory, but an interview with Robert Borden persuaded them to mute their approach. Another interview with the Prime Minister, Sir Wilfrid Laurier, persuaded the government to keep an open mind too. Laurier told Tyrrell he was considering the reappointment of Congdon. Tyrrell reinforced his earlier letter to Sifton. "I told him [the Prime Minister] that no one in the Yukon with any spirit of independence, Liberal or Conservative, would stand for the grafting methods of the late commissioner." It worked. Laurier agreed to await Thompson's arrival. And when the latter did arrive Tyrrell was on hand to guide him through interviews with the Prime Minister and the Leader of the Opposition and ensure that the new member took an "independent stand."

Politics at the turn of the century were not the clear, clean-cut electoral process that they are today. Stuffing ballot boxes, padding voters' lists, tampering with returns were the order of the day. Every general election was followed by a raft of court cases against both parties which in the end were usually withdrawn as part of a saw-off arrangement between political managers. Some years after the Yukon election a disgraced Attorney General of Manitoba told a unique royal commission investigating the corruption of the political process that "a nod is as good as a wink" and until the people demanded clean and honest politics they would continue to get crooked politics. In the Yukon in 1904 the people had demanded clean politics, and they got them. In the 1908 general election Congdon managed to stage a comeback and captured the seat. But in 1911 Thompson recaptured it and held it until 1921. By that time Tyrrell had long since left the Klondike and his brief sojourn into the political arena was but a memory.

Tyrrell's time in the Klondike was nearing an end. After his winter trip to Ottawa to arrange Thompson's reception he returned to Dawson for the rest of 1905. Then, for December 8 he wrote "I packed a valise with my bank books, papers and my suit against Bonanza Creek, the various papers and deposited it at the Bank of Commerce for safekeeping." He had not yet decided whether he would return so he left his cousin, Garrett Tyrrell, in charge of his house and interests and with as much baggage as he was allowed to take with him, paid $75.00 for a ticket and boarded the stage for Whitehorse." His career in the Klondike was over.

Back in Ottawa, almost exactly seven years to the day since he had resigned from the Survey he attended the annual meeting of the American Geological Society. At the meetings on December 29 and 30 he met many of his former colleagues on the Geological Survey. He still worried what they thought of him and his gold mining exploits. He wrote, "some of them doubtless considered that I had stepped downwards on leaving the Geological Survey to make a living by mining, but most of them were friendly." He need not have worried. He had achieved his purpose. It had been seven years since he had last had to live on less than $2,000.00 a year.

CHAPTER 11

Kirkland Lake

"I certainly would not participate in any wild goose chase." Tyrrell's words apply to his decision not to return to the Klondike although they were uttered long afterwards and in a different context. He was referring to a proposed mining venture of A. N. C. Treadgold's and, in his letter to his old friend R. G. McConnell, he went on to hedge that he might very well participate in such a chase provided there was "a good big fee" at the end. To have returned to the Klondike in 1906, however, would have been to set off on a wild goose chase without the promise of any substantial return. The Klondike had been good to him. Through it he had fulfilled the financial ambitions that had taken him out of the Survey. It had also provided him with a thorough, practical education in the business of mining. When he went in, he was a forty year old apprentice miner. When he came out he was a competent journeyman. The Klondike, however, was drying up. There was still gold there but it was thinly scattered, well worked over and difficult to retrieve. From its highest production of over a million ounces in 1900 the gold output of the Yukon had dropped steadily and sharply until by 1906 it was about a quarter of what it had been and still falling.

It was time to move on, to become part of the evacuation that would leave Dawson a virtual ghost town, a decaying remnant of a once glorious hey-day. The question for Tyrrell was where would he go now. There could be no return to his old career. For one thing he was now approaching the half century mark; and although he would continue to lead an active life for another half century, and would make yet another exploratory trip to the north, the rigours and hardships of annual expeditions were no longer appealing. More than that, however, to go back to the Survey (and he claims he was offered a job) would be to admit defeat and that Tyrrell could never do. It would be alien to his nature. The obvious answer to his problem was to continue as a mining consultant, but to remove the focus of his business from the Klondike.

The new boom area was northern Ontario. A couple of years before, in 1903, extensive deposits of silver and cobalt had been uncovered, and soon the names of Cobalt and Porcupine had caught the imagination of the mining community. In reaching his decision to join the new rush, Tyrrell typically decided that the first step was to have a look for himself. The world of mining was a world of speculation and promotion. That was his criticism of Treadgold. "I'm afraid," he wrote to McConnell, "the instinct of the promoter dwarfs everything else in his make up." His experience with Bronson and Ray made him cautious. Never again would he get caught up in a purely speculative adventure. He would work for others for a fee or he would participate in a venture if it were adequately capitalized, but he would neither be the front man for a fly-by-night operation nor be left with a pocketful of worthless paper. The mining industry was full of inherent dangers and elements of chance. But these could be recognized and evaluated and, Tyrrell insisted, they should be separated from the gambling instinct. If people wanted to gamble with mining stocks, that was fine with Tyrrell but it should be seen as being what it was and not confused with mining "any more than playing the shell game should be called 'Taking an interest in raising walnuts!' "

At Cobalt Tyrrell found the boom was real. In an article entitled "Value of a Mine," Tyrrell advised others that the essential element in deciding whether or not to invest in a venture was to weigh a mine's ore reserves against its market value. On a larger scale that was what Tyrrell was doing in Cobalt in 1906. Tyrrell liked what he saw there. He had already made his decision to leave the Klondike. Early in January he sold his interest in the B.C.H.C. and all associated rights to the Reverend A. S. Grant for $37,500.00. Shortly afterwards Treadgold bought his Hunker Creek properties for another $20,000.00. With the same thorough approach that he had used during his work on the Survey and in the Klondike he now set about making himself an expert on the Cobalt area and establishing his reputation for solid advice. This time, however, he would not stay in the area and operate a mine himself. Instead he hung his shingle on Ottawa's Sparks Street.

Before his consulting business was well under way, however, William Mackenzie once more entered his life and he was diverted from his course. This time the railway tycoon's offer of employment came to pass. In early May 1906 after spending a week cooling his heels in Mackenzie's waiting room until the great man was ready to do business, Tyrrell was employed as Mackenzie's mining adviser. The experience of waiting in an outer office day after day should have forewarned Tyrrell of the difficulties he would have as Mackenzie's employee. Mining was at best a side show for Mackenzie. His interest was in railways and it spilled over into Tyrrell's area only where the latter fitted with the exigencies of the iron track. There were the land grants to develop, exploit or divest. There was the need for bulk traffic for the line and ores were ideal for that purpose. There was the wisdom of diversifying to keep investors happy. But the key factor was always the railroad. Nevertheless $3,600.00 a year plus expenses was too good an offer to pass up. Tyrrell accepted the slight of sitting around in the waiting room and agreed to work for Mackenzie for one year.

His first assignment might also have warned him of the difficulties that lay ahead. "I have no instructions to give you in reference to mining matters," wrote Mackenzie "but I think it would be well for you to look around the Northern district." The warning lights did not flash, perhaps because looking around the north was precisely what Tyrrell would have been doing anyway. There was also the fact that Mackenzie's low priority on mining left Tyrrell with the illusion of freedom. His instructions were "use your own judgment entirely and look about and do what you think will be most likely to lead to good results." It was only later, after he had signed on for a second year, that Tyrrell realized that freedom without the support of his principal was an illusion leading nowhere.

During the summer, however, Mackenzie gave Tyrrell one specific job that did help ease his transition from the Klondike to Ontario. He sent him back to the Yukon. Mackenzie had taken out options on three mining companies that could cost him close to a million dollars for a 50 per cent interest in each. On two of the options he was committed to lay out $180,000.00 over the course of a year in addition to money he had already put up. The third option was costing him $20,000.00 a month to a maximum of $500,000.00. There were, however, escape clauses in each of the arrangements which allowed Mackenzie to terminate the options and possibly recapture some of his money from future operations. Tyrrell's job was to go up to the Yukon and investigate the properties to see whether Mackenzie should proceed or pull out.

The operations in the Yukon, Tyrrell was told, were under the control of three men. J. H. Conrad, the principal owner of the companies; J. P. Rogers, Mackenzie's local manager; and H. M. Lay, an accountant whose greater claim to fame was that he had married Mackenzie King's sister. This would be Tyrrell's introduction to the world of big money mining. His own operations in the Klondike had been small stuff. He failed to persuade Bronson and Ray to put up $5,000.00 a year, but now he was dealing with Mackenzie who was pouring $35,000.00 a month into the operation of these properties. With a mere fraction of that Tyrrell could have turned the Bonanza Creek concession into a paying proposition.

Even with big money, however, the Conrad operations were chaotic. One property was being mined at a cost of around $57.00 a ton while its product was paying back $30.00 a ton. When Tyrrell arrived on the scene he found the mining superintendent had not been around for a week, the manager had quit and Conrad was living elsewhere. Tyrrell's immediate advice to Mackenzie was "wait." Until the situation was sorted out it would be foolish to pour in any more funds. In the meantime he suggested that a "competent reliable" man be put in charge immediately.

The local management, with good cause, were suspicious of Tyrrell. He obviously was not there to serve their interests and they were desperately anxious to find out what was in the reports he was sending back to Mackenzie. All Tyrrell's messages, however, were going out in code. The technique was simple. Various code books were available and by deciding in advance which one would be used the telegraph system could be used with relative impunity. Code-breaking on a heavy volume of telegram traffic using this method is relatively simple, especially with modern techniques of cryptography. But at the turn of the century with a light volume of traffic such messages were secure unless someone happened to have access to the same code book. Mackenzie and Tyrrell guarded against this latter possibility by choosing an uncommon book that had little circulation in North America and was unlikely to be available anywhere in the Klondike.

Tyrrell suspected that Conrad, the mine owner, would manage to obtain copies of his telegrams by bribing the local telegraph clerk. When Conrad tried to borrow Tyrrell's code book on the pretext that he had left his own in Skagway, these suspicions were confirmed. Tyrrell, however, knew that Conrad had never been

218

given a copy of the code he was using. Tyrrell's refusal to lend Conrad his book confirmed the other man's worst fears and ended his co-operation. He became, Tyrrell said, "very obstructive and ugly" and from then on Tyrrell had to conduct his operations from a hotel room, renting a typewriter on which to type his report himself to ensure that Conrad could not get a copy of it.

With that one operation Tyrrell more than earned his salary for the whole year and a half that he stayed with Mackenzie. Based in large measure on Tyrrell's conclusions that there was no proven large body of payable ore and that the money was being spent "ignorantly and extravagantly," Mackenzie decided to pull out of the venture and to recoup what he could of his investment. Had the mine been close to his railway operations Mackenzie might have balanced his mining losses against the increased railway traffic as he was known to do in other cases. Without that advantage, however, the mines would have to have a good chance of success before he would be interested. Tyrrell established that Conrad's operations were not likely to fit that category and Mackenzie withdrew from the arrangement.

If Mackenzie had been able to supply his mining adviser with a steady flow of work of that calibre, Tyrrell would probably have stayed on the job for a long time. In fact the Conrad episode was the only real challenge in eighteen months of employment. Worse than that, it soon became obvious to Tyrrell that Mackenzie was not always anxious to have his advice. During the summer of 1907 Tyrrell identified a demand for a smelter in Cobalt to which the Ontario government would give its "hearty support and assistance." This was precisely the type of operation that Tyrrell wanted to see in the Canadian mining industry. It would do much to stabilize the business and reduce the wildcat atmosphere that had characterized it. He tried desperately to persuade Mackenzie to take on the project. With steadily increasing ore production in the area and government assistance in financing the smelter was bound to be a profitable undertaking. All his arguments, however, fell on deaf ears. Mackenzie would have nothing to do with the proposal.

At the other end of the scale, Tyrrell was equally anxious to dissuade Mackenzie from gambling in mines rather than investing in them. His last job for Mackenzie fell into that category. The fabulous Joe Boyle, whom Tyrrell had known in the Yukon, had also moved his centre of operations to northern Ontario. Boyle would later go on to fame and glory leading his own battalion of Canadian troops on the battlefields of World War I and afterwards as the favourite and probably the lover of Queen Marie of Rumania. In the meantime, though, he had a claim near Timagami which was showing a rich percentage of gold among the gravel and he offered it to Mackenzie for $30,000.00 cash. The gold was there all right but as far as Tyrrell could tell it was not very expensive. The gravel might even have been salted. Mine owners were known to add the gold dust to the gravel to lure an unwary buyer. To protect Mackenzie, Tyrrell suggested that Boyle give an option on the property so that it could be explored. When Boyle refused, Tyrrell recommended to Mackenzie that he forget about the deal. Mackenzie, however, had already made up his mind and told Tyrrell that he wanted to buy that claim. Tyrrell was furious. "In that case you shouldn't have sent me, you should have sent a clerk to buy it for you."

That was the end of the road for Tyrrell. He had already complained to Mackenzie's comptroller that he did not have enough to do and they had agreed to come up with a different arrangement – probably one that would have given Tyrrell a retainer in return for being available when needed. Instead Tyrrell decided to call it a day. Within a week he was back in Mackenzie's office handing in his resignation. By Tyrrell's account, Mackenzie was surprised, asking him if he had not been receiving his cheques regularly or if he wanted more money. But Tyrrell had made up his mind. Once again he was in the consulting business.

The haste with which he quit his job with Mackenzie meant he was back scrounging for work. He decided to stay in Toronto where he had moved when he took on the job with Mackenzie. Toronto was beginning to replace Montreal as the financial centre of the country and in large measure it was the willingness of that city's investors to put their money into the mining industry that was causing the transfer of fiscal power. In 1907, however, even in Toronto, risk capital was in short supply. The economy in general was in recession and as a result there was a slowdown in mining transactions. Work was therefore slow in coming to the new consultant. A year after he had hung out his shingle on Bay Street he was still having to send a circular letter offering his services in "the more remote parts of the country, or for that matter in any remote districts other than in tropical climates." The letters went on to promise that reports would be delivered "in the quickest possible time consistent with acuracy" – he misspelled "accuracy."

It was only a matter of time, however, until Tyrrell was well established in the Toronto mining community. His great exploits as an explorer were still remembered. His Klondike interlude was valuable both for the experience he was able to draw upon and for the contacts it provided. The sourdoughs of the Klondike formed an informal brotherhood. To have been there was to have an immediate entrée with thousands of others who had been there too. His new area of specialization, northern Ontario was a vast store-house of mineral wealth that was just beginning to yield its treasure. To these advantages Tyrrell brought his characteristic thoroughness. He made it his business to learn everything he could about the area. Within a few years his services were in such demand that clients not only paid him $100.00 a day plus expenses but agreed in advance to accept the advice he offered. Without such agreement Tyrrell refused to accept an assignment.

All Tyrrell needed now was a standing contract with a large company which would pay a handsome fee and, at the same time, leave him free to pursue his other interests. Such a contract came in 1910. Anglo-French Exploration Company, a major British mining endeavour, had until then not been active in Canada confining itself to its rich holdings in South Africa. Now, however, the company was interested in participating in the Canadian scene which was growing in activity and production. To that end Anglo-French Explorations wanted a "resident agent" in Canada and Tyrrell was a natural candidate for the job. Not only did he have the background, experience and standing in the Canadian mining community that the job would require, but he also had an international reputation as a scientist of note and a wide range of contacts in London who would vouch for him. Perhaps even more important in the eyes of a major mining corporation was his conservative approach in a field where flamboyance was the order of the day. Anglo-French had no need for ostentatious impresarios. They were knocking at the door daily. A solid expert, with an entrepreneurial bent, whose judgment could be relied upon was what they were after and Tyrrell was their man.

They offered him a retainer of $2,000.00 a year plus expenses when working for them and Tyrrell jumped at the chance. Had he been an employee he would probably have undergone the same disillusion with Anglo-French as he did with William Mackenzie. As a consultant, the relationship was made-to-measure. The fee, after the first probationary year, provided a secure base for his other activities.

The relationship between Tyrrell and the company had another side benefit. It brought with it an opportunity for frequent travel to Britain. Indeed, it began with a telegram summoning Tyrrell to London. Tyrrell at first objected to the peremptory summons but, with Doll's help, he quickly swallowed his pride and booked his passage aboard the *Royal Edward* from Montreal. Tyrrell had been in Britain before when he and Doll had travelled there in the winter of 1899-1900. That experience had been relished by both of them. For Doll it had been an occasion to return to the scene of an important part of her childhood. For J. B. it had been an opportunity to visit his ancestral home in Ireland and to make contact with the leading lights of his profession at the heart of the Empire. Ever since then, he had carefully nurtured those contacts by correspondence and by his participation in professional organizations whenever and wherever practical. Just the year before he had been elected to the Council of the British Institution of Mining and Metallurgy. In 1897 he had presented his notable paper on glaciation to the British Association for the Advancement of Science, and when the Association returned to Canada in 1909 he took on the responsibility for a major part of the Canadian planning that preceded the Winnipeg session. By adding these activities on top of his membership in and work for similar Canadian and American organizations, Tyrrell had developed a line of communications with the British scientific and mining communities. His arrangement with Anglo-French Explorations, gave him an opportunity to strengthen and deepen those ties.

In the years that followed he was a frequent visitor to London and the experience left its mark on him. A conservative in thought he was also a Conservative in politics, and, in the early decades of the twentieth century, to be a Conservative was to be committed to the idea of the Empire. There was before the world a glorious concept known as the Imperial Idea – a concept which sought to reconcile the growing national stature and aspiration of the Dominions with the continued existence of an Empire on which the sun would never set. That dream in the end failed to materialize and, in the inter-war years was replaced by the British Commonwealth, a holding operation that allowed the growth of Dominion autonomy while keeping the strategic and defence capacity of the old Empire in place for one more world war. In the post World War II period the old British Commonwealth was replaced by the new Commonwealth, which allowed the former countries of the British Empire to continue their co-operation in areas of mutual concern while recognizing that world power has changed hands and new strategic alignments replaced the old.

These developments were all in the future, however. For Tyrrell, as for many others in those early decades of the century, there was nothing incompatible between Canadian national growth and the welfare of the Empire. Indeed the two were ineffably linked. Through the intelligent development of its mineral resources and wealth, Canada faced a great future as a nation. As it did the Empire too could face the future with equanimity, no matter what difficulties arose. The arrangement with Anglo-French provided him with an opportunity to put his beliefs into practice.

The onslaught of war saw Tyrrell writing to the board of Anglo-French offering to release them from their arrangement with him because British currency controls would prevent the company from investing any new funds in Canada. His offer was rejected. Anglo-French had already made a considerable investment in Canada and wanted to retain Tyrrell's services to look after its interests. As a result, throughout the war he continued to travel across the Atlantic each year. The close contact reinforced his love and admiration for Britain and things British. Paradoxically it also brought out in him, as it did in many Canadians who had close contact with the heart of Empire, an abhorrence of the English attitude of superiority. "Canadian," he wrote, "is a new kind of monkey or Indian who is the best fighter in the world who of course is not fit to associate with *English gentlemen.*"

From the point of view of Anglo-French the arrangement with Tyrrell also paid off. In the first year of his relationship he identified Noah Timmins's Hollinger mines as a good investment and arranged for the company to take 20,000 shares in the company as its first major investment in Canada. Tyrrell also arranged with Timmins to give Anglo-French an option on 50,000 more shares. Despite Tyrrell's urging the company declined to exercise its option and in so doing underscored the value of the "resident agent" they had acquired. The next year, in London for a meeting of the Anglo-French board, Tyrrell was told that they now recognized that they should have followed his advice, indeed that it was a "tragedy" that they had not done so. The value of shares of Hollinger had since soared.

The voyage from Montreal to Bristol in 1910 was a momentous

one for Tyrrell. Not only was he sailing into a secure basic income and a relationship that would in the end be intricately bound up with his fortune but he was also in the course of the voyage to make a new contact – one which would provide him with a longed-for opportunity to return to exploration for a summer. Among the passengers on the *Royal Edward* was Sir James Whitney, the Premier of Ontario. Never one to miss an opportunity for a little lobbying, Tyrrell belaboured Whitney with the need for a branch line of the Toronto and Northern Ontario Railway into Porcupine to further open the north's mineral resources. For the most part, however, Tyrrell was willing to talk about the far north and the region of Hudson Bay while Whitney was a willing listener. The provinces of Quebec, Ontario and Manitoba were pressuring Ottawa for the extension of their borders to the north. The existing boundary of Ontario zigzagged from the mouth of the Albany River on James Bay across the north land to the Manitoba border above Lake of the Woods. Ontario contended that in moving into the north Manitoba's eastern border should simply be extended on its existing line slightly to the west of 95 degrees and Ontario should receive everything to the east of that line. Manitoba objected strenuously. It wanted access to Hudson Bay and salt water. If the postage stamp eastern border were extended northward it would miss the coast of Hudson Bay by a few miles and the province would be forever landlocked. In 1912 the border was set in Manitoba's favour. From its northeastern corner the new boundary extended not in a straight line to the north but at a forty-five degree angle to the northeast and the shore of the Bay. As a consolation prize Ontario was awarded the right to a ten mile strip of land on the south bank near the mouth of the Nelson River on which to build a seaport and to maintain a five mile access corridor to the proposed community.

It was here that Tyrrell's association with Whitney entered the picture. Ontario was anxious to lose no time in exercising its right to choose the site for this development. Premier Whitney, in search of a reputable figure to lead the expedition that would define the corridor and lay out the townsite, recalled his trans-Atlantic meeting with Tyrrell and invited him to lead the expedition through the District of Patricia. It was an opportunity Tyrrell could not resist. For all his activity and success as a mining consultant and the opportunities that his work brought to spend lots of time out of doors, he recalled with fond memories his great explorations of the past and longed once more for such an experience. Another twenty years down the road, reminiscing of their Barren Lands trip in a letter to his brother James, J. B. would recall those days as among his "happiest memories" and expressed the wish that he could return again "to the north where nature had provided a wonderful garden." Midway between his Barren Lands trip and that nostalgic letter, an opportunity had come.

The first part of the trip was the reverse of the one he had made at the end of 1893. Starting out from Winnipeg they travelled up the lake to Norway House and from there via the Hayes River to York Factory. Along the way Tyrrell was able to return to his old habits of collecting rock, and fossil and plant specimens without the inducement of a profit motive, but for the sheer joy of expanding knowledge. At one point he was to be found chopping down a stunted eight foot spruce tree to determine its age – it was 130 years old. Once on the banks of the Nelson they surveyed and laid out the plan for the new townsite of Port Nelson.

Apart from the fact that the expedition was completed safely, it was not much of a success in what was hoped for it. From his knowledge of the area Tyrrell was doubtful before he ever set out that the mouth of the Nelson could be turned into an effective seaport. His return visit to the district confirmed him in this belief and when he wrote up his report he emphasized the drawbacks of packed ice in the vicinity and the lack of deep water harbour facilities. He had also learned from first-hand experience that the smooth slippery clay of the seabed offered no grip for an anchor and the turning tides set up vicious currents that ripped boats from their anchorage and capsized small ones with no difficulty at all. When, despite these warnings, the decision was later made to proceed with the construction of the seaport Tyrrell was careful to make it known that he held little hope for the success of the venture. Events proved him right.

Nor was the expedition much of a success in identifying the five mile corridor. The work of surveying at the mouth of the Nelson and establishing the site for a bridge over the Hayes River occupied their time until late in August. In the course of their stay, however, Tyrrell did find time to delve into the history of the area. The remains of some of the old forts around York were examined with Tyrrell discovering for himself the site of Benjamin Gillam's fort built in 1683 and burned down by Radisson three years later. A 300 year old cannon ball left behind by Thomas Button who had first discovered and named the Nelson in 1612 – not after the famous admiral but after Button's old sailing master Francis Nelson who died there – was also uncovered, and the tombstones of the old graveyard were examined. As a memento of more recent history he visited Flamborough Head on the Nelson, the site of the first trading post in the area and, more recently, the scene of his desperate bid to cross the Nelson in 1893.

By the time he was finished at York Factory it was too late to set out across the new regions of Manitoba to identify the proposed corridor. Instead he contented himself with a canoe trip through the district of Patricia. From York Factory a Hudson's Bay Company boat took them to Fort Severn. From there they set out by canoe up the Severn and Fawn Rivers, through a maze of waterways similar to that to the north of Lake Athabasca, over the watershed of the Hudson Bay and the St. Lawrence drainage systems to Cat Lake and via Cat River to Sioux Lookout. The journey over the height of land from the Fawn River to Sioux Lookout contained close to 100 portages, some of them more than a thousand yards long. From Sioux Lookout, late in October, the way was easier. They took the train back to Toronto.

The result of Tyrrell's expedition was negative. To all intents and purposes it put an end to the ill-conceived seaport and land corridor idea. There were, however, some positive by-products from the mission. Tyrrell's report, like all the reports of his expeditions in years gone by, carefully went into the details of the geology and mineral prospects of the region he had explored. Another corner of the map was filled in. The major success of the trip, however, was that once again he uncovered new evidence of the ice age and its glaciers. Here in the district of Patricia, Tyrrell found, as he had done in the Barren Lands, that the *striae* of the ice age ran in every direction. Once more he was in the heartland of a great gathering ground of the glaciers. This one he concluded was the site of the last of the glaciers to form and advance southward over the land. Ontario may not have got the seaport it hoped for but once more the frontiers of prehistoric knowledge had been expanded.

Inevitably, however, the return to the shores of Hudson Bay was little more than an interlude in the life of J. B. Tyrrell. At fifty-three years of age he had been given a chance to return to the scene of former glories. He had welcomed the opportunity. It allowed him to recapture his lost youth. Ever since he had left the Survey part of him had longed for those times when he had led parties of men into the wilderness. The summer of 1912 had fulfilled that need.

In a larger sense, this whole period of his life was an interlude. Standing on Dick Low's fraction in 1898 he had been bitten

Tyrrell (centre) descending the Cat River in 1912. In his early fifties he adopted a more leisurely style of exploration. (TFRBL)

by the gold bug. He never recovered. During his years as a Toronto-based mining consultant he investigated and reported on other minerals for clients. Only one mineral, however, could arouse his interest – gold. Wherever that yellow ore was discovered in northern Ontario, Tyrrell was sure to be found. In the end his fascination led to his greatest coup in the world of mining and made him a millionaire. The undertaking revealed every aspect of his intense personality – his self-assurance, his strength of character, his dogged determination.

Gold had first been found in the Kirkland Lake area in 1911 but Tyrrell, always cautious of the wildcat, had carefully kept his various clients from becoming part of the new field and was proud of having succeeded. He was wrong. The Kirkland Lake camp would yield over a billion dollars in gold before it dried up. Yet at the time he was right. Prior to World War I, Kirkland Lake was a typical speculators' binge. Its stocks had soared but, by the time war broke out, most of them could not be sold for a nickel each. Fortunes were lost as a result but Tyrrell's clients were safe. Cautious as he might be, however, Joe Tyrrell was always open to conversion: and nothing could convert more quickly or more completely than production records. He had called Kirkland Lake a "fiasco," but by 1920 he had changed his mind sufficiently to accept a position on the Board of Directors of Harry Oakes's Lake Shore Mine. The flamboyant Oakes had been trying to entice Tyrrell into an involvement in Kirkland Lake since they first met in 1913 while Oakes was working his Lake Shore property by hand, but aside from a willingness to be engaged as a consultant in the area, Tyrrell had steered clear of all offers.

Oakes was the proverbial legend in his own time. He, like Tyrrell, had gone to the Klondike in 1898. Although they had never met there, that was enough to give them a common bond when Tyrrell walked onto the Lake Shore property. Tyrrell, as always, was gathering all the information he could about the workings in the area. Oakes was trying to prove a pet theory – that gold is often found under the bed of lakes. His plan was to sink a shaft by the side of the lake and then run a cross-cut underneath it.

As a general theory Oakes's hypothesis was nonsense. It must have made Tyrrell, the geologist, smile. In the specific case of Lake Shore, however, Oakes was absolutely right. There was gold under the lake and the mine produced a quarter of a billion dollars of bullion before it closed in 1968.

At their first meeting the two gold addicts struck it off. Oakes invited Tyrrell to share his dinner with him and the two of them swapped stories by the campfire late into the night. At first their conversation was of the Klondike and its sourdoughs. As the evening wore on the rest of Oakes's story unfolded. Eighteen ninety-eight had been his first gold rush. He had been too late, however. All the young New Englander ever got out of the Klondike was experience and a lasting case of gold fever. The Klondike reinforced in Oakes an already overwhelming obsession to make a fortune. He quit medical school in Syracuse to go to the Yukon, stopping off at Skagway to work as an "orderly" in the local "hospital" – a shack where venereal disease and alcohol poisoning vied with tuberculosis and pneumonia as the most common diseases treated by doctors with questionable credentials or a price on their heads.

For the next fourteen years he wandered around the world from one gold-field to another in search of his personal El Dorado. From Dawson he went west to Alaska before setting sail for the Philippines and the deserts of Australia. In a universe of extremes man can survive only within a narrow range of temperatures. He is on a razor's edge of tolerance between the almost infinite extremes of the sun's immeasurable heat and the inconceivable coldness of interstellar space. If the Arctic had introduced Oakes to the lower limits of man's razor's edge, the Australian deserts gave him a sample of the upper limits where day after day temperatures hovered midway to the boiling point.

For Harry Oakes the Australian desert was as barren of gold as it was of vegetation. New Zealand, with its more temperate climate, was little more than a stopping place before he tackled the equally arid Death Valley of California and the equatorial forests of the Belgian Congo. The search was in vain and he found his way back to Alaska. For four years he panhandled the northern gravels before setting out for Toronto to explore the new mining fields of Ontario.

The prospector was by now little more than a shell of a man filled, not with humanity, but only with an overwhelming compulsion to strike it rich. His eyes reflected the madness that drove his soul. His arrival in northern Ontario is shrouded in mythology. The most common accounts have him kicked off the Toronto train at Swastika either dead drunk or penniless and unable to pay his fare to continue the journey. Whatever the conductor's motive, his intervention marked the turning point in Oakes's life. A few miles west of Swastika was Kirkland Lake on whose shores Harry Oakes at last fulfilled his ambition and in doing so ended his mania.

When Joe Tyrrell met him he still had not made his fortune, but he knew it was within his grasp. Most of the potentially valuable staking had been done when Oakes arrived. He took to waiting in the wings until a claim was open for restaking and then making sure he, or someone on his behalf, was the first on the scene. By this process of land assembly – or more properly, land grabbing – he gained control of a major part of the gold-field and brought into production one of the world's greatest gold mines, Lake Shore. The company's stock which at times Oakes could not give away, reached a high of $64.00 on the open market. Not only that but Oakes attained that rare achievement of retaining control of the gold mine he had discovered until it went into production and started paying dividends.

Oakes's story absorbed Tyrrell's attention on that first night. From that encounter grew an association and friendship that lasted until Oakes was murdered in the Bahamas in 1943 – a death as engrossing and depraved as ever his earlier search for gold had been. The discovery of his battered and burned body, probably the handiwork of Mafia interests whose gambling ambitions for Nassau Oakes had thwarted, touched off a scandal that reached into the inner sanctuaries of the royal family because of the former King Edward VIII's involvement as governor of the colony. The investigation of the crime by corrupt American police called to the island, the accusation and trial of an innocent man, the public fascination at the death of a legendary multi-millionaire who had paid a half million dollars to become "Sir Harry," all added a touch of inanity to the mystery of his death.

If the end of his relationship with Oakes was abrupt, the beginning was cautious. Tyrrell liked his new companion but was still dubious about the value of gold in Kirkland Lake and was warning clients to stay clear. Oakes, recognizing the value of Tyrrell's expertise and reputation, tried to persuade him to join in his venture but Tyrrell declined. They kept in touch, however, and when Lake Shore was showing a return Oakes offered Tyrrell the use of the mine's directors quarters as a place to stay whenever he was in Kirkland Lake. A couple of years later when Tyrrell accepted a directorship on the Lake Shore board, his conversion to the value of the gold-field was complete.

Being a director of the mine also marked the beginning of Tyrrell's personal involvement in the gold-field. Soon that involvement would expand to the point where it consumed every ounce of his energy.

It began on February 10, 1924. On the train back to Toronto from a consulting job in Kirkland Lake, he sat beside William Sixt, superintendent of Kirkland Lake Gold Mine. Of all the lucky breaks in Tyrrell's career this chance meeting with William Sixt was without equal. Tyrrell had turned sixty-five on his last birthday and was beginning to think of retirement. He was a moderately wealthy man. Ever since he had been retained by Anglo-French he had earned over $15,000.00 a year. By prudent management and careful investment he had assured himself that he could look forward to a comfortable retirement. In preparation for that day, he had also purchased a farm north of Toronto on the Rouge River near the present site of the new Toronto Zoo. There, he was building up a sizable orchard. Total retirement was inconceivable to him but he could foresee the day when he could derive enough contact with nature from experimenting with new brands of apples, hatching pheasant eggs and raising turkeys.

Before that day came, however, he had one more challenge in store. Simply put, he had to take his first-hand expertise in ores and minerals and his wide second-hand knowledge of mine operations and apply them to a working situation by taking a faltering mine and turning it into an important producer. It would be the culmination of his life's work. Everything he had ever done had prepared him for the task.

Tyrrell knew the history of the tiny Kirkland Lake Gold Mine with its single claim. The property had been one of the first staked in 1911 before Harry Oakes had ever got on the fateful train whose conductor evicted him at Swastika. Six years later its worth had still not been proven and it was taken over by Beaver Consolidated Mining Company. The year before Tyrrell joined Oakes on the board of Lake Shore, however, Kirkland Lake was brought into production. On May 17, 1919, the first gold bar had been shipped from the mine. Tyrrell knew the value of that gold bar to the last cent and how much ore had been processed to acquire it. He also knew that soon afterwards the mine had started showing a return on its investment. By 1923 it was producing more than a quarter million dollars worth of ore a year. The ore body, however, was rapidly being depleted and, although the main shaft had been sunk to almost 1,000 feet, no new vein had been reached.

Tyrrell's cue came when Bill Sixt told him that the owners of the mine did not have enough money to dig any deeper and were in the market to sell it. Tyrrell immediately went back to

Kirkland Lake to examine the property. From what he saw there and from what he already knew of the area, he became convinced that gold would be found at the 1,800 foot level.

He moved fast. Within six weeks of his meeting with Sixt he had negotiated a deal with Beaver whereby Anglo-French, in association with Osler and Company of Toronto, and Tyrrell himself would buy into the company and in the process provide $700,000.00 of new capital. For Anglo-French the venture was a departure from their usual form. In all the years Tyrrell had been their "resident agent" their only major investment in Canada had been the early purchase of shares in Hollinger. When Tyrrell finally severed the relationship with Anglo-French, he wrote somewhat bitterly to G. R. Airth, the managing director, that during the first twelve years of their relationship, although he had offered them many good opportunities for investment in Canadian mines, "most and the best" of his suggestions had been ignored. In 1924, however, they joined Tyrrell's Kirkland Lake enterprise.

It was also a departure in form for Tyrrell himself. Instead of simply advising others where to put their money he was heavily investing his own money. It was not a gamble or a speculation. It was, however, decidedly a risk. The richest gold deposits of the area were found at deeper levels as they moved west from Lake Shore Mine. Next door to the Kirkland Lake Mine was the rich Tech-Hughes operation. Tyrrell conjectured that if the Kirkland Lake shaft was sunk deeper than the Tech-Hughes shaft, it should reach the rich ore. There were several hazards, however. First, he knew, the ore body not only drifted to the west but also to the south and there was a danger that it turned off before reaching the Kirkland Lake property. To hedge against this possibility he arranged with his southern neighbour, Chaput-Hughes, to explore into their property from underground at a depth which they could not reach with their own resources in return for a share of anything found. The second danger was that the gold would simply run out before it reached his mine or, alternatively would have turned so deeply into the ground that they could not reach it. The third danger was that having put up his own money, his partners would in some way renege on their commitment. Harking back to his experience with Bronson and Ray in the Klondike, Tyrrell was determined that he would not be thwarted in the same way again.

The arrangement he worked out with Beaver Consolidated was carefully designed to override this last prospect. The number of shares of Beaver Consolidated was increased by two million common and one million preferred. The old owners would keep their existing one and a half million shares while the new owners would buy some of the new ones for $470,000.00 and have options on the remainder which, if exercised would yield another $250,000.00. Thus Tyrrell was assured that at the least there would be close to half a million dollars on hand to do the job with the prospect of half as much again to complete it. He was not about to be thwarted by the money men again.

At the same time he also ensured that he would not be thwarted by any deviation from his proposed plan of action. The existing mine, although showing less and less return, was still a producing mine. His plan was to shut down production completely and concentrate on digging. He surmised, correctly, that as they bored their way through hundreds of feet of worthless earth, there would be a mounting pressure to start up production again to produce some return on investment. The one way to ensure that the work he planned was carried out was to have complete control of the operation himself. He already had power of attorney to act for Anglo-French in Canada. Now he secured his own appointment for a three year term as managing director of Beaver Consolidated and general manager of the Kirkland Lake Mine. For the next two years, although he continued to make his home in Toronto, he was more often to be found in Kirkland Lake checking every stage of the work and examining each piece of geological information he could find.

By June 10 everything was in readiness. All other mining activities were suspended and work was begun on sinking the shaft deeper into the bowels of the earth. By the end of the year they had reached 1,500 feet. By June 23, 1925, they were at 2,000 feet and a banquet at which silver medals were presented to the miners was held to celebrate the occasion.

Now they were ready to bore into the sides of the pit in search of ore. The whole depth had been dug without a single accident to the men. It had not been dug without a major battle between Tyrrell and his co-sponsors. As the work of sending tunnels off to the east in the direction of the rich Tech-Hughes property proceeded, the boardroom battles between the investors intensified.

In the spring of 1925 Anglo-French, unused to Canadian investment and anxious to protect its capital in the face of Tyrrell's obstinate conviction that his unorthodox theories would be proven true, began to doubt the wisdom of its course. The very difficulties that Tyrrell had feared had come to pass. It was here his foresight paid off. The agreement which set up the arrangement was watertight. He was in firm control of the Kirkland Lake operations. The money required to see the project through had also been paid into Beaver Consolidated in advance. So long as the funds lasted and he retained control he could not be diverted from his course; demands that he should resume production of the already established low grade and dwindling ore body could be ignored. All Anglo-French could do was open up another office in Canada and hire another agent to keep an eye on Tyrrell and, it was hoped, exercise some control over him. This they did under J. A. P. Gibb in the spring of 1925. Tyrrell, however, was not easily muzzled. His agreement with Anglo-French had for years past provided him with full power of attorney for the company in Canada. Whenever Gibb tried to speak for the company, Tyrrell pointed out that he, not Gibb, had in his possession a duly notorized piece of paper clearly authorizing him to speak for the company in Canada, which included being the company's voice on the board of Beaver Consolidated.

On October 19, 1925 they hit the main vein and it was rich. Indeed the spot where they first struck gold was fantastically rich, yielding over $130 a ton. That, however, was just a lucky break. As they explored further the ore was found to average about a quarter of that. Even so it was a valuable property that would yield a handsome return on everyone's investment. The find should have ended the fight. Instead it intensified.

It would take about a year from the first find before the mine was in production and earning money for its owners. Anglo-French, however, were too impatient to wait. As soon as news of the find reached the street a wave of speculation hit the market and the directors of Anglo-French, who had refused to exercise their options to buy more stock, began selling what they had at a substantial profit. For his own part, instead of selling his stock, Tyrrell exercised his options and increased his holdings in the company.

The find had vindicated Tyrrell's theory and he was putting his money behind the mine's continued success. But it did not end his trouble with the company. In the last weeks of 1925 the battle was carried across the ocean. Gibb had gone off to London for the first round on October 4. By comparison with Tyrrell, Gibb was a midget in the mining business. Even his timing was second-rate. While he was in London the ore was discovered at the mine. Tyrrell did not go over until early December, by which time the value of the find had been established and Gibb had returned to Canada. In the meantime Tyrrell had been doing his homework. A visit to Cochrane where Gibb had spent $10,000.00 of Anglo's money on a few buildings and some land clearing but had not turned up anything of value, gave Tyrrell ammunition for the fight. Even before he went over, however, he had joined battle. Letters to a number of Anglo's principal shareholders had spelled out the issue. Tyrrell had found a new mine for the company and it was only a matter of time until the returns started coming in. He did not go on, however, to urge patience. Instead he laid it on the line that, if the company's directors were not willing to see the deal through, it was time a new board of directors was elected who would do so.

In this fight, as in everything else he did, Tyrrell was tough – much tougher than the board of Anglo-French had expected. Instead of fighting them on their ground, the lone Canadian agent against the home office management, he had switched the ground on them. If they did not support him and see the enterprise through, then there were others who would. His notes for December, 1925, in London describe one "stormy meeting" after another. The fight centred on whether Anglo-French would have one or two agents in Canada. Had Tyrrell argued that either he or Gibb had to go, he would have been on weak ground. Instead he argued it was Gibb or the board. Whether Tyrrell could have pulled off the ouster remains unanswered. He never had to prove his threat. Probably he would have failed. The lone Canadian in London would have found himself up against the whole network of corporate and social inter-relationships. "Canadians are out of fashion here," he told Doll. He was not, however, without connections. He had been attending Anglo's affairs for fifteen years and had close contacts with some of the company's major shareholders. He even had one or two allies within the board. These were reinforced by his friends in the mining and scientific communities. He had carefully prepared these contacts for the present struggle. During the summer of 1924, just as Tyrrell began his digging at Kirkland Lake the British Association for the Advancement of Science had once again held its meeting in Canada. Tyrrell had made sure that a side trip to his new mine had been included in the itinerary of their usual excursion.

For every meeting with the directors in December 1925, he had a series of others with one or more of the principal stockholders. His network was more limited than that of his opponents, but it was not without strength. In the end a compromise was hammered out. Between Christmas and New Year's Eve, first at an informal luncheon and then at a formal board meeting, the details were settled. Tyrrell would return to Canada confirmed for another year as the sole representative of the company, and continue to carry full power of attorney. In the course of that year Kirkland Lake Gold Mines would probably be brought into production. At the end of the year Tyrrell would likely retire to be replaced by a new agent whom he would train.

On January 2, 1926 Tyrrell left London to board the *SS Montcalm* at Liverpool. This had been his twentieth visit to London. It was his last. He arrived back in Toronto on January 13 and the next day met with Gibb to inform him that he was fired. A month later Gibb was dead. The battle had taken its toll. Nor did Tyrrell escape unscathed. He himself suffered no illness but Doll, forever hotly engaged in his struggles, did. Within a few days of Gibb's death she had a nervous breakdown. It was months before she had fully recovered.

Despite the casualties, Tyrrell had won his objective. Although the pressure to begin production continued he was now able to carry the development forward and block out the ore vein before having to divert his resources of manpower and equipment. By the end of 1926 the mine was producing ore. Tyrrell was on hand to watch the weighing in of the first two gold bricks from November's production. Together they totalled almost 2,000 ounces for a value of over $42,000.00 Tyrrell was ecstatic. Before the year was over the mill would have extracted over $125,000.00 in bullion from the ore. By then, however, Anglo-French had passed from the scene.

The company had been selling off its shares on the open market and by mid-November had given up the control of Beaver Consolidated that it had acquired under the agreement negotiated by Tyrrell in March, 1924. They had not lost in the deal. Early on Tyrrell had wired his encouragement to the board, "I will make money for you if you will allow me to." Despite the fact that he had only been allowed to do so under duress, he was able to write to the company's managing director at the end of the year, "I have made money for you in the Kirkland Lake Gold Mines." This letter was his last official act in his sixteen year relationship with Anglo-French Explorations. It had been a profitable venture for both, although less profitable for Anglo-French than might have been the case. A year later Tyrrell was quoted in the *Financial Post* as sàying that they could have made a lot more if they had stuck it out. He estimated that the course they had adopted had "allowed $64 million to slip from their hands." He was exaggerating. Even so from its first production in 1919 until its closure in 1960, Kirkland Lake Gold Mines yielded $39,124,929.00 worth of gold from the earth.

Tyrrell's battles over the Kirkland Lake Mine were not limited to his fight with Anglo-French. The 1924 arrangement to buy into the mine had left the former shareholders of Beaver Consolidated with the largest block of shares in the expanded company. It had also left Frank Culver as the president of the company even though management control had been vested in Joe Tyrrell. In many ways Culver and Tyrrell were alike. They were both self-made men who had started out to read for the law. They had both quit to seek outdoor work for the sake of their health. Where Tyrrell had joined the gold rush to the Klondike, Culver had been in the 1905 stampede to Cobalt. By the mid-1920s they could both be described as "mine-owners and gentlemen farmers." In some ways they were too much alike. Conflict between them was inevitable. Although at first the injection of new capital which Tyrrell brought with him was sufficient to assuage Culver's chagrin as he watched control of his mine being taken away from him, with the passing of time Culver began planning his own return to power.

Once again the battle line was drawn on the issue of putting the mine into full production before Tyrrell was ready. While willing to start production late in 1926, Tyrrell wanted it done in a limited way. At the same time he was continuing with exploration and development. He pushed the shaft still deeper into the earth's crust.

Acting as the leader of the other disgruntled shareholders, Culver demanded that Tyrrell abandon his digging and concentrate on production. Tyrrell refused and, typically, concluded that Culver was "very jealous" of his success. Whatever his motivation, Culver was powerless until March, 1927. Until then Tyrrell was secure as managing director of the company and general manager of the mine. The three year agreement he had negotiated was ironclad. During the summer of 1926, however, word got to Tyrrell that Culver intended to "get rid" of him when the agreement expired.

The arrangement of March 1924 had left the old Beaver owners, with Culver as their leader, as the largest group of shareholders in the company, and Tyrrell knew that, undefended, he was vulnerable. Culver, however, only controlled one and a half million shares, less than 50 per cent of the total. Had he followed closely Tyrrell's fight with Anglo-French in far-off London Culver may have reconsidered the decision to take him on in his native environment. Had he listened to the old Klondike sourdoughs describe the war Tyrrell had waged against Congdon, he would undoubtedly have hesitated before issuing his challenge.

Apparently neither of these lessons was learned. Instead, knowing that Anglo-French had divested itself of much of its ownership, he decided that Tyrrell could be beaten. He miscalculated. Tyrrell fought back as ferociously as he had done the previous year in London. Once more he refused to fight on the enemy's ground. Instead of arguing over his reappointment he set out to do what he had threatened to do in London – overthrow the board and replace it with one that saw things his way.

This time Tyrrell was called upon to make good his threat. From late August through all of September and up until the company's annual meeting in mid-October the battle raged. It took the form of a bitter struggle for the proxies of shareholders who would not be at the annual meeting. When the vote was called, Tyrrell had won. Between himself and his supporters he had a clear majority and "the old board under Culver was turned out," and a new board "under Hanna was elected." D. B. Hanna had been one of Tyrrell's most ardent supporters in the fight. Thus, by the time Anglo-French relinquished their formal control of the company in November, Tyrrell was securely ensconced and able to ensure that Kirkland Lake Gold Mines could develop the way he wanted.

This battle too, took its toll on the health of the contestants. This time it was Tyrrell himself who was the victim. Within two weeks of the annual meeting, his doctor diagnosed a hernia that called for an immediate operation. He was still in bed recovering from the operation when his sixty-eighth birthday came and went. Age was beginning to have its effect. Still he was not ready to slow down and for two more years continued the active management of his mine, pushing the shaft down until it was the deepest in Kirkland Lake, its long finger reaching over a mile into the earth.

It was never the richest mine in the area for the quality of ore did diminish as it moved west and the base of operations was always small. When Tyrrell took it over the company still had only one claim and, although he expanded the property by acquisition, it never came close to the potential of the three leaders, Lake Shore, Tech-Hughes and Wright-Hargreaves which, among them, accounted for half the wealth of the whole camp. It nonetheless was in steady production after 1926 and by the 1930s was producing around a half million dollars a year and paying regular dividends. That in itself would have made Tyrrell a wealthy man. It was reinforced by the fact that he had bought his shares at 25 cents each. They had multiplied in value many times over. The depression, which left so many destitute, only increased Tyrrell's wealth. The price of gold in the late twenties was more or less unchanged from its value when he had moiled for it in the Klondike. The depression changed that. By the time the United States pegged gold at $35.00 an ounce it had more than doubled from the price it had fetched when Kirkland Lake Mines resumed production in 1926.

How long J. B. Tyrrell would have remained active in managing his mine – although there were other owners it had become his mine just as surely as the boat on the Yukon River in 1898 had become his boat – is problematical. A massive heart attack in 1928 when he was seventy years old decided the issue for him. He did not die. Instead he lived on for another twenty-nine years. He did however accept a less active life beginning by exchanging the job of general manager of the mine for that of president of the company, only resigning when forced to do so by old age – in 1955 – when he was ninety-six. Even then he stayed as a director of the company attending board meetings until within a year of his death.

His apple orchard on the Rouge River received more of his attention in the last quarter century of his life. He had built up the orchard during the 1920s, experimenting with new varieties in consultation with the federal experimental farms. During the depression he expanded his operation by picking up more land at a distress sale. His older son George, having first followed his father into a mining career and contracting severe lead poisoning as a reward, joined him on the orchard. Soon J. B. was concentrating only on the smaller, experimental work while George ran the entire commercial operation. By 1937 the main orchard had passed from J. B. to his son. George ran it well. In 1931, for example, he had taken no fewer than seven first prizes for his apples at the Canadian National Exhibition. But the price of apples was low and while George eked out a living on the large farm, his father continued his experimental grafting on the small one next door. Well on in his nineties he could be heard telling others that he could not die yet, he had to wait until spring to see if the latest grafts on the trees had taken. In fact he was ready to die.

In the first years of his retirement he continued to produce innumerable articles on his favourite subjects: the explorers Thompson and Hearne; the mining fields and their geology; the glaciers; his Irish ancestors. As the years passed the writings diminished. The honours did not: Toronto and Queen's presented him with honorary doctorates; the Geological Society of London added its most coveted Wollaston Palladium Medal to the already-awarded Murchison Medal; the Royal Society of Canada gave him its Flavelle Gold Medal. Along the way he had had a mountain and a lake named after him – not to mention a steamer plying the Yukon River. There were dozens more – even the National Geographic Society made him a life member. He in turn became a philanthropist, giving back endowments, scholarships, and prizes. The most notable of these was the Tyrrell Medal of the Royal Society of Canada. He did not, however, become a generous man. In 1941 his brother-in-law Tom Gibson fell ill and was confined to hospital in Kingston. It was before the days of medicare and the hospital bill was mounting rapidly. J. B.'s daughter, Mary, concerned for her uncle's well-being and peace of mind paid part of the bill. When her father found out he was furious. It was all very well, he told her angrily, to help Tom out if Tom were to live and benefit from her generosity. But if Tom were dying then the hospital could look after itself by getting what it could from Tom's estate. Mary should have nothing more to do with handling the bills.

He was not much more generous with his sons. In the middle of the depression his younger son Tom quit his job with Kirkland Lake Gold Mines because of the difficulties in working with his father-boss. Tom was a different type of man from his father. Slighter built, intellectually inclined, with a streak of the poet in him, he was a disappointment to the ageing explorer who had never abandoned the Victorian cult of manliness that had inspired his life. It was only when his son became a deputy minister in the Ontario government that Joe Tyrrell was willing to concede there were alternate paths to glory. Having established his worth in his father's eyes, Tom received $100,000.00 in his will. George, who had stayed next door on the orchard received $1,000. After all he had the farm!

This aspect of his personality, however, was balanced by a different kind of generosity. The generosity of obligation. As a wealthy man he was now able to resume the Squirearchy his father had been forced to abandon. The Squire of Weston's son became the Squire of Rouge River. In their old age he assumed the responsibility of providing a home for his parents' servants. Katie the cook, Jessie the maid and Fred the driver all came to stay.

The new Squire remarked, "Really our house is like a private hospital without the properly qualified nurses."

Slowly a certain pathos began to creep into his life. Doll after ailing for many years had died in 1945 but his strong body would not let go. The physical body, with its constant urge towards life, which had refused to succumb to scarlet fever, pneumonia, typhoid and heart attack, still refused to relinquish its hold. His day and generation had passed and he was left with his memories. He began writing them down in an unpublished and unpublishable memoir in which names of the great and near great are dropped freely. He wrote letters reminding people of his lost glory. On the surface the letters were self-effacing but the strangers who were among the recipients must have wondered. The president of Hudson's Bay Mining and Smelting Company received one of them. The president of the United States another.

Although his mind never yielded to senility the pathos mounted. It was time to die. He was ready to die. Repeated heart attacks seemed to promise release but still his body would not let go.

There is a poignant story of him late in life being shown his newest great grand-daughter then several months old. He took the child in one hand – that great right hand that had chipped rocks, paddled canoes, delved for gold and dug out dinosaur bones from millions of years before – and as the tears streamed from his eyes said simply "Poor wee thing, poor wee thing." It was time to go.

241

Epilogue

What is the measure of a man's life? Not the judgment of a particular action or the evaluation of a principle, or even of a full set of beliefs, but the measure of a man's whole life?

The task of making such measurement is too onerous. In day-to-day affairs a worker's performance is evaluated, a manager's decision-making capacity is analysed, a businessman's integrity is weighed, a doctor's competence is appraised. Perhaps with a few people – a parent, a child, a brother or sister – when they have died, the mind's eye tries to capture what they were all about; but for the most part the task is not attempted. Too little is known or revealed to venture into wholesale judgment. When the attempt is made it is often in the form of summing up the life in a word or a phrase – a crank – a crackpot – a scoundrel – a hero. And in the very act of judging the judge is convicted of narrowness of vision. No phrase can comprehend the complexities of a human life; no word can explain the seasons of the soul. When the word is multiplied by a hundred thousand and the phrase is expanded until it is called a biography, the problem is not reduced or dealt with. The question still remains. What is the measure of a man's life?

The biographer claiming otherwise and pretending, God-like, to weigh the life in the balance of eternity is no further ahead than he who would dismiss the life in a word or a phrase. A two hundred page book with forty lines to the page allows a half line (six or perhaps seven words) for each day of a life which lasts its supposed three score years and ten. How is a moment of joy or an hour of despair captured in seven words? There are days in a man's life that whole chapters could never adequately recapture and there are months and years that must perforce be written off in a sentence.

What emerges is not the whole story of a life, but rather *a* story of *a* life. A selection of fact, and perhaps some fiction, that it is hoped will capture a sense of the human spirit. If the biographer's subject is to come through as believable, as true to life's experience, there must be a mixture of the good and bad, a glimpse of what once made him tick, what drove his heart, inspired his actions, enlivened his mind.

There must always be an awareness that not only do the limits of space forbid the telling of the whole story but the evidence available is at best partial. Very few people commit to paper, or to any other lasting form of record, the odyssey of their innermost being through the world of fantasy and delusion into the intimacy of their sexuality and the true relations of the Child with the Parent. Whatever the picture that can be pieced together, it remains forever a fragment of reality inevitably coloured by the values of the biographer and his own, later, society. Yet the subject can only be understood in terms of the values of his day and in the context of his own ideals.

Any account of Joseph Burr Tyrrell's life written in the last quarter of the twentieth century would provide a fine example of these problems. Measured against current standards and concerns, responsibility could be placed on his shoulders for having opened up the wilderness of the Canadian north and thereby exposing its environment to the hazards of modern life – sewage infested rivers, concrete and steel barriers in the path of the caribou, the danger to ecological balances of even minor spills of oil, the uprooting of delicate plant life by the bulldozers of "progress." One can find in J. B. Tyrrell little awareness of the need to protect endangered species.

He would be equally out of touch with recent concerns about native rights. He was, to some extent, exceptional in his generation in that he judged an Indian, or a "halfbreed," or an Eskimo as an individual seeing in the qualities of the man, no matter the colour of his skin, the justification for his existence. There is no indication of any awareness that in heading into the northland, in mapping and exploring the west, in using the Indian chiefly as a manual labourer (although he did know a good guide when he saw one), he was imposing on one civilization the standards of another. He knew of the fears of the Indian people that his northern excursions would endanger their hunting grounds, but he never stopped to consider that their fears might be well-founded.

In his later life when he gave himself over to the exploitation of mineral resources, whether delving for gold himself in the Klondike, or advising others where they could find workable mineral deposits, or heading up foreign capital in turning Kirkland Lake Gold Mines into a paying proposition, there is similarly no apparent awareness of the implications of the fact that the resources were non-renewable and that not only should they be exploited but they should also be conserved.

Yet all of these are the problems and perspectives of the late twentieth century and it is hardly reasonable to expect a Victorian man to be aware of them. It is even less reasonable to expect him to have been deeply concerned about them. Other things occupied his mind. The land was unknown and he was determined to make it known. The mineral wealth was great and he was determined to tap it. He had a vision and a dream of Canada emerging to a place in the sun during the twentieth century and he gave his life to furthering that dream. If his life is to be measured, it must be measured in the context of these ideals. His success or failure lies in his effectiveness in implementing his dreams. The breadth of his life is to be seen in the range of activities in which he became involved: its depth lies in the importance of his work to his own generation and to the future. The principles and values by which he lived may themselves be questioned. In doing so, however, the questioner should be aware that the standards by which he judges will also some day come under question and may too be found wanting.

The provisos having been made, one fact stands out. By whatever criteria Joseph Burr Tyrrell's life is measured, if it is measured at all it will be found to possess an element of greatness. His deeds and accomplishments stand out larger than life. Whatever pettiness and smallness may have resided in him, it was outweighed by the magnificence of his achievements.

Note on Sources

The main source of primary material on J. B. Tyrrell is contained in the Tyrrell Papers which are held in the Thomas Fisher Rare Books Library of the University of Toronto as Manuscript Collection 26. These papers contain Tyrrell's correspondence, writings and various autobiographical accounts of his life. The diary of Robert Munro-Ferguson is also held at the Thomas Fisher Rare Books Library. Tyrrell's field note books, however, are in the Public Archives of Canada as part of Record Group 45 which contains the records of the Geological Survey of Canada.

Two previous biographies have been written of Tyrrell. The first was W. J. Loudon's *A Canadian Geologist* published in 1930. The second was the unpublished M.A. thesis *Joseph Burr Tyrrell, 1858-1957* written by W. E. Eagan for the University of Western Ontario in 1971. While both these works were useful in a number of areas, the latter was particularly valuable for the light it threw on Tyrrell's contribution to the field of glaciation and in providing the background discussion on that topic.

Tyrrell's wife and his brother both published accounts of parts of their lives. Edith Tyrrell's *I Was There*, published in 1938 by the Ryerson Press, was billed as her autobiography. It centred on her two trips to the Klondike to join her husband. James Tyrrell's book was entitled *Across the Sub-Arctics of Canada* and dealt with the first Barren Lands trip. It was first published in 1898 and was reissued in the Coles Canadiana Collection in 1973. It was also the basis for a chapter in Farley Mowat's *Tundra*.

Numerous other secondary sources were consulted but two among them stand out for special mention. Pierre Berton's masterpiece *Klondike* was invaluable in stimulating a sense of what the gold rush was all about. Canadians owe a massive debt of gratitude to Pierre Berton for his work in making Canadian history live. If Berton is the father of popular history in Canada, Professor Morris Zaslow of the University of Western Ontario is the father of northern history. His monumental history of the Geological Survey, *Reading the Rocks*, is without equal as a reference work.

At the Public Archives of Canada in addition to the Tyrrell field note books, various other collections (notably the Sifton Papers) were scanned for material although for this particular enterprise they were of little value. Several newspapers were consulted for various periods in particular the National Library's incomplete collection of Dawson papers for the gold rush years. Finally, of course, there was the quite massive list of J. B. Tyrrell's own publications. My own incomplete bibliography of these runs to more than eighty entries. They range from his large works on Samuel Hearne and David Thompson and shorter historical pieces to his scientific treatise, his Survey reports and his various articles on mining – both popular and otherwise.

The J. B. Tyrrell school in Toronto has an interesting collection of Tyrrell artifacts and interviews that the principal is willing to share generously.

INDEX

A

Aberdeen, Lady, 175
Aberdeen Lake, 20, 24-25
Aberdeen, Lord, 20, 25, 90,
  109, 111-112, 175
Adams, F. D., 89
Agassiz, Lake, 98, 134, 139
Agassiz, Louis, 134-135
Airth, G. R., 232
Alaskan boundary dispute,
  144-145, 158;
  see also sovereignty
Albany River, 52-54, 224
Alberta, Exploration of, 68-87,
  91, 100-104
American Geological Society,
  214
American Geologist, 98
Anglican Mission,
  Fort Churchill, 38ff.
Anglo-French Exploration
  Company, 221-223, 232-238
Ashe Island, 12
Athabasca, Lake, 11, 14-15,
  17-18, 36-37, 100-102
Athabasca Landing, 14, 54,
  100
Athabasca River, 100

B

Back (Sir George) Award, 140
Bad Lands, 81-82
Baggs, "Doc," 151
Baker Lake, 24, 54, 116
Bank of Commerce, 175, 194,
  201, 214

Barren Lands:
  1893 Expedition, 9-54,
  55-56, 59, 90, 100, 109,
  128, 133, 135-138, 140,
  149, 189, 202, 224-225
  1894 Expedition, 109-126,
  127-129, 133, 135-138,
  140, 149, 202
Batôche, 126
Beauvier, 15-17
Beaver Consolidated Mining
  Company, 231-238
Beddoe, W. A., 207-208,
  210-212
Belcourt, Napoleon, 199, 208
Bell, Robert, 12, 90, 110
Bennett, Lake, 160-161, 182,
  186
Beverly Lake, 24
Birch Lake, 20
"Bishop" the, 151
Blackfeet Indians, 84
Black Lake, 11, 13-14, 17-19,
  54, 101-102
Bonanza Creek, 164-166, 170,
  185, 200
Bonanza Creek Hydraulic
  Company, 175, 196,
  199-202, 206, 208, 214,
  216, 218
Borden, Sir Robert, 213
Bowers, "Reverend," 151
Boyle, Joe, 219-220
Brandon, 71, 96
British Association for the
  Advancement of Science,
  132, 134, 136-139, 194,
  222, 235
British Institution of Mining
  and Metallurgy, 222
Brock, Mrs., 193
Bronson, E. H., 175, 196,
  199-202, 206, 216, 218, 232

Brown, George, 58
Bruce, Rev., 94-95
Buchanan's boarding-house,
    Mrs., 88-89, 104
Buffalo Bill's Wild West Show,
    130
Burntwood River, 133
Button, Thomas, 225

C

Calgary, 76-78, 80, 179
Canadian National Exhibition,
    239
Canadian Pacific Railway, 39,
    71, 75-78, 92, 179
Canyon City, 155
Carey Lake, 20, 23, 25
Carey, Rev., 105-106, 113
Caribou, 23, 25-26, 111
Caribou River, 101
Carmack, George, 164, 170,
    185
Cartier, George-Etienne, 58
Cassiar gold rush, 144
Castle Grange, 60
Cat Lake, 226
Cat River, 226
Caughnawaga, 13
Cedar Lake, 116
Chapman, Edward, 65
Chaput-Hughes Mine, 232
Cheechako Hill, 164,
Chesterfield Inlet, 10, 24,
    28-30, 54
Chicago Exposition, 90, 189
Chilkat Indians, 156
Chilkat River, 155-156
Chilkoot Pass, 145-146, 150,
    154-155, 159-160, 176
Chipman Lake, 20-21
Chipman River, 11

Chippewyan folklore, 11, 16,
    18-19, 21, 87
Chippewyan Indians, 11, 14,
    16-19, 21, 24, 36-37,
    101-102, 121
Churchill, 10, 28-30, 34-36,
    39, 44, 54, 112, 118-120
Churchill River, 37, 39, 40,
    100, 119-120
City of Seattle, S.S., 150
Coal, 71, 75, 77, 79-80, 82,
    188
Coastal Mountains, 156, 181,
    203
Cobalt, 216, 219
Cochrane River, 116
Columbia River, 75
Concession policy, 185-186,
    199-201, 206-208;
    Royal Commission into, 201
Confederation, 57-58, 68-69
Congdon, Frederick, 207-214,
    238
Conrad, J. H., 218-219
Conrad Mine, 217-218
Conservative Party, 57-58,
    61, 64-66, 147-148, 211,
    213, 222-223
Corbett Inlet, 29-30, 116-118
Corrigal, James, 13, 35, 50
Cranberry Portage, 133
Cree Indians, 37, 44, 104
Cree Lake, 96, 101
Cross Lake, 122, 133
Crowfoot, 84-85
Crow's Nest Pass, 74
Culver, Frank, 237-238
Cumberland House, 116, 126

D

Dalton, Jack, 155-156
Dalton Trail, 149-150, 154-159

Daly Lake, *see* Wholdaia Lake
Daly, T. M., 20, 111
Dauphin, 56, 98
Dawson, 145-146, 149, 155,
  160-161, 163-164, 172, 182,
  184, 186, 188-192, 194-195,
  200-201, 205-206, 212, 215
Dawson Daily News, 207-208,
  210, 212
Dawson, George Mercer,
  70-76, 79, 81, 89, 91,
  109-110, 128-131, 133, 135,
  137-141, 148-150, 154,
  172-174
Dawson, Sir John William,
  70, 135, 137
Dead Horse Trail, 179, 181
Dennis Lake, 139
Diefenbaker, John, 110
Dinosaurs, 81
Dome, King Solomon's,
  168-171
Dominion Creek, 171
Dowling, Donaldson, 95-96,
  100-102, 110
Drumheller, 56
Dubawnt Lake, 23, 28, 40
Dubawnt River, 10, 17, 19-20,
  22-23, 52-54, 115
Du Brochet, 116
Duck Mountain, 96
Dyea, 145-146, 150, 154-155

E

Edmonton, 13-14, 78
Edna Eldorado, 192-193
Edward VIII, King, 230
Eldorado Creek, 164-165, 171,
  192-193
Elizabeth Falls, 17-19

Eskimos, 11-12, 21, 23-24,
  36-37, 59, 110, 115-116,
  224
Evans, Colonel, 204
Exploration, hazards of, 10,
  26, 101, 114
Exploration, techniques of, 9,
  17, 44-45, 71-72, 74, 79-80,
  122

F

Fairford, 94-95
Fairview Hotel, Dawson, 189,
  191, 193, 205
Fawn River, 226
Fenton, Faith, 205
Ferguson Lake, 116
Ferguson River, 116, 118-119
Ferguson, Robert Munro, *see*
  Munro-Ferguson
Fernie, 75
Fidler, Peter, 79
Financial Post, 236
Five Fingers Rapids, 161, 183
Flamborough Head, 119, 226
Flavell Gold Medal, 240
Flett, John, 13, 34-35, 50
Flin Flon, 133
Fond du Lac, 11, 13, 17, 36,
  100, 102
Fort Chippewyan, 14, 16, 23,
  36
Fort Churchill, *see* Churchill
Fort Garry, 126
Fort Macleod, 71, 76-77
Fort Prince of Wales, 11,
  40-43, 118-119
Fort Selkirk, 183
Fort Severn, 226
Foster, George, 130
Foster, "Slim Jim," 151-153

250

French, Louis, 13, 26, 31-32, 34-35, 50-51, 56
French, Michel, 13, 34-35, 38, 44, 49
French, Pierre, 13, 26, 31, 35, 50

G

Garnett ranch, 72-77
Geddes ranch, 77
Geikie River, 102
Geological Society of America, 90, 136
Geological Survey of Canada, 11, 51, 62, 65-71, 78-79, 87, 89-91, 108-112, 127-131, 139-142, 147-150, 172-175, 214
Gibb, J. A. P., 234-236
Gibson, Tom, 240
Gillam, Benjamin, 225
Glaciation theory, 98, 134-139, 226, 240
Glove, E. J., 156
Golden, 75
Gold rush, *see* Klondike
Gordon Expedition, 1885, 12
Governor-General's Foot Guards, 130
Grahame, steamer, 14
Grand Rapids, 50, 114, 116
Grant, Rev. A. S., 192, 210-211, 216
Grass River, 133
Green, Tom, 193, 195

H

Haines Mission, 154-155
Hannah, D. B., 238

Hayes, Captain, 120-121
Hayes River, 39, 44, 49, 119-120, 225
Hearne, Samuel, 10-11, 23, 40-44, 116, 118, 240
Hearne, Samuel, Journals of, 40-44
Hegg, Eric, 155
Hendry, Anthony, 79
Hollinger Mine, 223, 232
Hudson Bay, 22, 24-25, 28, 32, 39-40, 116-118, 224, 226
Hudson Bay Railway, 120, 133
Hudson's Bay Company, 11, 14, 37-38, 40, 44, 49, 59, 69, 88, 99-100, 112-113, 118-121, 126, 226
Hunker Creek, 168, 194, 196, 198, 201, 206, 216

I

Ile a la Crosse, 100, 102-103
Indian River, 171
Indians, *see* Chippewyans, Iroquois, Cree, Blackfeet, Stony, Chilkat, Stick, Mohawk; *see also* métis: 56, 84, 94, 103-104, 110, 122-126, 244
Iroquois Indians, *see* French, Pierre, Louis and Michel
Irvine, Joe, 167

J

Jarvis, Inspector, 158

Tech-Hughes Mine, 232-233, 238
Telegraph Creek, 146-148
Telzoa River, *see* Dubawnt River
Teslin Lake, 146-148
Teslin Lake railroad, 146-148
Thelon River, 10, 24-25
The Pas, 116, 125
The Sun, 210
The World, 208-210
Thicket Portage, 133
Thlewiaza River, 116
Thomas, Roderick, 178-180, 182
Thompson, 133
Thompson, Dr. Alfred, 211-214
Thompson, David, 79, 92, 98, 100-101, 240
Thompson, David, Journals of, 98-100
Thompson, Sir John, 111
Timmins, Noah, 223
Toronto, 58, 220-221
Toronto and Northern Ontario Railway, 224
Toronto, University of, 61, 240
Toronto World, 127
Treadgold, A. N. C., 154-155, 164-171, 215-216
Tripp, "Old Man," 151
Tyrrell, 240
Tyrrell, Elizabeth Burr, 59-60
Tyrrell, Garrett, 214
Tyrrell, George, 239-240
Tyrrell, James W., 12, 15-19, 21-22, 25-26, 32, 34-35, 44, 46-48, 51, 54, 89, 108, 140
Tyrrell, J. B.,
    as historian, 40-44, 99-100, 118-119, 239-240;
    character, 22, 52, 54, 59-63, 65, 106, 153, 160, 167,

184, 208, 212, 244-245;
    family, 12, 59-61, 66;
    financial affairs of, 129-132, 147, 149-150, 168, 175, 184, 196-198, 201, 216, 221, 232, 234, 238, 240;
    health of, 62, 64, 94-95, 238-239, 241;
    elitism of, 61-62, 240-241;
    Irish ancestry, 14, 60;
    legal battles, 191-192, 201, 206-214, 235-238;
    maps by, 52, 90-91, 140-141;
    marksmanship of, 28, 31, 55-56, 59;
    courtship and marriage, 105-109;
    orchard of, 231, 239;
    personality, 10, 16, 20, 25, 50, 58-59, 68, 76, 78, 96, 109, 119-120, 135, 138-141, 143, 146, 161-162, 172-174, 186-187, 190-191, 215-216, 240-245;
    reputation, 9-10, 55-56, 137-138, 174, 184, 243
Tyrrell, Mary, 129, 191, 202-205, 240
Tyrrell, Mary Edith (née Carey) 105-109, 113-115, 128-132, 138, 142, 178, 180, 189-190, 201-206, 222, 235
Tyrrell Medal, 240
Tyrrell, Tom, 240
Tyrrell, William, 60, 64-65

U

Uniformitarianism, 135
Union Pacific Railway, 58

255

Upham, Warren, 98
Upper Canada College, 61
Upper Canadian Society, 56, 61

V

Vermilion River, 98

W

Wade, Fred C., 145, 175, 198
Wallace, Clark, 66
Walsh, Major, 145, 172
Westasecot, James, 44, 46, 49,
  120-122
Westbourne, 95
Western settlement, 56
Weston, 58-60
Whiskey traders, 71-72
Whiteaves, J. F., 66, 70, 94
Whitehorse, 204, 214
Whitehorse Rapids, 182, 203
White Pass, 144-146, 151, 155,
  159-160, 176, 179, 181, 203
White Pass and Yukon
  Railway, 178, 180, 203-204
White Pass City, 181
Whitney, Sir James, 224

Wholdaia Lake, 10, 20-22, 40
Wilkinson, Bill, 192-193
Winchester rifle, 31, 113
Winnipeg, 10, 44, 71, 94,
  113-115, 119, 139, 222, 225
Winnipeg Free Press, 127
Winnipeg, Lake, 28, 44, 50, 92,
  94, 96, 114, 116, 122, 133,
  136
Winnipegosis, Lake, 92
Wollaston Lake, 102-103
Wollaston Palladium Medal,
  240
Wolseley's Nile Expedition, 13
Wolverine Lake, *see* Chipman
  Lake
Wood, Inspector, 145, 182
Woodcock Rapids, 17-18
World War I, 223, 228
Wright-Hargreaves Mine, 238

Y

York boats, 49
York Factory, 39, 44, 47, 49,
  119, 225-226
Yukon, *see* Klondike
Yukon River, 146, 159-162,
  168, 170